Failed Illusions

COLD WAR
INTERNATIONAL HISTORY
PROJECT SERIES

James G. Hershberg
series editor

Brothers in Arms
The Rise and Fall of the Sino-Soviet Alliance,
1945–1963
edited by Odd Arne Westad

Economic Cold War
America's Embargo against
China and the Sino-Soviet
Alliance, 1949–1963
By Shu Guang Zhang

Confronting Vietnam
Soviet Policy toward the
Indochina Conflict, 1954–1963
By Ilya V. Gaiduk

Kim Il Sung in the Khrushchev Era
Soviet-DPRK Relations and the Roots of
North Korean Despotism, 1953–1964
By Balázs Szalontai

WOODROW WILSON CENTER PRESS
STANFORD UNIVERSITY PRESS

Failed Illusions

Moscow, Washington,
Budapest, and the
1956 Hungarian Revolt

Charles Gati

Woodrow Wilson Center Press
Washington, D.C.

Stanford University Press
Stanford, California

EDITORIAL OFFICES
Woodrow Wilson Center Press
Woodrow Wilson International Center for Scholars
One Woodrow Wilson Plaza
1300 Pennsylvania Avenue, N.W.
Washington, DC 20004-3027
Telephone: 202-691-4010
www.wilsoncenter.org

ORDER FROM

Stanford University Press
Chicago Distribution Center
11030 South Langley Avenue
Chicago, IL 60628
Telephone: 1-800-621-2736

2 4 6 8 9 7 5 3 1

Library of Congress Cataloging-in-Publication Data

Gati, Charles.
    Failed illusions : Moscow, Washington, Budapest, and the 1956 Hungarian
revolt / Charles Gati.
        p.   cm. — (Cold War International History Project series)
    Includes bibliographical references and index.
    ISBN-13: 978-0-8047-5606-8 (cloth : alk. paper)
    ISBN-10: 0-8047-5606-6 (cloth : alk. paper)
    1. Hungary—History—Revolution, 1956.   2. Hungary—Foreign relations—
Soviet Union.   3. Hungary—Foreign relations—United States.   4. Soviet
Union—Foreign relations—Hungary.   5. United States—Foreign relations—
Hungary.   I. Title.   II. Series.
DB957.G36 2006
943.905′2—dc22
                                                                            2006015215

The Cold War International History Project

The Cold War International History Project was established by the Woodrow Wilson International Center for Scholars in 1991. The project supports the full and prompt release of historical materials by governments on all sides of the Cold War and seeks to disseminate new information and perspectives on Cold War history emerging from previously inaccessible sources on "the other side"—the former Communist bloc—through publications, fellowships, and scholarly meetings and conferences. The project publishes the *Cold War International History Project Bulletin* and a working paper series and maintains a website, cwihp.org.

In collaboration with the National Security Archive, a nongovernmental research institute and document repository located at George Washington University, the project has created a Russian and East-bloc Archival Documents Database at Gelman Library, from Russian and other former Communist archives donated by the project, the National Security Archive, and various scholars. The database may be explored through a computer-searchable English-language inventory. For further information, contact the National Security Archive, Gelman Library, George Washington University, Washington, D.C. 20037.

At the Woodrow Wilson Center, the project is part of the Division of International Studies, headed by Robert S. Litwak. The director of the project is Christian F. Ostermann. The project is overseen by an advisory committee that is chaired by William Taubman, Amherst College, and includes Michael Beschloss; James H. Billington, Librarian of Congress; Warren I. Cohen, University of Maryland at Baltimore; John Lewis Gaddis, Yale University; James G. Hershberg, George Washington University; Samuel F. Wells, Jr., associate director of the Woodrow Wilson Center; and Sharon Wolchik, George Washington University.

The Cold War International History Project was created with the help of the John D. and Catherine T. MacArthur Foundation.

To my Toby, inimitable and irreplaceable

Contents

Series Preface

James G. Hershberg

1956: Even after half a century, the year still resonates with drama and meaning—not merely for historians, who recognize it as pivotal in the tales of communism and the Cold War, but also for the millions of people still struggling to comprehend, even escape and transcend, the legacies of Stalinism (political, economic, social, moral, psychological, et cetera) in Russia as well as the other lands of the former Soviet realm. It was only in 1989–91 that the world witnessed the sudden, stunning implosion of the Kremlin's empire in Central and Eastern Europe, and then of the Union of Soviet Socialist Republics (USSR) itself, along with its controlling Communist Party. Yet in many crucial respects, the trajectory to that outcome—to the ultimate collapse of a vast and once seemingly indestructible (except in a thermonuclear cataclysm) edifice of power, subservience, and stifled resistence—was foreshadowed, even ordained, more than three decades earlier.

Although Stalin died in March 1953, his towering image and prestige persisted for almost three years before his record and reputation, and consequently that of the political structure the dictator had fashioned and personified, came under frontal assault. Nineteen fifty-six was

James G. Hershberg is associate professor of history and international affairs at George Washington University and editor of the Cold War International History Project Series. From 1991 to 1997 he was the first director of the Cold War International History Project at the Woodrow Wilson International Center for Scholars.

bookended by two crucial events that, collectively, fatally undermined the Stalinist system's legitimacy, even if it would take a while, and a few twists and turns, for the historical implications to work themselves out. In February, at a closed-door session of the twentieth Congress of the Communist Party of the Soviet Union (CPSU), Nikita Khrushchev denounced Stalin for assorted crimes, above all the murderous purges that had doomed millions to the *gulag* or more immediate extinction, and condemmed the "cult of personality" that had allowed the *vozhd* (boss) to perpetuate these acts.[1] This devastating "secret speech" didn't stay secret for long, but instead rapidly leaked, sparked a spiraling debate throughout the communist world that never really ended, and lit the fuse of an explosion that detonated in the fall.[2] When a revolt erupted in Hungary in late October—initially inspired by a defiance in Poland that aimed lower and, as a result, remained peaceful[3]—and rapidly escalated into violent clashes with hard-line communist forces, the same Soviet leadership that had so recently moved toward de-Stalinization now felt compelled to employ massive military force to crush the rebellion and install an obedient regime. In the process it squashed the hopes Khrushchev had raised of a looser, more open form of communism ("with a human face," as Dubcek would later put it before his own variant, the Prague Spring, was likewise quelled by Soviet invasion).

In the short, even the medium term, Khrushchev had succeeded in restoring discipline within the restive bloc. But the very fact that Moscow had resorted to such brutal methods—disdaining international borders to bully a small country, killing thousands, arresting (and then countenancing the secret trial and execution of) Imre Nagy and his reformist communist associates whom the chaotic events had propelled into power—permanently stained its enterprise in East-Central Europe with Budapest blood. The revolt and its suppression also presaged a pattern, almost sunspot-like in predictability, of periodic resistance to test

---

[1] For a crucial new interpretation of the enigmatic Soviet leader's part both in de-Stalinization and the invasion of Hungary, see William Taubman, *Khrushchev: The Man and His Era* (New York: Norton & Co., 2003).

[2] The metaphor is not original: a post-1989 Romanian compendium of formerly secret communist documents on these events is simply, aptly entitled *Explozia 1956*.

[3] Of course, the tense but nonviolent "Polish October" that brought Władysław Gomułka to power in a popular nationalist-communist upsurge followed by a few months the bloody suppression, in June 1956, of anti-regime protests in Poznan.

the limits of Soviet tolerance—in Czechoslovakia in 1968, in Poland in 1970 and 1980–81—until finally, in 1989, the people in the streets of Warsaw, Budapest, Leipzig, East Berlin, Prague, Timisoara, Bucharest, and elsewhere in the Warsaw Pact discovered that the latest Kremlin leader, Mikhail Gorbachev, unlike his predecessors, lacked the stomach, the heart, or the Stalinist mentality to send in the tanks when the local communists could no longer maintain their grasp on power.

The outlines of the story have long been apparent, but the end of the Cold War and the ensuing flood of newly available sources enable historians to reassess the events of 1956 from a fresh historical perspective and with an enormous amount of previously unavailable information. And no one is better poised to take advantage of this opportunity than Charles Gati, long recognized as a leading expert and commentator on contemporary Central European history and politics, and author of some of the field's most important books and articles. *Failed Illusions* is in many ways the culmination of a career's, and a life's, engagement with the fates of both his native and adopted countries: Gati fled Hungary when the Soviets invaded, and ended up in the United States, where he embarked on a distinguished academic path that took him to Union, Columbia, and finally Johns Hopkins, with occasional forays into government service.

In this lucid, trenchant, provocative, insightful, at times moving, and authoritative (yet astonishingly concise!) volume, he reassesses the Hungarian Revolution by combining the immediacy of an eyewitness (he was a cub reporter in Budapest in 1956) with the experience, expertise, and wisdom earned in decades of inquiry. Whether digging into long-closed communist archives in Hungary and Russia, using the Freedom of Information Act to pester the CIA into opening its internal reports, prodding veterans of the events from multiple countries, distilling the voluminous scholarship, or incisively entering into the crowded and contentious historiographical debate, Gati offers fresh perspectives. Exploring the complex, intertwined dynamics of top-level decision-making in Budapest, Moscow, and Washington as well as broader historical, social, and political forces underlying the events, he tackles enduring mysteries and controversies both factual and interpretive: What caused the revolt, and who led it? Was it doomed from the start, or could it have succeeded? What impact did the post-Stalin succession struggle in Moscow have on the emergence of the Hungarian crisis? How should the roles of figures such as Khrushchev, Nagy, and Kádár be evaluated? What finally triggered the Soviet invasion, after initial hesitation and vacillation, and what were that fateful act's most important consequences? What part did the Americans play in the crisis—Eisenhower and the Dulles brothers with their doctrine of "liberation" and "rollback," the CIA, and Radio Free Europe—and does this story have any relevance for Washington's subsequent efforts to "democratize" or otherwise reshape distant lands?

Failed Illusions should stir considerable debate, especially in Hungary where the events it covers remain politically charged, and attract immediate recognition as a major contribution to scholarly and public understanding. Naturally, it complements Gati's own *Hungary and the Soviet Bloc* (1987) and joins post-communist works by such scholars as Mark Kramer, György Litván, Csaba Békés, János Rainer, and Malcolm Byrne as essential reading for anyone fascinated by the Hungarian crisis and revolution.[4] But its dazzling integration of multi-archival, multi-lingual research, cutting-edge scholarship, and sage erudition also qualifies it to become one of the vital texts of the new Cold War international history[5]—as well as a contribution to the broader literature of twentieth century communism and totalitarianism.

In 1996, after attending a conference in Budapest marking the fortieth anniversary of the pivotal year—and wondrously recounting in *The New York Review of Books* how extraordinary it was that those events could now be freely debated and dissected in a post-communist Hungary and reconstructed through a subtle interlacing of oral history

---

4 Among important English-language post-1989 works, see, e.g., Mark Kramer, "New Evidence on Soviet Decision-Making and the 1956 Polish and Hungarian Crisis," and "The 'Malin Notes' on the Crisis in Hungary and Poland," *Cold War International History Project Bulletin* nos. 8–9 (Winter 1996/1997), pp. 358–84, 385–410, and his eagerly-awaited forthcoming manuscript on 1956; Csaba Békés, *The 1956 Hungarian Revolution and World Politics* (CWIHP Working Paper no. 16; Washington, D.C.: Wilson Center, 1996); György Litván, János M. Bak, and Lyman H. Legters, eds., *The Hungarian Revolution of 1956: Reform, Revolt and Repression, 1953–1963* (New York: Longman, 1996); and Csaba Békés, Malcolm Byrne, and János M. Rainer, eds., *The 1956 Hungarian Revolution: A History in Documents* (Budapest: Central European Press, 2002).

5 Illustrative works based on extensive research in multiple newly available communist archives include books and articles by such authors as Vladislav Zubok, Chen Jian, Odd Arne Westad, Mark Kramer, Norman Naimark, Ilya Gaiduk, Zhai Qiang, Hope Harrison, Piero Gleijeses, Zhang Shuguang, David Holoway, and Vojtech Mastny, as well as forthcoming works by younger scholars such as Sergey Radchenko, Lorenz Luthi, and Douglas Selvage.

testimony and fresh documentation—Timothy Garton Ash ruminated about how the "kaleidoscope" of historical interpretation would have shifted by the time the fiftieth anniversary arrived in 2006.

"How much more, and how much less, will we then know about the revolution?" he asked. "It is precisely the mark of great events that their meaning constantly changes, is forever disputed, with some questions never finally answered. Questions such as, What happened in France in 1789?"[6]

Failed Illusions is not the last word, nor does it answer all questions and resolve all disputes. There is no such thing as "definitive" history, least of all when endlessly complex events such as revolutions and wars are at at issue. But Charles Gati has given us a great book on a great event, a profound and sage response to the question, "What happened in Hungary in 1956?"

---

6 See Timothy Garton Ash, "Forty Years On," in *History of the Present: Essays, Sketches, and Dispatches from Europe in the 1990s* (New York: Random House, 1999), pp. 183–92, originally published in *The New York Review of Books*, November 14, 1996.

1

Introduction to the Argument

> You must not deprive a people of their illusions.
>
> —Count Kunó Klebelsberg, Hungary's minister of culture in the
> 1920s, denying a historian permission to publish newly discovered
> documents showing that a much-admired hero of the 1848–49
> Hungarian revolution against Austria was an Austrian agent.

· 1 ·

Reduced to its essentials, the 1956 Hungarian revolution parallels the story of David and Goliath. Oppressed for a decade by the Soviet Union and its local Communist acolytes, Hungarians rose to assert their right to independent existence. The revolution consumed both the Kremlin and world opinion, but it failed; after thirteen days of high drama, of hope and despair, the mighty Red Army prevailed. The Hungarian government surrendered, its members arrested, kidnapped, or co-opted. The Soviet empire survived, the Cold War continued. Soon enough, the cautious, post-Stalin search for détente resumed. Though in its 1956 year-end issue *Time* magazine honored the Hungarian freedom fighter as its Man of the Year, by the end of 1957 the choice fell on the Soviet leader Nikita S. Khrushchev, also known as the "Butcher of Budapest."

Fifty years later, a more complex story can be told, one that contradicts neither Hungarian heroism nor Soviet brutality. The opening of most Hungarian and many Russian archives since the collapse of communism, and greater access to secret American documents, point to a more differentiated picture of who did what, how, and why, and in particular why the 1956 revolt failed. The coincidence of new evidence and the passing of time make a partial reassessment of many aspects of 1956 both possible and imperative. Of course, Khrushchev and his cohorts cannot be exonerated or vindicated, but what they knew and what they feared can now be better understood and better explained.

As for the record of the United States, it turns out to have been far worse than previously known. New information shows how disingenuous the United States was when it kept the Hungarians' hopes alive—without making any preparations at all to help them either militarily or diplomatically. The initials "NATO" could summarize its approach: No Action, Talk Only. The Dwight D. Eisenhower administration's official declaratory policy of rollback and liberation, including the passing of politically inspired and self-satisfying "Captive Nations" resolutions, amounted to hypocrisy mitigated only by self-delusion; the more evident goal was to satisfy the far-right wing of the Republican Party led by Senator Joseph McCarthy and roll back the Democrats from Capitol Hill—rather than liberate Central and Eastern Europe from Soviet domination. During the revolt itself, Radio Free Europe (RFE) kept encouraging its Hungarian listeners to keep fighting for *all* they sought and more—whether those goals were realistic or not.

The passing of time makes it also less compelling to view uncritically the Hungarians' bravery—without considering the choices they made. In particular, it is not necessary, if it ever was, to endorse everything they did, including the pursuit of maximalist demands that united the Kremlin's different factions against them. Moved by understandable fury against their Communist oppressors in Moscow and in Budapest, the insurgents neglected to contemplate the likely consequences of their actions. Much as their romantic idealism was so appealing, it was also unwise. And even if the young fighters could not and should not have been expected to be politically adept, shrewd, or calculating, older and presumably more experienced hands in the new government should have insisted that the rebels temper their youthful enthusiasm. Despite repeated talks between them, there is no evidence that members of Imre Nagy's revolutionary government ever asked young freedom fighters to look at a map, consider where the Soviet Union was, and, in view of geopolitical realities, exercise restraint. Granted the goodwill and patriotism of Nagy and his colleagues, and recognizing that guiding history's first major anti-Soviet revolution to victory was a most difficult, perhaps even a hopeless, task, there is still no need to obscure their bungling performance.

▪ 2 ▪

In the past, the most widely known scholarly accounts of the behavior of the Hungarians,[1] and also to a lesser extent of the United States,[2] were respectful and restrained—criticism was offered even toward the United States sotto voce—so as not to divert attention from Soviet culpability and Hungarian bravery. After all, it was widely believed, Washington, in contrast to Moscow, could be blamed only for reckless idealism and the Hungarians for excessive zeal and naivete. Fifty years later, Americans and Hungarians alike should be ready to take a more realistic and therefore more self-critical look at what they did—how their mistakes contributed to the revolution's downfall—and what else they could have done.

Such debatable, and indeed controversial, conclusions rest on four seldom-stressed facts and considerations:

First, relatively few Hungarians actually fought against Soviet rule, and their ultimate goal was to reform the system, not to abolish it. In a country of less than 10 million, those who took up arms against the Soviet oppressors numbered no more than 15, 000 (although practically all Hungarians stood shoulder to shoulder with them). Because the revolution's main objective was independence from the Soviet Union, the freedom fighters were deeply nationalist, anti-Soviet, and anti-Russian—but not antisocialist. To the extent that they had a chance to develop a common political platform, it was a mix of independent communism as seen in Tito's Yugoslavia, West European social democracy, and, perhaps, what

---

[1] See, e.g., Ferenc A. Váli, *Rift and Revolt in Hungary: Nationalism versus Communism* (Cambridge, Mass.: Harvard University Press, 1961); and Paul E. Zinner, *Revolution in Hungary* (New York: Columbia University Press, 1962).

[2] Bennett Kovrig, *The Myth of Liberation: East-Central Europe in U.S. Diplomacy and Politics since 1941* (Baltimore: Johns Hopkins University Press, 1973).

came to be known twelve years later in Czechoslovakia as "socialism with a human face." Indeed, one of the few remaining mysteries of 1956 is how the revolution absorbed reformist goals.

Second, the revolution lacked effective leadership. On October 23, 1956, when the revolt began, the crowd, composed of students and demonstrating peacefully, demanded Nagy's return to power. The students admired him for what he had done as the country's reform-minded, anti-Stalinist prime minister in 1953–55, but they did not know very much about him; they did not know that he had collaborated with the Soviet secret police in Moscow in the 1930s, that it was the Soviet Politburo that appointed him as head of Hungary's Communist government in June 1953, and that he was dismissed at the urging of the same Soviet Politburo in April 1955.

During the first few days of the revolt, Nagy disappointed his followers. Reinstated as prime minister, he initially opposed the freedom fighters' demands. Then, in effect going from one extreme to another in a few days, he fully embraced even the most radical demands—without telling the insurgents that quitting the Warsaw Pact and declaring Hungary's neutrality would almost certainly invite a Soviet military crackdown. Nagy's fearless, uncompromising behavior before a kangaroo court that sentenced him to death in 1958 should not obscure the fact that, however well-meaning he was, he lacked the political skill to make the revolution victorious; in particular, he failed to steer his country between the freedom fighters' maximalist expectations and Moscow's minimalist requirements.

Third, the Soviet leadership in Moscow was not trigger-happy. Too much should not be made of the Kremlin's interest in finding a political rather than a military solution to the crisis; every imperialist country prefers to get what it wants peacefully, without bloodshed. In this sense, no reappraisal is in order, because what matters in the end is what Moscow did rather than the alternatives it considered. Still, the Soviet Politburo's now-available deliberations suggest that if Nagy had led rather than followed—if he had calibrated the insurgents' demands and then convinced Moscow that its own interests would be better served by granting his government a modicum of autonomy—Hungary, in exchange for supporting Soviet foreign policy, might have obtained limited pluralism at home.

This possibility—*admittedly only a possibility*—takes account of the revolution occurring against the background of three pertinent realities. The first, in 1955, was the surprising Soviet decision to withdraw its military from Austria, Hungary's western neighbor, which allowed that country to embrace neutralism between East and West as well as pluralism and free-market economics at home. The second critical reality was the historic Twentieth Congress of the Communist Party of the Soviet Union in February 1956, at which Khrushchev denounced Stalin, anticipating substantial changes in international communism. The third reality favoring Soviet concessions was the fact that Hungary, unlike Poland, where anti-Soviet sentiments were also rising, had little or no strategic significance for the Kremlin. Thus, if Hungarian demands had been less radical, Khrushchev might have allowed Hungary to evolve toward semi-independent existence so that if necessary he could deal with Poland more effectively and at the same time protect his anti-Stalinist platform at home.

Fourth, the United States was both uninformed and misinformed about the prospects for change—even as its propaganda was very provocative. Documents made available to me in 2005 under a Freedom of Information Act request by the Central Intelligence Agency (CIA) reveal that the outbreak of the 1956 revolt took Washington by surprise. Evan Thomas disclosed several years ago that in Vienna, the nearest Western European capital, the CIA had no Hungarian-speaking official.[3] The U.S. Legation in Budapest had but one fluent Hungarian speaker who, during the revolution, was busy accepting petitions from various Hungarian groups and individuals.[4] Earlier in the 1950s, the CIA did not have an active program in or toward Hungary, which was assigned *the* lowest priority among the satellites of Central and Eastern Europe.[5]

---

[3] Evan Thomas, "A Singular Opportunity: Gaining Access to CIA's Records," *Studies in Intelligence* 39, no. 5 (1996): 19–23.

[4] The CIA declined to identify him. As it turns out, however, the man is question is alive and well. He is Geza Katona, eighty-eight years of age as this is written in 2005, and he lives in a Washington suburb. In a lengthy telephone interview with me on the record on August 27, 2005, he related his experiences as a CIA officer in Budapest, working under official cover, from 1952 to late 1957. Katona was born in the United States of Hungarian parents. (See chapter 3 below for more details.) In his inaccurate, misleading, and biased book, David Irving identifies Gaza [*sic*] Katona as a U.S. diplomat serving in Budapest; see *Uprising!* (London: Hodder and Stoughton, 1981).

[5] "Hungary, along with the Balkan satellites, had the lowest priority. Indicative is the fact that there were no Hungarian-speaking case officers" at critical places. CIA, *Clandestine Services Historical Series*

Some, though certainly not all, of the information available to the U.S. government about Hungarian domestic conditions came from profascist Hungarian exiles in West Germany and Austria whose contacts at home were missing the main story of the mid-1950s: that the most promising opposition to the Stalinist dictatorship came not from the country's oppressed, unhappy citizens but from Nagy and his anti-Stalinist supporters in or close to the governing elite, many of them disillusioned Communists.

Radio Free Europe (RFE)—the unofficial voice of America—did reach many Hungarian listeners and readers, too. As part of its psychological-warfare program, at times called Operation Focus, RFE launched helium-filled balloons over Hungary that, among others, dropped a cartoon identifying Nagy as the Kremlin's stooge, saying in effect that when you've seen one Commie you've seen them all. . . . In broadcasts to its huge and receptive Hungarian audience, RFE should have cautiously supported Nagy's reformist course in 1953–55 but did not; it should have enthusiastically, and with great effect, supported Nagy during the second week of the revolt but did not. RFE failed to encourage a gradualist, "Titoist," or simply anti-Stalinist outcome that had a chance, however slim, to succeed; instead, it egged on the most radical insurgent groups to fight on until all their demands were met. In the end, and tragically, the United States did not find the proper balance between the admirable goal of keeping the Hungarians' hopes alive and the dubious goal of encouraging them to fight a hopeless battle against the Soviet Union. Thus, the proper question, then or now, is not why the United States refused to fight for Hungary in what could have become World War III; the proper question is why the United States refused to press through its propaganda outlets and diplomatic channels for realistic if small gains.

Why wasn't *something* better than *nothing*?

· 3 ·

Because there is a link between the subject and the author, it may be useful to disclose more about my background and about what I thought *then* of what I witnessed.

(CSHP 323): Hungary External Operations 1946–1965 (MORI DocID: 1161462; parts declassified at my request in December 2004), 82.

I began my journalistic career in 1953, when the daily *Magyar Nemzet* (Hungarian Nation) hired me as a cub reporter. At the age of eighteen, I was the youngest member of the staff. Why Iván Boldizsár, the editor-in-chief, offered me a job remains something of a mystery. Just out of high school with poor grades, I had neither any work experience nor a college education. I could produce no clippings that would have helped him evaluate my skills as a journalist. I submitted no references. I had no pull, no connections. I was not a member of the Communist Party. Of neither working-class nor peasant stock, I did not qualify under the Communist version of affirmative action. (Classified as a petit-bourgeois, my father used to own a small electrical supply store that was closed by the Nazis in 1944 and confiscated by the Communists in 1948.)

During my hour-long interview, which came about as a result of a brief handwritten letter to Boldizsár, I do not recall saying anything wise or witty. I told him that while I lacked proper academic and political credentials, I was nevertheless a born reporter: curious, critical, and a good writer. "Are you a socialist?" he asked. Not knowing exactly what he wanted to hear, I mumbled, opportunistically: "I'd like to be." He nodded and smiled. Mindful of changing political winds after Stalin's death, and of the recent appointment of the anti-Stalinist Nagy as prime minister, he might have wanted a nonparty youngster on the staff. More likely, perhaps, I happened to apply for a position just when he was authorized to hire a neophyte.

I was assigned to the cultural desk to do prepublication and preproduction interviews with writers, playwrights, actors, painters, composers, and musicians. From the beginning, I loved my job and the status that went with it. From the flunky I was in high school a few short months before, I had jumped to the staff of the country's second largest and only prestigious national daily, written and edited for the noncommunist intelligentsia. I had a free pass to the opera, two free tickets to concerts held at the famous Ferenc (Franz) Liszt Academy of Music, and, in the course of my work, I met practically all the leading figures of the world of film and theater, including quite a few of the incredibly attractive actresses of my adolescent fantasies.

By far the most unforgettable moment at *Magyar Nemzet* was the phone call I received one day in 1954 from Zoltán Kodály, perhaps the greatest composer of his time who was once Béla Bartók's partner and soul mate. Aside from Ferenc Puskás, the soccer star, Kodály was the only world-famous Hungarian who did not leave the country before the Iron Curtain fell in the middle to late 1940s. For this reason, the Communist regime kept him in high regard. Somewhat reclusive, Kodály almost never spoke to reporters; but now, to my total amazement, the maestro himself was on the line. He had read my long article that morning in which I traced the application of the Kodály Method of teaching music to students at every level of education, from kindergarten to high school to college, and he thought it was an excellent piece. After a brief pause, I asked him sheepishly if he would be willing to talk to me some day about other aspects of his work. His answer was music to my ears: "Come over for tea this afternoon at 5:00."

In the next two years, I visited Kodály in his spacious and elegant apartment on several occasions—same time, same room, same chair, same tea. Once I drew his attention to the refrain in his new cantata—*"Ne bántsd a magyart!"* (Don't harm the Hungarian!)—wondering if it was meant to convey not only a patriotic but an anti-Soviet message as well. He nodded (I thought) but did not say anything. In fact, he preferred not to discuss political topics. To outlast the dictators, he was cautious. To look at himself in the mirror, he did not conform. Life 101 under Stalin had taught him how to survive; Life 101 after Stalin taught him how to balance the needs of conscience with the instinct for survival. He did not fight the regime. He did not collaborate with the regime. He composed music, but his cantatas contained subtle, even hidden, political messages the censors did not dare edit or delete.

After Stalin's death in 1953, the circumstances of life in midcentury Hungary defied either exact categories or easy definitions.

My two years at *Magyar Nemzet*—I was hired in 1953 and fired in 1955—coincided with Nagy's first premiership. The new prime minister was very popular among my colleagues at the paper. He wanted to decentralize the economy rather than privatize it. He favored socialist legality, which in plain language meant less repression rather than the introduction of the rule of law. He sought a more humane political order, with a small party or two playing a supporting role, rather than a Western-style multiparty democracy. He hoped that the Patriotic People's Front, which became the formal sponsor of *Magyar Nemzet* and was run by Ferenc Jánosi, his son-in-law, would become a new center of power, checking the Communist Party's dominant position without undermining its so-called leading role. I heard that he was a Titoist or a national Communist, but I did not know at the time what that really meant, except that it was far more promising than what we had under the Stalinist Mátyás Rákosi. It goes without saying that Nagy's program was neither anticommunist nor (yet) anti-Soviet.

Nagy and my colleagues, though lacking a precise or even a clear vision of the future, were crystal clear about their opposition to Stalinism and their hatred of Rákosi and his Stalinist gang. In private, they framed the issue in personal terms. On one side was the *öreg*, the old man, or *Imre bácsi*, Uncle Imre, as Nagy was affectionately called; on the other was the *kopasz*, the bald one, Rákosi—the bald murderer. With only a few exceptions, everyone at *Magyar Nemzet* rooted for the *öreg* and despised the *kopasz*.

In that majority was my political mentor, István Radó, the night editor. My senior by almost fifteen years, he took an interest in me and we became friends. A victim of Rákosi's brutal purges, he almost never talked about the horrors he had experienced for four years as a political prisoner. (In that respect, he was a lot like others, discussed in chapter 2, who were released in 1954–55, during Nagy's premiership.) I knew he had joined both the small anti-Nazi resistance and the tiny illegal Communist Party during World War II, and I knew his wife had left him for another man while he was in jail. By the time we met, he was a quiet, gentle soul, something of a loner. The shattered dreams of his youth kept haunting him, but he was no longer a Communist revolutionary. In his outlook and in his demeanor, he turned into a sad, softspoken man. Only when it came to Rákosi and his cohorts, and to the ÁVH (Államvédelmi Hatóság, or State Security Authority), the dreaded secret police, did Radó reveal the suppressed passions that struggled against his calm personality. I remember thinking that I was spared his worst experiences in the 1940s because I was much too young then to be swept up in the political whirlwinds that engulfed Hungary and indeed all of Europe at that time.

By the spring of 1955, I was no longer too young to get by without a bad political experience. In April, as a result of Rákosi's machinations and Moscow's fear of Hungary slipping away, Prime Minister Nagy was ousted. In a month or so, I was in the first group of twelve staffers to be fired; a second group of nine others, including Boldizsár, the editor, soon followed. For its strong support of Nagy's anti-Stalinist "New Course," *Magyar Nemzet* was decimated.

My dismissal was undeserved. I had overheard a lot of political gossip, and I had a sense of what was going on, but I understood little of what I knew. Politics was not my beat. My interviews with composers and ballerinas were largely free of political content. So why was I fired? I put the notice of dismissal in my coat pocket and walked aimlessly from the publisher's office toward the Danube, crying. At twenty, my journalistic career seemed over. I did not have a college education and I did not have a usable skill. I was going to lose my precious draft deferment. What would I do now? A few miserable weeks passed before I learned that my punishment was not as severe as I had feared. I was not classified as an enemy; I was not blacklisted. My punishment was limited: I was deemed an outcast forbidden to hold a full-time job. As a freelancer, I was permitted to write for trade publications and some other lesser known, low-circulation weeklies and monthlies.

After the initial shock wore off and I regained my bearings, I began to view my pink slip as a badge of honor. In a country that puts losers on the pedestal—Hungarians love to celebrate their failed heroes—I was acquiring the respected status of an innocent victim. Though I lost my free pass to the opera house and no longer had an office with a desk and the prized telephone I used to share with four other reporters, and though I had to hustle to make a living as a freelancer, what mattered more and what made life even exciting was that I was no longer a political innocent. I belonged to a movement now, although I did not fully understand what it was about. I just *felt* the same way everyone I respected felt. Being in the movement meant that I picked up and passed on political gossip in the Hungária coffee house and at the Lukács swimming pool—the latter a unique spot that combined swimming with politicking—and that I regularly attended sessions of the Petőfi Circle, a newly formed meeting place for soul searching for the anti-Stalinist intelligentsia. In fact, I began to go there when the sessions attracted no more than a dozen people; by mid-1956, thousands showed up. Not once did I speak up, however. I was less interested in the discussion, much of which I did not understand anyway, than in an attractive redhead who was a regular from the beginning.

More than a year passed this way—from the spring of 1955 to the summer of 1956—when Moscow, to please Tito's Yugoslavia, suddenly decided to dump Rákosi. The ups and downs, all dictated by Moscow, were confusing and nerve-racking: From late 1944 to 1953, Moscow favored the Stalinist Rákosi. From 1953 to 1955, it preferred the anti-Stalinist Nagy. From 1955 to 1956, it once again supported the Stalinist Rákosi. But then, in the summer of that year, it dropped the Stalinist Rákosi again, without reinstating the anti-Stalinist Nagy. . . . Still, I was encouraged, even delighted. Moscow had forced Rákosi, the bald murderer, to pack up and become an exile in the Soviet Union. At the same time, more and more Hungarians, mainly in Budapest, had begun to believe that something had to give, something good had to happen. The only specific expectation I can now recall was that the Communist Party would readmit Nagy to its ranks and eventually he would be returned to his position as the country's prime minister.

Good things began to happen to me, however. In August 1956, I wrote a radical article that the editors of the weekly *Művelt Nép* (Cultured People) immediately accepted for publication and published on page 3 at the beginning of September. The article dealt with the teaching of foreign languages at the high school and university levels. I was very proud of myself for being the first in the country to argue publicly that students should have a choice of taking Russian, English, German, or French—rather than being required to take Russian. I received a few congratulatory notes. Long before Bob Dylan, the times they were a-changin'.

Also in August, Iván Boldizsár, the editor who always landed on his feet, was "rehabilitated" and authorized to start *Hétfői Hírlap* (Monday Herald), a new weekly. The idea was to bring out a Sunday evening paper with an anti-Stalinist agenda—and with extensive summaries on its last page of the afternoon soccer games. On their way home from the stadiums, Boldizsár explained to me, the fans always stopped in their favorite tavern to argue about the teams and curse the referees. By the time they finished their second or third *fröccs* of wine and soda, and ran out of argument, they would want to read *Hétfői Hírlap* with news of the other games and of politics as well. I badly wanted to work for the new paper. I did not know at the time—I found out several decades later, while studying once-secret documents in Hungarian archives—what a cunning political operator Boldizsár was, how he betrayed his closest friends and colleagues; all I knew then was that he was a legendary editor who gave me my first job and that he was a Nagy supporter. And so when he invited me to sign up as a general assignment reporter, I accepted his offer on the spot and rushed home to tell the good news to my parents. Sharing my joy at being exonerated, and of having a full-time job once again, my father gently reminded me that I should have asked what my pay would be.

Within a few weeks, a special committee of the Journalists' Association "rehabilitated" me, too, stating after a two-minute hearing that my dismissal in 1955 was without cause. The hearing took place less than a month before the revolution began. The chairman of the committee was Géza Losonczy, one of Nagy's two or three closest associates.

The revolution that began on October 23 and ended at dawn on November 4 caught me by surprise and left me confused. The first day, I marched with thousands of university students through the streets of Budapest, going from Pest via the beautiful Margaret Bridge to Buda, shouting slogans about independence from the Soviet Union and solidarity with Poland, where promising changes were under way. We demanded Nagy's return to the country's leadership. By evening, the joy I felt during the afternoon march gave way to apprehension. Witnessing the first shots at the radio station, I did not understand what was going on. I was baffled by the sudden appearance of young fighters. Who were these people? Where did their weapons come from? It took me another day or two to begin to sense something that was both curious and confusing: that *the movement for the reform of the system was being pursued simultaneously with a revolution against it*. I recall being both very excited and somewhat uneasy about what was happening around me.

I was puzzled by Nagy and remained so for about a week. On October 23, during the battle at the radio station, the party co-opted him by making him a member of the Politburo and by returning him to the prime minister's office that he had occupied from 1953 to 1955. That was the good news. The bad news was that for almost a week he either vacillated or acted as if he were a hard-line member of the Old Guard. His Marxism and party discipline blinded him to the ongoing revolution. He allowed Ernő Gerő, Rákosi's alter ego, to serve as the party's first secretary and then approved Gerő's replacement by János Kádár, a centrist on the Communist political spectrum who would soon betray Nagy.

For five long days, the new government was composed almost entirely of discredited party hacks, at a time when Nagy, with the whole country behind him, could have consolidated his authority. With most noncommunist politicians of the 1945–47 coalition era in exile or forgotten—and no noncommunist counter-elite available to fill key positions—Nagy was the only credible politician on the scene. Yet, instead of taking advantage of new circumstances, he failed to surround himself with his own reformist supporters. For too many days, he did not respond to the demands of the street. Listening to Moscow's high-level emissaries, the Politburo members Anastas Mikoyan and Mikhail Suslov, and his hard-line Hungarian Communist colleagues, Nagy was insensitive to the mighty winds of radicalism outside party headquarters, where he spent day and night with his one-time comrades, recent critics, and current enemies.

My disappointment in Nagy was matched by my ambivalence about the young insurgents I encountered on the streets of Budapest. I certainly shared their demands for independence and freedom, and I was exuberant about witnessing the fall of Stalin's hideous statue. Yet I was also troubled by and upset about individual acts of violence that I saw almost every day. Although these awful incidents usually occurred in response to provocations by remnants of ÁVH thugs, hanging these creatures on lampposts was not my idea of change or justice. The other thing that bothered me was the apparent belief among the insurgents that everything was now possible. To my mind, it was one thing to shout "Russians, Go Home!" as I did too; it was something else to liberate Hungary by trying to defeat the Soviet Union. I felt that their demands were excessive; that they were going too far too fast. Put another way, I was put off by the freedom fighters' admirable but dangerous romanticism as much as I was put off by Nagy's inability to understand and then lead the revolution that was under way.

For these reasons, and embarrassingly, I did not do very much at all for several days. I wrote a brief article, listened to the radio, read the papers, and talked with friends. I had a potentially dangerous encounter with a group of armed revolutionaries who occupied my weekly's printing shop. When news of the "occupation" reached our office, one of the editors asked me—because I was young, I suppose—to go downstairs to the printing shop and convince the insurgents to leave. My legs trembling, I told them *Hétfői Hirlap* was on their side. They took a look at the last issue I carried with me, we shook hands, and they left. No problem.

After a frustrating week of hope and despair, the Soviet government issued a conciliatory statement—published on October 31 but made available on October 30—that promised negotiations for the removal of Soviet forces from Hungarian territory. Nagy, encouraged by the Soviet declaration, announced the end of one-party rule. Because Mikoyan and Suslov, the two Soviet Politburo members, were in Budapest until the day before, I took it for granted that Nagy had made his dramatic announcement with the Russians' approval. Listening to him on the radio, he sounded confident. What I did not know then was that, having withdrawn most of its military from Budapest, Moscow was sending new troops to eastern Hungary from Soviet territory; in short, some were leaving but others were coming. As Nagy more or less successfully kept the details of ominous Soviet troop movements out of the papers to avoid panic, I believed the Soviets were leaving. By November 1, I was beginning to think the revolution was victorious and Hungary would be free and independent; that was the day when Nagy embraced a major popular demand by declaring Hungary's neutrality and pledging the country's withdrawal from the Warsaw Pact. I did not know that Nagy's declaration—an act of desperation—was largely in response to the arrival of new Soviet troops in eastern Hungary. In less than twenty-four hours, between October 30 and 31, the Kremlin had completely changed its mind.

By accepting at face value what was being said in Budapest and in Moscow rather than paying attention to what was being done in eastern Hungary, I revealed my lack of political experience. So did everyone else I knew. My father, who remained skeptical, was an exception. Because he was often worried about something, despite his generally cheerful nature, I thought I knew better and so paid no attention to what he said.

We lived in a dream world during the first three days of November. Budapest was calm. I was happy. I was proud to be Hungarian! Nagy had needed time to find himself, my friend Radó said, adding that compared with the French Revolution ours was quite nonviolent. It dawned on me that I had overreacted both to Nagy's initial timidity and to the freedom fighters' excessive radicalism. I was witnessing a momentous historical event marked by instances—many instances—of sacrifice, courage, and integrity. I began to phrase a report in my head about a store on Lenin Boulevard that was not looted even though it was ripped open during the fighting. Seeing camaraderie around me lifted my spirits and spiked my ambivalence.

I felt that way, in particular, during the third great day of freedom—Saturday, November 3—when my editor told me to spend the day at the mighty Parliament Building. Little did I know that it would be the last day of free Hungary. A young reporter of barely twenty-two, I explored the sumptuous, labyrinth-like corridors and hallways of this outsized, glorious building on the Danube built at the turn of the century, finding nothing unusual or newsworthy there. What I knew or thought I knew was that somewhere in the building Hungarian and Soviet negotiators were discussing the withdrawal of Soviet military forces from Hungarian territory and they were making progress. I was told the talks would continue and possibly conclude in the evening. By Sunday, I believed, my country would regain its independence, achieving the twelve-day-old revolution's major objective. By Monday, with the city's buses and streetcars scheduled to run again, I hoped I would not have to walk so much anymore. It did not cross my mind that the date and the place would so very soon—at dawn the next day—earn a page in history for deception and disgrace.

What caught my attention were two Western television crews getting ready for Prime Minister Nagy's midafternoon press conference. I had never even seen a television set, let alone a crew in action. Having been isolated from the West both physically and psychologically all my life, I was puzzled by the lights and the cameras, unable to figure out how something filmed here would be seen in living rooms far away. I jotted down a few words about this curious thing called television, wondering how to explain it to my readers the next day. I worried that I would not have anything else to report.

My editors at *Hétfői Hirlap* had sent Péter Halász and myself to the Parliament Building to cover the day's events. A senior correspondent, Halász was to do the serious political stuff, while I was assigned to write a *szines:* tidbits of mood and color, political gossip, brief items about the atmosphere. Our deadline was Sunday noon; the paper was to hit the streets at dinnertime. As it happened, neither Halász nor I could file our stories. Few papers were published on Sunday. *Hétfői Hirlap* never appeared again.

Strange as it may now seem, I suspected nothing as I walked the corridors of the Parliament Building on November 3, trying to catch a glimpse of Nagy—I did not succeed—and trying even harder to collect colorful tidbits of all the comings and goings for the report I expected to file the next day. In midafternoon, when I learned that Nagy's press conference was canceled, I remained calm. He must be busy, I thought. His two deputies—Géza Losonczy, the man who chaired the Journalists' Association's special committee that had rehabilitated me in September, and Zoltán Tildy, the country's noncommunist president in 1946–48—showed up instead. Their plea to Moscow for good neighborly relations was as pointed as my inability to comprehend their message to us, which was that the situation was desperate. Why did I not listen more carefully? I was present at the government's last, historic press conference, and I failed to decode either the words or the body language that strongly suggested the Russians were coming. My behavior was strange because all my life, living under authoritarian and totalitarian rule, I had to read between the lines—a skill one learns when the press is not free.

That Sunday—on November 4, 1956—Soviet troops, having reached Budapest, captured the Parliament. I could not have been more surprised. Caught up in the prevailing mood of euphoria, I did not believe—I did not want to believe—that the post-Stalin Soviet leadership would crush the revolution. Denying the existence of bad news, I suffered from what social scientists call cognitive dissonance. Others might call it stupidity.

At 5:30 A.M. on Sunday, one of my cousins called to say I should turn on the radio. Right away. When I did, the voice on Radio Free Kossuth was familiar and the speech short: "This is Imre Nagy speaking, the president of the Council of Ministers of the Hungarian People's Republic. Today at daybreak Soviet troops attacked our capital with the obvious intention of overthrowing the legitimate Hungarian government. The government is at its place. Our troops are fighting. I notify the people of our country and the entire world of this fact." Speaking from a studio in the Parliament Building, Nagy read his five-sentence declaration for the first time at 5:20 A.M. It was repeated several times, and I listened to it several times, but I could not figure out what he was actually telling us. Are we at war? Is this the end? I was confused, stunned, and despondent. In the next hour or so, the station also broadcast various appeals for Western help, and then it went dead. Meanwhile, Nagy and his immediate family, together with more than a dozen officials and their families, accepted the Yugoslav Embassy's offer of asylum. As I learned many years later, that offer, made in collusion with the top Soviet leadership, was intended to trap and neutralize Nagy's government.

Two weeks after Moscow crushed the revolution, I left Hungary, going first to Austria and then in a few weeks to the United States. I became one of some 182,000 refugees from Soviet-dominated Hungary. My parents, though I was their only child, did not discourage me from leaving. They stayed up all night before I left, watching me as I wrote a few notes of farewell to relatives and friends and put a few belongings together for my escape from uncertainty to uncertainty. Emerging from the kitchen, my mother came around to stuff her freshly baked sweets—the best in the world—into my small backpack. "Look up Uncle Sanyi in New York," she said. At dawn, when it was time to say goodbye, my father tried to hold back his tears but he could not. "Write often," he said, his voice quavering with emotion. We embraced. We kissed. As I left, they stood on the small balcony of our Barcsay Street apartment and waved. I walked backwards as long as I could see them, hoping they could also see me for another few seconds. (As I recall this scene some fifty years later, holding back my tears as my father once tried to do, I still see them waving on the balcony, and I always will.)

I did not fully appreciate until much later—when I had my own children in America—how unselfish my parents were to let go of me.[6]

· 4 ·

Now, five long decades later, having studied the scholarly literature and explored once-secret archives about 1956, I am surprised to find how little I knew or understood back then of what was happening around me. I thought there were many, many more insurgents than I now know to be the case. I assumed back then that the Soviet leadership was more united than it was. I have come to realize fully only recently the negative impact of the United States on the course of events both before and during the revolt. After the Soviet crackdown, I mistakenly expected the West to retaliate, *really retaliate*, against Moscow for the rape of Hungary.

I find it particularly telling now that Moscow and even Washington came to see the failure of the Hungarian revolt as something of a success. The Soviet Union claimed to have saved Hungary and the cause of socialism from Western machinations—even though Khrushchev's anti-Stalinist momentum, with its promise to reform the bankrupt Communist movement, was arrested after the Soviet intervention. It

---

[6] My editor insists I relate at least some of what has happened since. Here are a few details: I was always able to correspond with my parents regularly, but we never discussed political topics. For at least a couple of years after I left, I wrote four or five long letters to them every week, and my mother replied as often and at great length. Later on, there were fewer letters sent or received, but we exchanged at least two shorter letters or one long one every week for more than two decades. Because I have saved their letters and my mother saved mine, and because I brought the whole correspondence to New York after they passed away, I have these letters stored in several boxes that I moved as I moved around. (I have not yet read them.) As I think of my wonderful parents and our extensive correspondence, I often wonder what would have happened if we had had e-mail available at the time. I also recall, and I am sad when I do, that I did not have enough money when they were alive to call them every now and then. The good news I should report is that, as some 182,000 people left Hungary when I did, relatives were seldom prosecuted or persecuted; my parents were left alone by the Communist authorities. In 1963, my mother was allowed to visit and stay in the States for three months; my father had to stay behind to make sure she would return. In 1965, by then with an American wife and two American-born sons, I returned to Hungary to see them. After that, my parents were both allowed to visit me and my ever-growing family, and they always went back. We talked time and again about their settling in the United States. At their age, it would have been very hard to start a new life in America, though my loving and idealistic father often said he would lease a hot dog stand in New York just to be near me. What else can I say? My mother passed away in 1970, my father almost ten years later. My large American family of five children and (at last count) four grandchildren, led by my wife Toby, stop by my parents' grave every time we visit Budapest to honor their memory. During both the Holocaust and Communist rule, they protected me the best way—the most unselfish way—they knew how.

was hardly a mark of Soviet success that only Soviet force could sustain Communist rule in Hungary and by implication elsewhere throughout Central and Eastern Europe. As for the United States, it claimed the free world's moral victory over communism despite that fact that its inability to assist Hungary—by advancing at least one diplomatic proposal, for example—spoke louder than its anticommunist propaganda. True, the United States soon and abruptly abandoned the hollow slogans of liberation and rollback, but Washington never came clean by publicly acknowledging the damage it had done. "Poor fellows, poor fellows," said President Eisenhower privately of the Hungarians as he campaigned for reelection. He added, pathetically: "I think about them all the time. I wish there were some way of helping them."[7]

As for the Hungarians, members of the so-called democratic opposition—few in number but persistent and quite realistic in their assessments of 1956—preserved the revolt's memory in their samizdat publications in the 1970s and 1980s. But a seemingly large majority of the population suffered from collective amnesia during the era of somewhat more moderate "goulash communism" after 1962 or so. Meanwhile, Hungarian exiles in the West kept the issue of Soviet domination on the agenda of Western chancelleries. The connecting tissue between Hungarian bravery in 1956 and the 1989 collapse of the Communist regime was the ceremonious reburial of Nagy and his associates on historic Heroes' Square in Budapest in June 1989. With communism on its last leg, many Hungarians recalled that their sacrifices had not been in vain.

Yet, in 2006, fifty years later, most Hungarians have yet to come to terms with the complexities of what they did or did not do and what actually happened in 1956. Words like "defeat" or "failure" or "loss" seldom appear in public discourse because in the popular imagination the revolution was victorious—until it was betrayed by an uncaring world. This conclusion reflects one of the recurring myths of Hungarian political culture: that those who bravely fight for hopeless causes and lose deserve more admiration than those who opportunistically seek, and obtain, small gains.[8]

---

[7] C. L. Sulzberger, *The Last of the Giants* (New York: Macmillan, 1970), 336.

[8] For three highly stimulating essays related to this point, see György Litván, "Mítoszok és legendák 1956-ról" [Myths and legends about 1956], in *Évkönyv 2000* [Yearbook 2000] (Budapest: 1956 Institute, 2001), 205–18; Csaba Békés, "Győzhetett volna-e a magyar forradalom 1956-ban?" [Could the

With the rise of angry divisions in Hungarian society since 1989, moreover, current political considerations have come to distort popular explanations of who did what in 1956 and why the revolt failed. Reading history backward has become an integral part of a deeply polarized political scene. Today's ex-Communist socialists identify with Nagy and claim to be his heirs and of 1956 too—as if their predecessors had had nothing to do with suppressing the revolt, supporting the Soviet intervention, and in 1958 organizing the juridical murder of Nagy and hundreds of revolutionaries. By contrast, today's anticommunists—some of them political impostors and turncoats who before 1989 cooperated with the Communist regime—do not know what to make of Nagy's Communist past, disparage his associates, and passionately deny the revolution's socialist goals.

Alas, the behavior of Hungarians—and Americans—in 1956 does not lend itself to simple explanations. Consider the answers to these questions: Was Nagy at one point a Stalinist true believer and a Soviet secret police informer? Yes. Was he a popular—if also a Communist— prime minister between 1953 and 1955? Yes. Were many of his supporters disillusioned Communists who had once loyally served Stalinist causes? Yes. Did they prepare the ground for an anti-Soviet revolution? Yes. Was Nagy both a patriot and a Communist during the revolt and in captivity afterward? Yes. Did he and his associates lead that revolution ineffectively, even incompetently—but to the best of their ability? Yes. As for the United States, did Soviet aggressive behavior after World War II call for vigorous U.S. countermeasures? Yes. Did the U.S. government hope to liberate the Soviet satellites in Central and Eastern Europe? Yes. Did Washington prepare for the moment when some sort of diplomatic or economic, let alone military, assistance would be requested? No. Did key officials in the White House and elsewhere believe the slogans they uttered, or were they hypocrites? A few were true believers, most hypocrites. Did U.S. propaganda mislead the Hungarians? Yes. Did the United States let them down? Yes.

Hungarian revolution have been victorious in 1956?], in *Mitoszok, legendák, tévhitek a 20. századi magyar történelemből* [Myths, legends, delusions in 20th-century Hungarian history], ed. Ignác Romcsis (Budapest: Osiris, 2002), 339–60; and Péter Kende,"Elkerülhetetlen volt-e a magyar forradalom, és mi volt a haszna?" [Was the Hungarian revolution unavoidable, and what was gained by it?], *Világosság* 37, no. 10 (October 1996): 3–22.

Even the Soviet Union and Yugoslavia displayed uncommonly complex characteristics in the 1950s, when, at times, bad guys did amazingly good things too. Khrushchev brutally suppressed the Hungarians, while Yugoslavia's Tito, that shrewd hypocrite par excellence, conspired with the Kremlin, notably with Khrushchev, to ensnare and capture Nagy. Of these two scoundrels, Tito also pursued an independent Communist course that helped destroy the unity of what used to be international communism, while Khrushchev pursued an anti-Stalinist course at home that made life in the Communist world, especially in the Soviet Union, more bearable for millions of people.

Trying to cope with such a political muddle, I find the key players—notably some Hungarians and Americans—to have been both idealistic and self-serving, naive and cynical, brave and cowardly, agreeable and obstinate, principled and opportunistic. It is in this incongruous mixture of human and political qualities that readers of this book should expect to find new insights about the uplifting spirit and tragic outcome of the 1956 Hungarian revolt. To understand what happened and especially why the revolt failed, the celebration of valor should be accompanied by a recognition of ambiguities and inconsistencies. Contrary to Count Klebelsberg's advice cited at the beginning of this chapter, responsible scholarship *should* try to deprive people—Hungarians, Americans, or Russians—of their historic illusions.

· 5 ·

Although Hungarians earned admiration in all corners of the globe, the revolt failed. In 1956, Hungary did not realize either the goal of independence or the goal of freedom in a politically pluralist and economically socialist environment.

Discussing the revolt and its failure, I focus on four themes in this book: the critical role of Nagy and his well-meaning but inexperienced associates (chapter 2); America's lack of preparation for what transpired before and during the revolution (chapter 3); the nature and impact of Soviet infighting and unpredictability, especially in 1956, after the historic Twentieth Congress of the Soviet Communist Party (chapter 4); and the intricate set of relationships that developed among the four key actors of the drama of 1956—the insurgents, the Nagy government, the

Soviet leadership, and the United States (notably Radio Free Europe) (chapter 5). Implicit in these themes is the argument central to this book, developed in chapter 6, that failure was not the only option: The Soviet Union's brutal intervention culminating in Hungary's domination for decades to come was not preordained. In the epilogue (chapter 7), I look at 1956 from the perspective of 1989.

This argument differs from what I believed as a young man in the mid-1950s. Largely on the basis of new evidence, I have come to believe that a stronger dose of realism in 1956 could have made a difference. For the tragic failure of the revolt—a product of excessive romanticism in Budapest, unwarranted belief in the power of rhetoric in Washington, and especially the confusing signals from Moscow that eventually yielded to the imperial impulse—could have been circumvented by more gifted and less idealistic leaders in Moscow, Washington, and Budapest who knew both what was desirable *and* what was possible.

2

The Inadvertent Revolutionary

Today, probably a return to the policy of the New
Course and the application of the June [1953]
principles to the economic, political, and social life
of the nation could still check the growing crisis and
avert catastrophe. But it is doubtful whether a return
to the June principles would suffice as a solution
tomorrow. . . . There is a danger that the masses,
having lost their faith, will reject both the June way
and the Communist Party, and it will become
necessary to make a much greater retreat in order
to keep the situation under control.

—Imre Nagy, *On Communism*

· 1 ·

Responding to the Hungarian economy's poor performance and growing unrest in large industrial centers, the Soviet leaders decided to act.
In June 1953, barely three months after Joseph Stalin's death, during
the course of a secret summit with a Hungarian delegation in Moscow,
they chose an experimental, more reasonable course for that country.
They made it clear as well, and at great length, what the Hungarians

must and must not do. They selected Imre Nagy as Hungary's new prime minister, telling him to ease the burden of compulsory agricultural deliveries in the countryside and curtail some of the unnecessarily intrusive activities of Hungary's dreaded secret police. He was to embark on a "New Course" that would include small but under the circumstances still significant changes. It was understood that Nagy should not introduce a free market or a multiparty system; what he was to initiate was not even called a program of "reforms," because that would have signified Western-style social democracy. To make sure Nagy did not go too far, the Kremlin allowed the Stalinist Mátyás Rákosi to stay on as head of the Communist Party.

Nagy's fortunes began to decline soon after the summit, and his tenure as prime minister ended in less than two years. Following the removal in June 1953 and the execution in December 1953 of secret police chief Lavrenti Beria, one of Nagy's two strongest Soviet supporters, Rákosi stepped up his efforts to discredit the New Course. Once Georgi Malenkov, Nagy's other chief patron, was demoted in January 1955, Nagy promptly lost the Kremlin's trust; at Rákosi's insistence, he lost all his government, party, and academic positions. Later that year, accused of nationalist deviationism and worse, he was even expelled from the Communist Party he had joined some thirty-five years earlier.

As prime minister, Nagy made a difference. Though, by Western standards, the actual changes he introduced were modest, he was the first Communist leader in the world to convince his people that the system could be so altered as to make their country both freer and more prosperous. Even though Nagy was a Communist and a Muscovite, Hungarians liked him because he spoke in a language they understood, sought both economic and political change, and was something of a Lone Ranger surrounded by scheming, wily "real" Communists. In the economic realm, his emphasis on investing in the production of consumer goods rather than heavy industry was most welcome in a country seriously troubled by shortages. Most important, he offered political salvation—the prospect of escape from a sinful, Stalinist past—to his intellectual followers, for whom Stalin's death was a time when the certainties of their old illusions about a Communist utopia began to yield to new illusions about the reformability of communism.

In the spring of 1955, after Rákosi repeatedly denounced him to the Kremlin, Nagy became a private citizen. During the next eighteen months, as detailed in chapter 4, he was free to move about when his health allowed him to do so—and he made the most of it. He could be seen in downtown Budapest enjoying a brisk walk, cordially greeting a rapidly growing number of well-wishers. With his large moustache, innocent, round face, inevitable pince-nez, old-fashioned hat, black umbrella, and courtly, jovial demeanor, he did not look like the devout Communist he was. As two of his devoted supporters reported, "his popularity was so great that bus drivers stopped between stations to pick him up."[1] Meanwhile, his presence hinted at his availability as an alternative to Rákosi.

This chapter traces Imre Nagy's career from the time he was a Communist émigré in the Soviet Union to the outbreak of the 1956 revolt. Section 2 describes the dramatic June 1953 summit in Moscow where the Kremlin picked Nagy as Hungary's new prime minister. Section 3 seeks to answer the question of why the Soviet leaders trusted Nagy to implement a post-Stalin program of action, a question that invites a discussion of his relatively moderate views (called right-wing deviationism) and his activities as an informer to the Soviet secret police in Moscow in the 1930s. Section 4 offers an account of Nagy's role in Stalinist Hungary from 1945 to 1953, which centered on agricultural and political issues, including the land reform of 1945; support for the persecution of the Communists' real or imagined adversaries; and, despite reservations about the rapid pace of collectivization, active involvement in the implementation of the party's catastrophic agrarian policies. Section 5 deals with Nagy's tenure as prime minister in 1953–55, which made him a popular figure among the attentive public—and the nemesis of the Communist Old Guard. This was the time when changes in the economy improved living standards and when in the name of "socialist legality" the government released political prisoners en masse, including former Communist leaders purged as Titoists.

---

[1] Tamás Aczél and Tibor Méray, *The Revolt of the Mind: A Case History of Intellectual Resistance behind the Iron Curtain* (New York: Praeger, 1959), 396.

This was the beginning of the era, aptly identified as the "revolt of the mind,"[2] when Nagy's followers, initially small in numbers, started to come to terms with their own responsibility for Communist rule. The high priest of soul searching was Imre Nagy, a man Hungarians both respected and admired for the reforms he introduced as prime minister and for his stubborn refusal to fall in line after his ouster. Yet Nagy, without whom 1956 almost certainly would not have happened, was a studious ideologue, a superb polemicist, and an experienced practitioner of Communist elite politics—but not a revolutionary leader. His past—detailed in this chapter—did not prepare him for the twin tasks of coping with the complexities and then leading a popular uprising. A reformer who turned into a reluctant and indeed inadvertent revolutionary, Nagy could not guide the revolt to a successful conclusion.

▪ 2 ▪

Dissatisfied with Hungary's Stalinist diehards, and worried about signs of instability, the Soviet Politburo appointed Imre Nagy as Hungary's new prime minister in June 1953. Invitations to a Soviet-Hungarian summit in Moscow had been handed out in Budapest by General Secretary Rákosi just a day or two before the meeting was to begin on June 13, but the Kremlin, not Rákosi, chose the Hungarian participants. This was a bit unusual, and so was the composition of the delegation. Rákosi was ordered to appear with his deputy, Ernő Gerő, another hard-working Muscovite; Imre Nagy, then a deputy prime minister known for agricultural expertise and also a Muscovite; four younger party leaders (Rudolf Földvári, András Hegedüs, István Hidas, and Béla Szalai); and István Dobi, Hungary's figurehead president, who had once been a leader of the anticommunist Smallholder Party and concurrently a secret Communist Party member. Strangely absent were Mihály Farkas and József Révai—two of Rákosi's closest colleagues—who made up, with Gerő, the foursome that ran the country. On the long flight from Budapest to Moscow, there was no discussion of what to expect and the atmosphere was subdued.[3]

---

[2] Ibid.

[3] András Hegedüs, *Élet egy eszme árnyékában: Életrajzi interjú* [Life in the shadow of an ideal: Memoir interview] (Vienna: Zoltán Zsille, 1985), 188–97.

Members of the Hungarian delegation apparently did not know that the Soviet leaders had told Rákosi a few weeks earlier, in May, to give up his prime ministership (though not his position as party chief), but the bald dictator stalled; he was not used to and did not want to get used to sharing authority with another Hungarian. He agreed in principle but could not come up with an appropriate replacement, leaving the Russians furious. Nikita Khrushchev had told him in May that "the leadership of the party and the state should not be concentrated in the hands of one man." Vyacheslav Molotov had complained that Rákosi had wanted a replacement "who would have no voice in the making of decisions." As Malenkov recalled later, during their May encounter, "we [had] asked [Rákosi], 'Whom do you recommend as your deputy?' He could name no one. He had objections to everyone. Everyone was suspect except him alone."[4] To break Rákosi's resistance, the Soviet leaders decided to bring him back to Moscow and embarrass him in front of his colleagues and subordinates.

The summit lasted three days. The Soviet delegation included every important leader of the day: Malenkov, Khrushchev, and Molotov, as well as Beria, N. A. Bulganin, and Anastas Mikoyan. With Malenkov and Beria in the lead, they let it be known in no uncertain terms that Rákosi could retain only one of his key positions. "It's not that we don't trust Comrade Rákosi," declared Beria, but new leaders were needed. "We look critically at Hungarian conditions," said Malenkov, and "our impression is the Hungarian comrades underestimate the shortcomings."[5]

---

[4] Imre Nagy, *On Communism: In Defense of the New Course* (New York: Praeger, 1957), 250–51. Cf. Károly Urbán, "A Nagy Imre-kormány megalakulása (1953)" [The formation of the Imre Nagy government (1953)], in *Nagy Imre és kora* [Imre Nagy and His Age], ed. József Sipos and Levente Sipos (Budapest: Nagy Imre Alapítvány, 2002), 39–80.

[5] Unless otherwise indicated, this account of the summit is based on the very detailed transcript prepared by the Hungarian Politburo member Béla Szalai, who also served as chief of staff of the Secretariat of the Prime Minister's Office. The transcript—deposited at the Hungarian National Archive (Magyar Országos Levéltár, or MOL, 276.f. 54/246.ő.e.)—was published by György T. Varga, comp., "Dokumentumok: Jegyzőkönyv a szovjet és a magyar párt- és állami vezetők tárgyalásairól (1953, Június 13–16)" [Documents: Transcript of Negotiations between Soviet and Hungarian Party and State Leaders (June 13–16, 1953)], *Múltunk* 37, nos. 2–3 (1992): 234–69. The translation is mine. For an abbreviated version of the transcript in English, translated by Mónika Borbély and Csaba Békés, see *The 1956 Hungarian Revolution: A History in Documents*, ed. Csaba Békés, Malcolm Byrne, and János M. Rainer (Budapest: Central European Press, 2002), 14–23. For an earlier version, translated by Mónika Borbély, see "Transcript of the Conversation between the Soviet Leadership and a Hungarian United Worker's Party Delegation in Moscow on 13 June 1953," *Cold War International History Project Bulletin*, issue 10 (March 1998): 81–86. See also Hegedüs, *Élet egy eszme árnyékában*; Nagy, *On*

Malenkov began the formal proceedings by saying they would focus on three issues: economic development, personnel, and arbitrariness in state administration (by which he also meant excessive terror). Then, following his outline, he stated that Hungarian agriculture was not doing well. The collective farms did not meet their production quotas. The courts sent peasants to jail when they could not make their compulsory deliveries to the state. The authorities kept harassing the population by constant investigations, arrests, and imprisonments. The purges harmed both the country and the party. Beria blamed Rákosi for doing everything by himself, deciding who would be arrested and who would be tortured, instead of leaving such matters to the investigative apparatus. Beria said that Rákosi was not only the party's general secretary and the head of the government but also served as the actual boss of the ÁVH (Államvédelmi Hatóság, or State Security Authority), the infamous secret police.[6] Realizing, perhaps, the irony of Beria, of all people, admonishing the Hungarians about excessive reliance on terror, Malenkov interjected: "In our country we're correcting the mistakes we've made in this respect."[7] To make sure the Hungarians fully understood the message they were getting, Beria told them, ominously: "The Soviet Army is still in Hungary today, but it will not be there forever."

Beria also commented on agriculture, relating the issue for the first time to Imre Nagy: "Comrade Imre Nagy was expelled from the Polit-

---

Communism; and Mária Palasik, "Látlelet a magyar függetlenségről" [Diagnosis of Hungarian Independence], *Kapu,* May 1989, 4–10. (Palasik's brief account is based on notes taken by Rudolf Földvári, another Hungarian participant.) For a comprehensive description of Nagy's life and times that will long remain the standard by which all other biographies will be judged, see János M. Rainer, *Nagy Imre: Politikai életrajz* [Imre Nagy: Political biography], 2 vols. (Budapest: 1956-os Intézet, 1996 and 1999); the June 1953 summit is described in vol. 1, 509–20. For an early attempt to reconstruct this encounter in Moscow without access to archival sources, see Charles Gati, *Hungary and the Soviet Bloc* (Durham, N.C.: Duke University Press, 1986), 129–33. No transcript has yet surfaced from Russian archives.

[6] From October 1946 to September 1948, the political police force was called Államvédelmi Osztály or ÁVO (Department of State Security); in 1948, its name was changed to Államvédelmi Hatóság or ÁVH (State Security Authority) and its functions expanded.

[7] The irony of ironies was that at the very moment when Malenkov and Beria were both complimenting and complementing each other, Malenkov and Khrushchev were launching a massive conspiracy to remove, arrest, and eventually execute Beria. For a superb account and interpretation, see Mark Kramer, "The Early Post-Stalin Succession Struggle and Upheavals in East-Central Europe: Internal-External Linkages in Soviet Policy Making, Part 2," *Journal of Cold War Studies* 1, no. 2 (Spring 1999): 3–38. Kramer notes: "Following a discussion of the matter on 12 June, the two [Malenkov and Khrushchev] began actively preparing to dislodge their rival." Thus the meeting with the Hungarians attended by Malenkov, Khrushchev and Beria began on June 13, one day *after* the conspiracy by Malenkov and Khrushchev against Beria had commenced.

buro [from 1949 to 1951] because he favored the slower development of cooperatives. This was wrong. The comrades in charge of the Central Committee and the cabinet do not know the villages and do not really want to know the villages." Beria made it clear that the "comrades" he was alluding to did not understand the countryside because they were Jewish. This is why, he said, "it would be better for the prime minister to be Hungarian. Comrade Stalin had [already] told Comrade Rákosi to promote Hungarians."[8] In what appeared to be a summary of the Kremlin's message, Beria said: "If Comrade Nagy becomes the prime minister, let Comrade Rákosi stay on at the head of the party as a comrade who has rich experiences and who has kept faith with the party. *Comrade Nagy is qualified to be prime minister (party loyalist, Hungarian, knows agriculture)*" (italics added).

Although everyone seemed to agree with that conclusion, Molotov took the floor to talk more about Rákosi's know-it-all attitude and about the "wave of repression" that engulfed Hungary. Marshal Bulganin focused his criticism on the Hungarian armed forces. Mikoyan addressed himself to economic plans that were unrealistic, noting that Hungary did not have the resources to make large investments in heavy industry, for example. "Comrade Rákosi has become very conceited," Mikoyan told this veteran of the international Communist movement to his face. When Khrushchev took the floor, he echoed Beria's attack on Rákosi and praised Nagy. "It is my impression," declared Khrushchev, "that there is no collective leadership, that a leading collective has not come into being. Comrade Nagy criticized the leadership [in 1949]; for this reason he was expelled from the Politburo. What kind of respect is that for [different] opinions?"

When it was his turn to reply to his critics, Rákosi was silent about Khrushchev's utterly hypocritical remark about his, Rákosi's, unwillingness to tolerate different views; instead, Rákosi exercised self-criticism—though he did not humble himself, not yet. He said the economic plans would be revised to reduce investments in heavy industry and improve living standards, a general amnesty would be announced, and he

---

[8] "Jewishness" in the Soviet Union officially denoted both a religion and a nationality; thus a Soviet Jew was identified in his passport as Jewish, not Russian or Ukrainian. By contrast, after World War II a Hungarian Jew was identified only as Hungarian, with no mention of his "Jewishness." Following Soviet practice, Beria and his colleagues considered Rákosi Jewish rather than Hungarian.

would give up his position as prime minister. He also gave a long account of the "Jewish question," noting—quite accurately—that after World War II a fairly large number of Jews had joined the party because they identified with the fight against fascism, not because they supported the construction of a Communist society. On the whole, he said, Jews were unreliable. Some of them still occupied influential positions, especially in the press, and they would be removed. However, he did not bother to mention that Hungary's notorious foursome, including himself, were of Jewish origin.[9] Nor did he endorse Nagy's appointment as prime minister until Malenkov asked him pointedly if he agreed to Nagy's "nomination."

Rákosi defended himself by noting that everything he had done or was doing was in line with Moscow's, including Stalin's, instructions. He tried to shift blame from himself, but the Soviet leaders made it clear that he was responsible for Hungary's political or economic problems. Molotov was blunt: "You wanted to have a prime minister who would have had nothing to say about decisions." Malenkov left Rákosi with no options: "What we're saying is that there must not be three Jews [the reference here is to Rákosi, Gerő, and Farkas] in the leadership." The follow-up from Beria was brutal and ominous: "As an old Bolshevik, you, Rákosi, must know that we really know how to break someone's back."[10]

Interestingly, Gerő, Rákosi's alter ego, sized up the situation far better than Rákosi. He agreed to Nagy's appointment as prime minister. He agreed that the Hungarians had made serious mistakes in agriculture. He agreed that the state apparatus was too large. With respect to the secret police, he agreed that the Hungarian leadership did not pay sufficient attention to the application of "sadistic methods" and the "violations of the rule of law." Showing he was a political pro sensing which way the wind was blowing, Gerő assumed some responsibility for what had gone wrong even as he dissociated himself, however slightly, from Rákosi. He understood that as the Kremlin decided to introduce a new course but allowed Rákosi to keep his position as head

---

[9] Aside from Rákosi, the reference here is to Gerő, Farkas, and Révai. These four leaders and others, too, were born Jewish, but they hated their parents' and grandparents' Jewish values and traditions. Cf. Gati, *Hungary and the Soviet Bloc*, 100–7.

[10] The Szalai transcript does not include this particularly vivid Beria quote, which appears in Hegedüs, *Élet egy eszme árnyékában*, 192, and in a similar way in Palasik, "Látlelet," 9.

of the Communist Party, he, Gerő, had to please the Soviet comrades without alienating Rákosi. Privately, however, Gerő was perplexed. He confided in his younger colleague, Földvári, that he did not understand the Russians' critique. "They supported our activities up to the present," he said, but "now they expect the opposite from us."[11]

As for Imre Nagy, the Kremlin's new favorite, he liked everything he was hearing from the Soviet comrades. When it was his turn, he offered extensive remarks about economic mismanagement, particularly in agriculture, and he criticized the concentration of power in the hands of Rákosi, Gerő, and Farkas. He said it was wrong for Rákosi to run the ÁVH. As a final dig at the bald dictator—to show that Rákosi was still trying to circumvent Moscow's comradely advice—Nagy revealed that just before this gathering Rákosi had offered him not the prime ministership but the insignificant Ministry of Adult Education. The imperious Beria turned to Rákosi: "You could find another person for that job."

The two delegations met for the last time on June 16. The unstated purpose of this ninety-minute session was to intimidate Rákosi so that he would not sabotage the decisions just made. Malenkov introduced a new issue that had to do with a supposedly suspicious contact between the United States and Rákosi. He said that at a recent British reception in Budapest, in the presence of the U.S. chargé, there was a discussion about the possibility of a meeting between Hungarian officials and U.S. president Dwight Eisenhower. Implying that something sinister was happening behind Moscow's back, Malenkov wanted Rákosi to know that he was being watched. When it was his turn, Beria came up with another intimidating comment. He spoke of a recent encounter, one between Rákosi and four Soviet advisers in Budapest. There, according to Beria, Rákosi gave the advisers only twelve minutes to do their advising while he took up almost two hours to give the Soviet comrades his advice; instead, Rákosi should have listened to *their* comradely advice rather than taking up their valuable time with *his*. Together, the implication of this Mafia-like browbeating was that Rákosi should stop treating Americans well and Russians poorly. When Rákosi tried to explain

---

[11] Rudolf Földvári, "Egy ungvári kéretlen 'vendéglátás'" [Uninvited 'Hospitality' in Ungvár], *Új Tükör*, no. 53, 1989, 6–8. For a more detailed account of what Földvári witnessed, see also his interview (#231) in the Oral History Archive of the 1956 Institute in Budapest.

what, in fact, had happened, Beria accused him of "obstinacy that would lead to even more serious mistakes."[12]

With that, the summit came to an end. As the Soviet leaders returned to their main preoccupation, which was to discredit each other in their relentless struggle for power at home, the Hungarians were seemingly confused. Leaving the conference room in the protocol-conscious Kremlin, Nagy politely prompted Rákosi to be the first to step outside. But Rákosi pushed Nagy ahead: "You go, Imre, you're the leader now."[13] As it happened, Rákosi was totally insincere. He did not, in reality, accept Nagy's promotion; his schemes against Nagy began immediately after their return to Budapest. After all, he was down but not out. As a well-known and loyal veteran of the international Communist movement, the Soviet leaders were still counting on him to look out for their interests in Hungary.

▪ 3 ▪

Who was Imre Nagy, the Kremlin's new man in Budapest? Why was he praised and promoted?

The Soviet leaders knew his past when they chose him to initiate Hungary's New Course. They knew him or of him since the time he fought with the Red Army in the Russian Civil War.[14] They knew him

---

[12] At a smaller gathering, away from the plenary session, Beria reportedly confronted Rákosi with even harsher warnings, accusing him of trying to become "the Jewish king of Hungary." Referring to "Turkish sultans, Hapsburg emperors, Tartar kings, and Polish princes" who had all once ruled Hungary, Beria—according to two of Nagy's prominent supporters who must have heard it from Nagy—remarked: "But, as far as we know, Hungary has never had a Jewish king. Apparently, this is what you have become. Well, you can be sure that we won't allow it." Tamás Aczél and Tibor Méray, *Revolt of the Mind*, 159. Of the three members of the delegation who subsequently tried to recall this comment about the "Jewish king," Hegedüs and Földvári claim not to have heard it, while Dobi says he did. If the comment was made, it was not made at the plenary meeting in front of the two delegations.

[13] Hegedüs, *Élet egy eszme árnyékában*.

[14] According to a melodramatic account that circulated in the early 1990s, Imre Nagy was in Yekaterinburg in July 1918 with a Red Army regiment that executed Nicholas II, Russia's last tsar. This story got a boost from Edvard Radzinsky's bestseller, *The Last Tsar: The Life and Death of Nicholas II* (New York: Doubleday, 1992). Radzinsky wrote on p. 383: "The detachment [for the tsar's execution] was assembled. Six Latvians from the Cheka [the NKVD's predecessor]—two had refused to join it. One who did not refuse, according to legend, was Imre Nagy, the future leader of the 1956 Hungarian revolution. Nagy's eventual death (executed without trial by Soviet troops invading Budapest) fits our story well." Note the author's reference to his source ("according to legend") and note also his factually incorrect reference to Nagy's execution (which, in point of fact, took place after a secret trial conducted by Hungarians in 1958, not by Soviet troops invading Budapest in 1956). I had an oppor-

as a political émigré who became a Soviet citizen and who lived in Moscow with his wife and daughter in the 1930s and joined Soviet forces in World War II. They knew he was a "real Hungarian," not Jewish, which seemed to matter to them greatly. They knew that Nagy, an agrarian expert with what used to be called a right-wing-deviationist bent, disapproved of the rapid pace of collectivization in the Soviet Union in the 1930s and in Hungary in the late 1940s. They knew that he always favored a go-slow approach to the full consolidation of power and to the building of a socialist and then a Communist society, advocating collaboration with noncommunists if common goals could be found. Given his extensive reporting to the Soviet secret police, at least some of the Soviet leaders—notably Malenkov and Beria, who did most of the talking at the June 1953 summit where Nagy was promoted— had to know that Nagy was an informer while living in Moscow.

Although some of the Soviet leaders knew Nagy's past, they could not know what he was going to do. Mistakenly, they assumed that Nagy's loyalty to the Soviet Union would trump his idealistic commitment to making socialism work. Mistakenly, they did not expect Nagy to introduce changes that would stretch the limits of the Communist one-party state. Mistakenly, they appear not to have considered that Nagy, a true believer, was also a very stubborn man who did not always or easily or quickly conform. Once, when he was told that his views differed from the latest party line favored by the Communist International (Comintern), he famously replied that he would not necessarily "spring to attention" before the International.[15] Conversely, Nagy's mistake was that he failed to realize after 1953 that, as a result of decreasing support for Malenkov's domestic agenda in the Soviet hierarchy, the leeway for reform in Hungary had been greatly narrowed.

---

tunity to ask Radzinsky about his story after the publication of the American edition of his book, and he could not name his source. Still, various "anticommunist" Web sites continue to print this legend that appears to have originated in Moscow as part of a Soviet-style disinformation campaign intended to besmirch Nagy's legacy. For a particularly revealing example of this Soviet-style campaign that claims to draw on materials from the archives of the KGB, see P. Kuzmichev, "Eszli ne zakruvat' glaza . . . " [If one doesn't close one's eyes . . .], *Literaturnaya Rossiya*, December 20, 1991, 22–23.

[15] For decades to come, Nagy was attacked for his "spring to attention" phrase as proof of his contempt for party discipline. For a comprehensive survey of Hungarian communism that includes discussion of such obscure factional disputes and more—written well before the archives opened but still unparalleled in its scope and sophistication—see Bennett Kovrig, *Communism in Hungary: From Kun to Kádár* (Stanford, Calif.: Hoover Institution Press, 1979).

When the Soviet leaders ousted Nagy in 1955, they did not fully appreciate his popularity with his countrymen. They did not anticipate that Nagy's dismissal would light the fires of an anti-Soviet revolt the following year. How could they foresee such a role for a man who lived his formative political years in the Soviet Union where, despite the gruesome experience of Stalin's purges, he remained an idealist loyal to the Communist cause and who then returned to Hungary to help install a Soviet-type system?

During his exile in Moscow between the two world wars, Nagy was one of thousands of foreign Communist émigrés from around the world impatiently preparing for their eventual homecoming. They analyzed economic trends in the West, hoping for a worldwide depression that would mobilize the industrial proletariat against capitalism. They analyzed the global political correlation of forces, wondering when this country or that would become ripe for revolution. They denounced each other for signs of right-wing or left-wing deviationism, or of infidelity to the cause or to the Soviet Union. Gyula Háy, a Hungarian playwright and himself one of the émigrés, subsequently described the way they were: "They [the émigrés] had nothing of consequence to do but they behaved as if they had. They practiced assiduously something they referred to as politics, plotted one another's downfall, and they generally pranced and cantered and whinnied like superannuated parade horses at the knacker's gate."[16]

In this setting, Nagy was not considered a particularly skillful player. He was a serious but not very original theoretician who believed the transition to socialism should be gradual, the process should be allowed to take a long time. Specifically, Nagy implicitly favored Nikolai Bukharin's position on the need to prolong concessions to small-scale private economic activity.[17] He was uncomfortable with the premature abandonment of Lenin's (and Bukharin's) go-slow New Economic Policy in the late 1920s.

---

[16] Julius Hay, *Born 1900: Memoirs* (La Salle, Ill.: Library Press, 1975), 218–19.

[17] For an insightful essay comparing Bukharin and Nagy that was widely circulated in Budapest in samizdat in 1988—and scheduled for publication in the quarterly *Századvég* but never published— see Miklós Szabó, "A magyar Buharin" [The Hungarian Bukharin]. See also György Földes, "Buharin és Nagy Imre" [Bukharin and Imre Nagy], *Múltunk* 27, no. 4 (1992): 15–25.

Because of his interest in agriculture, Nagy's first job in Moscow was with the Comintern's International Agrarian Institute. He signed in on April 24, 1930, under his new Russian name of "Vladimir Iosifovich (Imre) Nagy."[18] The new first name, Vladimir, was the same as Lenin's and so were the initials (V. I.). Later that year, on September 4, Nagy enlisted with the secret police then called OGPU (1922–34), which became the NKVD (1934–43), and is best known to this day as the KGB (1954–91).[19] Though he signed a certificate accepting the obligations of a relationship with the OGPU,[20] there is no written evidence of his cooperation with that organization.[21] There is extensive written evidence, however, that in 1933 Nagy became an active informer for the NKVD, the OGPU's successor agency.[22] For example, when five years

---

[18] Rainer, *Nagy Imre*, 158.

[19] OGPU stood for Unified State Political Directorate; NKVD for People's Commissariat of Internal Affairs, and KGB for Committee for State Security.

[20] Nagy's enlistment certificate, a copy of which is in my files, was translated by and attached to Johanna Granville, "Imre Nagy, aka 'Volodya'—Dent in the Martyr's Halo?" *Cold War International History Project Bulletin*, issue 5 (Spring 1995): 34–37. For a careful discussion of the evidence regarding the relationship between Nagy and the Soviet secret service, see Rainer, *Nagy Imre*, 199–212. An outstanding and conscientious scholar, Rainer doubts the authenticity of several documents that surfaced in Moscow in 1989. He states quite convincingly that they were intended to harm Nagy's reputation and discredit Hungarian dissidents and politicians then fighting for Nagy's and the 1956 revolution's rehabilitation. Nevertheless, Rainer affirms the existence of Nagy's service to the secret police. For another perspective that seems to assume all of the documents to be authentic, see Granville's commentary, ibid., and her subsequent book, *The First Domino: International Decision Making during the Hungarian Crisis of 1956* (College Station: Texas A&M University Press, 2003), 23–24.

[21] Interestingly, he was assigned the code name "Volodya," which was of course the nickname of his newly adopted Russian first name of "Vladimir." As some knew Imre as Vladimir now, the code name Volodya was a curious choice that did not speak well for the imagination of the Soviet secret police.

[22] My view of Nagy's NKVD ties—a subject of controversy in Hungary— is that he was an active informer, but the precise scope of his collaboration and the consequences of his reporting for the victims are debatable. This view is based on (1) eleven of Nagy's NKVD reports and statements in my possession, of which five are handwritten; (2) five additional handwritten Nagy reports identified by Rainer (*Nagy Imre*, 202) that I do not have but briefly reviewed in Moscow (for a description of my encounter in the archives of Russia's Foreign Intelligence Service, see Charles Gati, "New Russia, Old Lies," *New York Times* [op-ed], July 11, 1992); and (3) three documents translated by Granville in *Cold War International History Project Bulletin*, issue 5 (Spring 1995)—I deposited copies of all documents I have obtained with the '56 Institute for the Study of the Hungarian Revolution in Budapest.

Even though I find the evidence of Nagy's relationship with the NKVD convincing, I dissociate myself from some exaggerated allegations that have been made: (1) In his June 16, 1989, submission of the "Volodya" file to Gorbachev, Vladimir Kryuchkov, head of the KGB, made it appear that Imre Nagy's reports were so extensive and so consequential as to make him responsible for the exile, imprisonment, and execution of dozens if not hundreds of his comrades in the 1930s and early 1940s. It is impossible to believe that the NKVD acted solely or primarily on the basis of what a minor, non-Russian informer had reported. (2) Former senior KGB operative Pavel Sudoplatov claims that Nagy was a "full-time [Soviet] agent." My query to Sudoplatov and his son, conveyed by Jerrold Schecter in 2004, produced no evidence to support their contention. Cf. Pavel Sudoplatov and Anatoli Sudopla-

later, on March 4, 1938, Nagy was mistakenly arrested by an NKVD unit unaware of his relationship with the organization, an NKVD captain who knew of his status promptly demanded his release by offering the following information: "'Volodya' was recruited on January 17, 1933, and he has since provided valuable material about the anti-Soviet activities of a number of people from the ranks of the Hungarian emigration." In his subsequent report, the NKVD captain added: "After we demanded to know why [on the basis of what materials] 'Volodya' was arrested, he was freed [four days later] on March 8 of this year."[23]

Of Nagy's numerous submissions to the Soviet secret police denouncing his émigré colleagues, at least the handwritten ones should be seen as authentic. Among them are three lists of people engaged in "anti-Soviet" activities. The first one is dated 1936 (month and day not indicated); the second and third reports are dated April 20, 1939, and June 15, 1940, respectively. Together, the lists contain the names of 203 political émigrés Nagy denounced to the authorities, of whom many were Hungarian exiles and dozens became victims of the purges sweeping the Soviet Union.[24] There is another handwritten report, dated June 30, 1938, in which Nagy complains about being followed despite his

---

tov, with Jerrold and Leona Schecter, *Special Tasks: The Memoirs of an Unwanted Witness—A Soviet Spymaster* (Boston: Little, Brown, 1994), 452. (3) After World War II, three top Hungarian Communist leaders—Mátyás Rákosi, János Kádár, and Károly Grósz—missed few opportunities to bring up the issue of Nagy's extensive ties to the Soviet secret police, notably to Beria. Even in 1985, for example—more than twenty-seven years after Nagy's execution!— Kádár still brought up Nagy's association with Beria at a summit meeting with Mikhail Gorbachev. That's how important history was, and is, in Hungarian politics! (Information given to the author by Valerii Musatov in the course of several interviews in Moscow and Budapest between 1991 and 1996. Musatov was present at the 1985 meeting in his capacity as the official in charge of Hungary for the Central Committee apparatus of the Soviet Communist Party.) See also Valerij Muszatov, "Kádár János és M. Sz. Gorbacsov találkozója Moszkvában, 1985. szeptember 25-én" [Meeting between János Kádár and M.S. Gorbachev in Moscow, September 25, 1985] *Történelmi Szemle*, No. 1–2, 1992, 133–149. In fact, while there is no direct evidence to link Nagy to Beria, there were similarities between Malenkov's ideas and career and Nagy's ideas and career. Thus, a less sensational, and more accurate, conclusion is that Nagy was respected, promoted, and for years protected by various departments and individuals in Moscow that dealt with personnel and security matters.

[23] A copy of this document dated March 10, 1938, is in my files. I obtained it in Budapest in November 2004 from Gyula Thürmer, a high-ranking Hungarian Central Committee official who in June 1989 headed a small delegation to Moscow to receive this and other documents from the KGB. Cf. fn. 22 above. For an English version that includes a mistake (translating the Russian "arestovan" as "recruited" rather than "arrested"), see Granville, *First Domino*, 37.

[24] Rainer, *Nagy Imre*, 202–12. In 1992, during a visit to the archive of the Russian Foreign Intelligence Service, I looked at and very briefly reviewed these three reports and Nagy's curriculum vitae prepared in 1940, but I took no notes and I was not allowed to copy them. In fact, the "archivist" dealing with me threatened me with a revolver if I did not stop pressing my case for more information.

cooperation with the police.[25] Finally, there is Nagy's twelve-page-long, handwritten curriculum vitae, in which he fingered numerous Hungarian friends, comrades, and relatives, as well as colleagues and neighbors in the Soviet Union he had named earlier. It should be noted, too, that in 1941 when Nagy volunteered to join the Red Army against Nazi Germany, he served in a special NKVD unit.

There are several possible reasons why Nagy signed up with the OGPU in 1930 and the NKVD three years later. In 1930, it was probably a condition of employment. Although the Agrarian Institute's publications were unclassified, institute employees, especially foreign Communists residing in Moscow, had to be dependable party cadres. One way to prove one's trustworthiness was to cooperate with the police. A second possibility is that Nagy himself initiated the relationship to show his loyalty to "the homeland of socialism" or—more likely—to protect himself from his political enemies in the Hungarian Communist Party who considered his gradualist, Bukharin-like orientation treacherous. By agreeing to cooperate, Nagy proved his reliability to the Soviet comrades and thus developed some leverage, real or imagined, over radical Hungarian exiles who often slighted and even condemned him. He probably excused his cooperation with the secret police by telling himself that he must survive through this "Stalinist detour" so that he could some day help restore and uphold Lenin's and Bukharin's true Bolshevik principles.[26]

Whatever his initial motives, Nagy had a more obvious reason for continuing his reporting activities in the second half of the 1930s: fear of arrest, torture, and execution. As millions—including Lenin's closest associates, such as Bukharin—disappeared and perished during the Great Purge, Nagy presumed that he too could be arrested and liquidated. Indeed, all members of the exile community feared arrest; some, like László Rudas, a philosopher who was taken away and released twice, kept a packed suitcase by the door of his apartment "just in

---

[25] Ibid.

[26] In his nuanced and perceptive essay, written before the opening of the archives, the late Miklós Szabó (see fn. 17 above) was the first to suggest that Imre Nagy was more calculating and more opportunistic than commonly assumed. According to Szabó, Nagy, subscribing to the notions of Marxist determinism, might have believed that Stalinism was but a transitional phenomenon and Leninism as reflected in Bukharin's and his own gradualist views would eventually prevail.

case."[27] These Muscovites lived in a curious mental state that combined permanent anxiety and boundless idealism. Their Communist faith blinded them to the realities they were experiencing, because they believed in the promise of a Communist paradise with all their heart.

One reality they could not easily deny was the devastating impact of Stalin's purges on the Hungarian Communist Party. By 1940, fewer than fifty loyal activists who were still alive could be counted in Moscow (while at most a couple of hundred activists could be identified in Hungary itself). At the end of the year, when Rákosi arrived in Moscow after sixteen years in Hungarian jails and took charge of the Hungarian party, he found that he did not have personnel in sufficient numbers to implement his ambitious plans for postwar Hungary.[28] Most of the cadres living in Moscow were intellectuals, like the Marxist philosophers György Lukács and László Rudas, people who could be useful in writing position papers but useless when it came to making things happen. So weak was the Hungarian party that the Comintern transferred Mihály Farkas, an ethnic Hungarian from Slovakia and supposedly a talented organizer, from the Czechoslovak party to the Hungarian's. Others with some practical experience were Gerő, Ferenc Münnich, and Sándor Nógrádi, all three veterans of the Spanish Civil War and Comintern or NKVD operatives. Small in number, these professional revolutionaries were nevertheless ready and willing to fight and die for the Soviet Union. They were also anxious to return to their own homeland and shape its future after the war.

However, the Hungarian Muscovites were barely consulted, and the United States and the United Kingdom were not consulted at all, when the postwar Hungarian government was formed in Moscow in No-

---

[27] Interview with Rudas's daughter, Miklós Molnár, in Budapest in the summer of 1998. During a walk in Moscow in mid-1937, when Béla Kun, the celebrated leader of the 1919 Hungarian Commune, was still free, he ran into Jenő (Eugene) Varga, the Hungarian-born Soviet economist. Kun asked Varga how he was. "For the moment, free," was Varga's acerbic reply as he tried to make a joke of their predicament. Kun's humorless reaction (to his wife): "To think that even an intelligent man like Varga can say such stupid things!" Within a few days after this encounter, the Comintern and then the NKVD interrogated Kun, and he was executed in November 1939. Unsurprisingly, given the mentality of this Communist Mafia, Varga, a friend going back to 1919, was among those who turned against Kun. Bennett Kovrig relates the encounter in *Communism in Hungary*, 128; his source is Mrs. Kun's Hungarian-language memoir.

[28] Mátyás Rákosi, *Visszaemlékezések 1940–1956* [Memoirs 1940–1956], 2 vols. (Budapest: Napvilág, 1997), vol. 1 passim.

vember and December 1944.[29] With Molotov in charge, undoubtedly implementing Stalin's directives, the Kremlin sought a broad-based coalition composed of noncommunist politicians and especially military officers of the disintegrating authoritarian regime of Miklós Horthy, Hungary's regent between the wars. Understanding that a Communist government could not effectively govern Hungary or contribute to the anti-German war effort, Molotov bluntly told a delegation Horthy had sent to the Soviet capital to negotiate the terms of surrender what kind of provisional government Moscow wanted: "The institution to be created should be democratic, with the participation of every party. It may be that *Moscow-based Hungarians* could be useful, too, but especially those should be regarded as suitable who are respected in Hungary. Jews must be counted out"[30] (italics added).

In the provisional government so formed, General Béla Miklós, a Horthy-ally, was selected as the new prime minister. Rákosi did not go home; the Kremlin told him he was to stay in Moscow for now because

---

[29] To some extent, at least, Soviet policy did follow the thrust of the Soviet-British so-called percentage deal reached in Moscow on October 9–11, 1944. The "deal" provided for the distribution of Soviet and British influence in five countries after the end of World War II: Greece, Romania, Bulgaria, Yugoslavia, and Hungary. In the end, Soviet influence in Greece was set at 10 percent, in Romania at 90 percent, in Bulgaria at 80 percent, in Yugoslavia at 50 percent, and in Hungary at 80 percent. Neither the British, represented by Prime Minister Winston S. Churchill and Foreign Secretary Anthony Eden, nor the Soviets, represented by Stalin and Molotov, defined the meaning of "influence"; and thus the real meaning of this controversial and indeed cynical "deal" has never been clarified. Because of heavy bargaining by Molotov, the final result Eden and Molotov concluded on October 11 concerning Hungary was substantially different from the initial agreement reached by Churchill and Stalin on October 9. That agreement by Stalin and Churchill provided for only 50 percent Soviet influence in Hungary. Subsequently, several "package deals" offered by Molotov sought to make it 75–25 in favor of the Soviet Union, with Eden—fighting for British influence in Yugoslavia—accepting Molotov's Hungarian offer. In the end, the British apparently agreed to 80 percent Soviet influence in Hungary. For a more detailed account, see my *Hungary and the Soviet Bloc*, 28–33. A copy of the deal is in Churchill's file at the Public Records Office in London (PREM 3/66/7, PRO). For the record of what happened on October 10 and 11, see "Record of Meeting at the Kremlin, Moscow on 10th of October, 1944, at 7 p.m." (PREM 3/43/2) and "Record of the Meeting at the Kremlin on 11th October, 1944, at 3 p.m." (PREM 3/434/2). See also John Lukacs, "The Night Stalin and Churchill divided Europe," *New York Times Magazine*, October 5, 1969, 36–50; and Vojtech Mastny, *Russia's Road to the Cold War* (New York: Columbia University Press, 1979), 208–12.

[30] Molotov used the words "Moscow-based Hungarians," "persons in Moscow," or "Hungarians residing on Soviet territory" rather than "Communists" or "Muscovites." He did not want to alienate or frighten Horthy's anticommunist emissaries. He hoped the Hungarian military would organize the army against Hitler and lend legitimacy to the new postwar order. (Given Molotov's stand on the exclusion of Jews from the government, it is worth noting that his Jewish-born wife had been exiled to the Gulag on Stalin's order and was still there in 1944 while her husband was Stalin's de facto deputy.) For the Molotov quotation, see Péter Gosztonyi, "Az Ideiglenes Nemzeti Kormány megalakulásának előtörténetéhez" [To the Prehistory of the Founding of the Provisional National Government], *Uj Látóhatár* 15, no. 3 (August 1972): 228–29.

his presence in Hungary might frighten his countrymen. Gerő, Révai, Farkas, and Zoltán Vas were allowed to return, but Moscow did not agree to their joining the government. For the time being, the Communists tried to conceal their real identity. One of the secret instructions given to returning party cadres said that "leaders of the party shall not thrust themselves into prominence: whenever possible, the party's objectives must be implemented through others, many times through another party." Such cunning tactics were quite effective. Even the well-informed and normally skeptical *The Economist* of London assured its readers on December 30, 1944, that the composition of the new Hungarian coalition had proved the accuracy of "Mr. Molotov's promise" that Moscow would not attempt to influence the "domestic structure" of countries under its "temporary supervision." Such was the extent of Western naivete at the time.

As for Nagy, the Kremlin included him in the new government as minister of agriculture and also in the Communist Party's Politburo for the same three reasons the Kremlin would give in 1953 for his appointment as prime minister. First, Nagy could easily pursue the Kremlin's then-favored gradualist tactics that called for obscuring the goals of the dictatorship of the proletariat and of communism itself. Second, given his association with the NKVD and everything else they knew about him, the Soviet leaders considered him a loyal and reliable Communist. And third, he did not have a Jewish background.[31] For the very few who knew him, he was a curious choice: a relatively moderate Communist who was also an informer for the dreaded NKVD. As Moscow sought to play down the ties of "Moscow-based Hungarians" to the Soviet Union, Nagy was also an ideal choice because he was not widely known as a Muscovite; indeed, he was all but unknown in his native land.

---

[31] In November 1944, when Rákosi was in Moscow and Zoltán Vas already in Hungary, Rákosi told Vas in a letter that he should not count on being a member of the party's top leadership because the "Christian Imre Nagy" was slated to play a more prominent role. Cf. Charles Gati, "A Note on Communists and the Jewish Question," chap. 4 in *Hungary and the Soviet Bloc*, 100–7. For a comprehensive account, see István Deák, "Jews and Communism: The Hungarian Case," in *Dark Times, Dire Decisions: Jews and Communism*, ed. Jonathan Frankel, Studies in Contemporary Jewry, Avraham Harman Institute of Contemporary Jewry and Hebrew University of Jerusalem (Oxford: Oxford University Press, 2004), 38–61.

■ 4 ■

Even though the Red Army occupied all of Hungary, the Kremlin ruled out a formal Communist takeover for years to come. Countering the views of some of the militant, and impatient, home Communists—those who had spent the war years in Hungary and were anxious to proclaim the "dictatorship of the proletariat" right away—Gerő said: "Some Communists think the order of the day in Hungary is the establishment of socialism. That is not the position of the Hungarian Communist Party. It is not a correct viewpoint to urge the construction of socialism on the rubble of defeat."[32] Révai added: "I declare that we do not regard national collaboration [by several political parties] as a passing, political coalition, as a tactical chess move, but rather as a long-lasting alliance."[33] Révai explained the party line by stressing international considerations: "England and America would not recognize a Communist government. Those who want socialism and the dictatorship of the proletariat [now] make the anti-German policy more difficult."[34]

Stalin's coalition formula for Hungary did not produce the expected results. At home, the anticommunist Smallholders' Party received a stunning 57 percent of the vote in the free elections in November 1945—way ahead of the Social Democrats' 17.4 percent and the Communists' 17 percent—and it could not be easily tamed. In the West, Stalin's go-slow approach did not impress either. In mid-1946, already, a top-secret U.S. intelligence assessment prepared for President Harry S Truman put Hungary (and even Czechoslovakia) in the same category as all of the Soviet Union's new dependencies in Eastern Europe.[35] Washington had little or no interest in fine distinctions; differences among the new Soviet satellites were too subtle to appreciate. With the

---

[32] As quoted in Kovrig, *Communism in Hungary,* 157.

[33] *Délmagyarország* (Szeged), December 5, 1944.

[34] Mihály Korom, *Magyarország ideiglenes nemzeti kormánya és a fegyverszünet (1944–1945)* [Hungary's provisional national government and the armistice (1944–1945)] (Budapest, 1981), 286.

[35] Central Intelligence Group, Office of Research and Evaluation, ORE 1, "Soviet Foreign and Military Policy," July 23, 1946, in *The CIA under Harry Truman,* ed. Michael Warner (Washington, D.C.: History Staff, Center for the Study of Intelligence, Central Intelligence Agency, 1994), 75–85. In what was an obvious oversimplification, the CIG report stated that Communist control has been achieved in Hungary "in the same degree and manner" as in "Poland, Rumania, and Bulgaria." In point of fact, the Sovietization of Central and Eastern Europe was a differentiated process. The future of Czechoslovakia remained somewhat open until early 1948 and Hungary until 1947. See my *Hungary and the Soviet Bloc,* "Part One, Communists in Coalition, 1944–1948," 13–123.

wartime alliance over, the Cold War was about to commence. In late 1947, Stalin created the new Communist Information Bureau, or Cominform, a minor-league variant of the Comintern, which formally terminated the short-lived postwar era of what it mockingly called "parliamentary pirouetting." The gradualist Popular Front tactics that began in 1935 and applied selectively after World War II, too, were being brought to an end.

For Nagy, 1945 was a very good year, probably the best before his elevation to the prime ministership in 1953. In the Politburo, he was ranked after the Muscovite Foursome—Rákosi, Gerő, Farkas, and Révai—but usually ahead of such home Communists as László Rajk and János Kádár. As minister of agriculture in what was still a broad-based coalition government in 1945, Nagy had an opportunity to fulfill his life's dream of implementing the Land Reform Act of 1945, which provided for the expropriation, and subsequent division and distribution, of estates larger than 1,000 *hold* or 1,420 acres. He was in his element doing something truly revolutionary. Hungary's landless millions could own and cultivate their land for the first time in history—before being forced into collective farms in the early 1950s, a policy Nagy quietly opposed behind the scenes and then helped implement. For now, however, he was comfortable with the Kremlin-ordered policy of cooperation with noncommunists. He seemed less consumed than his colleagues with the struggle for power and the deceitful intrigues it entailed. He was different from his Politburo comrades in some other ways, too. For example, he did not object to his daughter's romance and eventual marriage to a Protestant minister, and he even attended her religious wedding ceremony in 1946 without Politburo permission.[36]

The Muscovite Foursome, who disparaged him professionally and disliked him personally, kept trying to undermine Nagy's reputation in the Kremlin. After Nagy had advised Soviet authorities in the fall of 1945 that the Red Army's lawless behavior made it difficult for the Hungarian Communist Party to gain a measure of legitimacy, Rákosi was furious. He informed Moscow that Nagy had offended Soviet authorities in Budapest by asking them to return food supplies they had

---

[36] I discussed aspects of Nagy's life with Erzsébet Vészi, Nagy's daughter, during the course of several conversations in the early and again in the late 1990s. She related this particular episode on July 11, 1991.

seized. Rákosi said Nagy would have to be reprimanded.[37] Because he could have handled the case in Budapest, Rákosi's complaint to Moscow was unusual. Why did he turn to the Kremlin in Nagy's case? The answer is that Nagy, who had neither friends nor allies in the Hungarian party, did have high-level protectors in Moscow.

To undermine the Kremlin's trust in Nagy, Rákosi complained to Moscow that Nagy not only offended the Red Army but also colluded with "Horthyite bureaucrats" in his ministry and neglected party work. Without saying so directly, Rákosi was asking for permission to reprimand Nagy. Sending the letter to Georgi Dimitrov, who used to head the Comintern, had special meaning as well. Dimitrov had played a key role in selecting the Communist leaders of postwar Central and Eastern Europe, and he was still an influential liaison to the ultimate authority on such matters under Stalin—Georgi Malenkov, the secretary of the Soviet Communist Party's Central Committee in charge of personnel in general and Hungarian personnel in particular.[38] Though there is no direct evidence that Rákosi knew of Dimitrov's or Malenkov's special ties to Nagy stemming from his years as an NKVD informer,[39] Rákosi did know that it was the Kremlin that had initiated Nagy's rise from relative obscurity in late 1944 by appointing him a Politburo member and minister of agriculture. It seems, then, that this

---

[37] "Rákosi Mátyás 1945. szept. 3-i jelentése Dimitrovnak" [Mátyás Rákosi's report to Dimitrov on Sept. 3, 1945], *Múltunk*, nos. 2–3 (1991): 287. The former head of the Comintern, Dimitrov was still in Moscow at this time; he was not yet allowed to return to his native Bulgaria, where noncommunists would have seen his presence there as a sign of their country's imminent Sovietization. On Dimitrov's relationship with Stalin, see Alexander Dallin, Fridrikh Igorevich Firsov, and Vadim A. Staklo, eds., *Dimitrov and Stalin, 1934–1943: Letters from the Soviet Archives*, Annals of Communism Series (New Haven, Conn.: Yale University Press, 2000).

[38] According to Miklós Kun, a well-known Hungarian historian with excellent access to Russian archives and officials, "until 1946, Hungarian personnel matters were generally decided by Georgi Malenkov." See Lajos Izsák and Miklós Kun, eds., *Moszkvának jelentjük—Titkos dokumentumok 1944–1948* [Reporting to Moscow—Secret Documents 1944–1948] (Budapest: Századvég, 1994), 288. A grandson of Béla Kun, Miklós Kun notes that at about the same time the Kremlin assigned Finland and Estonia to Andrei A. Zhdanov, Lithuania to Mikhail A. Suslov, and Romania to Andrei Ya. Vyshinsky.

[39] According to a document of uncertain authenticity dated June 1941—with no day of the month indicated—Malenkov was the recipient of reference materials about Nagy forwarded to him by Vsevelod Merkulov, the NKVD's deputy director under Beria. At that time, Malenkov was a department head in the Soviet party's Central Committee responsible for personnel issues. There is no explanation as to why Malenkov or a lesser official in his department had requested or needed information about Nagy from the NKVD. Even if one were to assume this 1941 document to be genuine, it does not by itself prove Nagy's *personal ties* to Malenkov. For the text in English of Merkulov's report addressed to Malenkov, see Granville, "Imre Nagy, aka 'Volodya,'" 37.

is why Rákosi contacted Dimitrov and this is why he waited seven days before proceeding to have Nagy chastised. Then, having either learned or sensed the extent to which Dimitrov or Malenkov cared to protect Nagy, Rákosi decided to censure Nagy but did not feel free (yet) to demote or dismiss him.

For Rákosi, who jealously guarded his prerogatives and insisted on being the only point of contact with the Kremlin, Nagy remained a source of constant irritation. He resented that Nagy's forecast about the November 1945 elections turned out to have been accurate and his own turned out to be wildly overoptimistic. Adding to Rákosi's dismay was that Marshal Kliment Voroshilov, chairman of the Allied Control Commission in Budapest, and his Russian colleagues, shared Nagy's outlook as they also predicted the Smallholders' landslide victory. After the elections, too, Nagy continued to be a thorn in Rákosi's side. During the struggle among the coalition parties for key portfolios, Rákosi was unable to have the Smallholders agree to the appointment of the tough home Communist, László Rajk, as minister of internal affairs. Rákosi was shocked when Marshal Voroshilov personally intervened, "suggesting" the more congenial Nagy as a compromise candidate for the post. The Smallholders found "Voroshilov's man" somewhat less objectionable and agreed. The barely hidden Soviet message to Rákosi was that Nagy, a potential rival, remained at or near the top of Moscow's list of trusted Hungarians.

Nagy did what a Communist minister of internal affairs was expected to do.[40] He did not interfere with the activities of the Communist-led political police that used any and all means to prosecute and persecute those the Communists called "collaborationists" (who cooperated with the Nazis during World War II) and "reactionaries" (who favored either a Horthy-type authoritarian or a Western-style democratic regime). On the main issue of his brief, five-month tenure—which was, in today's terminology, "ethnic cleansing"—Nagy also followed the party line. The issue had to do with collective punishment: the expulsion of all Hungarians of German origin—some 450,000 people or

---

[40] According to his daughter, Nagy did not enjoy being minister of internal affairs. In the late 1940s, after she told her father she was bored working for the Institute of Cultural Relations and would like to transfer to the Ministry of Internal Affairs, his reply was curt, almost rude: "Don't even think about it." See fn. 36 above.

about 5 percent of the population—to Germany. The decision was not his or his government's. The victorious allies had made that decision at the 1945 Potsdam summit, but Nagy and his ministry prepared the regulations and the guidelines concerning definitions and implementation. One position paper prepared in the ministry strongly and convincingly objected to a policy of wholesale expulsion based on ethnic origin, comparing the plan to the deportation of Jewish-Hungarians in 1944. But Nagy, reflecting the Communist Party's stance, did not bulge. The regulations issued by the ministry eventually provided only for minor exceptions on the basis of an individual's participation in Hungary's small anti-Nazi resistance movement.[41]

Still, Nagy could do nothing right so far as Rákosi was concerned. In March 1946, the general secretary succeeded in having Nagy replaced as minister by Rajk, his original candidate for the position. This time, Rákosi explained to Moscow only after the event what he had just done. In a disingenuous but seemingly compassionate note, he said that Nagy was having problems with his heart and with his liver, and therefore could not keep up with the heavy workload in the ministry. Nagy needed rest. Rákosi's letter could be read as a sympathetic account about Nagy, who, Rákosi explained, would not only remain a Politburo member but also take part in policy implementation, as a member of the party's Secretariat. In what was almost an afterthought, however, Rákosi added that "later on we will make him an ambassador in an important neighboring country." Of course, as János Rainer has pointed out, the prospective ambassadorial post would have removed Nagy as a player in Budapest.[42]

Was Nagy removed because of ill health? He did have complaints, but his health was not as bad as Rákosi made it out to be (and wished). Was it because he was too weak as minister of internal affairs? True,

---

[41] The writer who argued against ethnic cleansing was István Bibó, the noncommunist head of the Department of Public Administration in Nagy's ministry. Bibó was a major legal scholar and a brilliant political analyst and theorist. Judicious by temperament and centrist by conviction, he was the Hungarian Isaiah Berlin: articulate, insightful, and eminently reasonable, very possibly the best political analyst Hungary has ever produced. His finest essays are available in English in István Bibó, *Democracy, Revolution, Self-Determination (Selected Essays)*, ed. Károly Nagy (New York: Columbia University Press, 1991). Despite his disagreement with Nagy over ethnic cleansing in 1945–46, Bibó joined Nagy's cabinet toward the end of the 1956 revolution as a representative of a small noncommunist party.

[42] Rákosi's letter to Rezső Szántó, who was the Hungarian party's liaison with the Soviet leaders in Moscow, dated March 22, 1946, as quoted by Rainer, *Nagy Imre*, 318–19.

Nagy was much more interested in agriculture than in state administration, but he served the Communist cause loyally and effectively in the Ministry of Internal Affairs. The real reason for Rákosi's success in pushing Nagy aside in the spring of 1946 can be found in his skillful exploitation of the icy political winds blowing from Moscow. For, in his famous preelection speech of February 9, 1946, Stalin had just called for new sacrifices at home and no concessions abroad. A little less than a month later, Winston Churchill spoke of a new Iron Curtain dividing Europe. More important for Nagy, the hard-line Andrei Zhdanov was ascendant within the Soviet hierarchy as the fortunes of the somewhat more pragmatic Malenkov began to decline. With Malenkov, still a Politburo member, assigned to work in Siberia and then Central Asia, the Kremlin's Hungarian portfolio was transferred to Zhdanov and his acolyte, Mikhail Suslov. Rákosi must have been delighted. By mid-1946, he addressed his memoranda to Suslov rather than Malenkov (though the latter continued to be on the Soviet distribution list for Hungarian correspondence).[43] Because Malenkov was no longer strong enough or at the right place in the leadership to be an effective patron, and neither Zhdanov nor Suslov interested in Nagy's political fate, Rákosi could more easily move Nagy around.

For several years, Nagy continued to occupy high positions in the hierarchy. He was, except for a period of eighteen months in 1949–51, a full member of the Politburo. He served as speaker of Parliament. Because of his disagreement with the Rákosi-led majority on economic issues in 1947, he was sent off in 1948 to teach economics at the University of Budapest. In 1949, he differed from the majority on the pace of forced collectivization.[44] However, after the party rejected his go-

---

[43] Izsák and Kun, *Moszkvának jelentjük*, 95–97, and especially Kun's concluding essay on 283–93.

[44] Addressing the party's Central Committee in March 1949, Rákosi ominously if plausibly compared Nagy's go-slow approach to Bukharin's. After the session, Nagy replied at length. Rákosi forwarded a copy to Moscow where it was discussed on several occasions and at a high level. See Rainer, *Nagy Imre*, 401–21. In September, Nagy, almost certainly with the Kremlin's approval, lost his position in the Politburo. Without being identified so by name, he was identified as a right-wing deviationist. Nagy's relationship with Ferenc Donáth, then head of Rákosi's secretariat and Nagy's nemesis on agrarian issues, was both more complicated and quite telling of how members of this Communist Mafia related to each other. In 1951, Donáth was purged with János Kádár, among others, and sentenced to fifteen years in jail; he was freed in 1954. In 1951, Nagy was a Politburo member who did not speak up on Donáth's behalf. In 1954, Donáth was released while Nagy was prime minister. In 1956, Donáth became Nagy's political ally; in 1958 he was a defendant during the trial of Nagy and his associates. Because of their dispute in 1949, the two could never become friends, however.

slow approach, he exercised self-criticism as "the party" told him he should. In 1952, when he became minister for food collection, he agreed to put into practice the very policies he had opposed—collecting agricultural produce and livestock by any means at the disposal of Hungary's brutal police state.

As for other matters, Nagy meticulously followed the party line. When in 1947 a group of anticommunist political and military leaders called the "Hungarian Community" (*Magyar Közösség*) were found to have held discussions about the country's future, and about how to limit the Communists' power, Nagy was among the first to condemn publicly their "conspiracy" against the state. He was quiet at the time of the purges of the late 1940s and early 1950s when innocent victims of the police state—ranging from church leaders to politicians on the left, including Communists Rákosi or Moscow decided to dump—disappeared without a trace. In 1951–52, Nagy even headed the Central Committee Administrative Department that played, at least in part, a supervisory role over his old Ministry of Internal Affairs and the political police. In short, Nagy, whatever his private scruples might have been, was a Stalinist militant who understood that his party must not tolerate dissent within its ranks. He accepted the principle of "democratic centralism," which meant that after some discussion by the leaders behind closed doors the majority's decision was binding on all.

From the winter of 1947–48 until Stalin's death in March 1953, Hungarians experienced five years of totalitarian nightmare. Economic steps included the nationalization of factories and trade, combined with the introduction of central planning. By 1952, the economy—burdened with huge defense expenditures and immense investments in heavy industry for which raw materials were locally unavailable—was on the verge of bankruptcy. Looking for scapegoats for the regime's failures, the secret police were as active in the countryside against unproductive peasants as they were against all "enemies" of socialism. The peasantry, declared Rákosi, "must be forced to make greater sacrifices for the building of socialism."

Copying Stalin's pattern of forceful collectivization in the 1930s, [45]

---

[45] In the next two paragraphs, I paraphrase sections of my chapter, "From Liberation to Revolution, 1945–1956," in *A History of Hungary*, ed. Peter F. Sugar, Péter Hanák, and Tibor Frank (Bloomington: Indiana University Press, 1994), 368–83.

Rákosi ordered an unrelenting struggle against kulaks (peasants who owned at least 25 *hold*, or about 35 acres) and against so-called middle peasants (who owned 10 to 25 *hold*). But force did not produce economic results. Despite, or because of, all the threats, intimidation, and terror, combined with impossibly high delivery quotas and a tax system that actually discouraged production, collective farms accounted for no more than one-fifth of the country's arable land in the early 1950s, while the average independent peasant produced less than what his own family needed. So poorly did the collective farms perform, and the state paid so little for their products, that by 1952 the average income of peasant families belonging to such farms dropped to 30.8 percent of what it had been as late as 1949.

Elsewhere in the economy, the nationalization of factories employing ten workers or more was ordered in 1949; by the following year, essentially all private enterprise ceased to exist. Barbers and plumbers, newspaper vendors and psychiatrists all worked directly either for the state or for state- or city-controlled cooperatives. The proudly proclaimed objective was to turn Hungary into a "country of iron and steel." The unrealism of totalitarian economic policy was reflected in the decision to build a metallurgical complex at the newly named town of Sztálinváros (Stalin City)—but the party neglected to consider the fact that the needed iron ore and coking coal were locally unavailable. Rákosi claimed that "the new socialist man" would overcome all such technical obstacles and difficulties. By 1952–53, the Hungarian economy —burdened with extravagant investments, immense defense expenditures, and inefficient and highly politicized central decisionmaking— was bankrupt. The age of totalitarian economic transformation was a total failure.

One of the most notorious show trials taking place then was that of József Cardinal Mindszenty who, having been drugged and tortured, confessed to leading an "antistate" conspiracy for which he was sentenced to life imprisonment. The most prominent Communist who was also purged to instill fear among all was László Rajk, the former minister of internal affairs who replaced Nagy in 1946; he was executed in 1949. Another to be tried and imprisoned was János Kádár, the man who had replaced Rajk and who—together with the sadistic Miháy Farkas—had once personally subjected Rajk, his old friend, to some of the most gruesome forms of psychological and physical torture.[46] Hundreds, perhaps thousands, of perfectly loyal Communists were arrested and purged between 1949 and 1952, accused of such made-up crimes as spying for the United States and Yugoslavia and for leading "antipeople" conspiracies, as well as for dissolving the Hungarian Communist party in 1943. The number of Communist and socialist victims of the Communist terror—twenty-eight were executed or died in jail[47]— paled in comparison with others who were jailed, deported, or otherwise punished; the latter included anticommunists as well as noncommunists from the 1945–47 coalition era who tried to cooperate with the Communists. Between 1950 and early 1953, the courts dealt with 650,000 cases, of whom 387,000 or 4 percent of the population were found guilty.[48] The reign of terror turned out to be harsher and more extensive than it was in any of the other Soviet satellites in Central and Eastern Europe.[49]

Why not Nagy? Why wasn't he purged? All top leaders of the party, including Rákosi, Gerő, Révai, Farkas, and others in high positions, disliked him. He was something of a loner, an apparatchik without allies in the party hierarchy. He held opposing views on agriculture. To purify the party of potential enemies and to show vigilance at a time of Stal-

---

[46] The full text of this event is in *Kádár János bírái előtt: Egyszer fent, egyszer lent 1949–1956* [János Kádár before his judges: Once up, once down 1949–1956], ed. László Varga (Budapest: Osiris, 2001), 157–70. For excerpts in English, see "The Interrogation of László Rajk, 7 June 1949: The Transcript of the Secret Recording," ed. Tibor Hajdú *New Hungarian Quarterly*, Spring 1996, 87–99; Hajdú's excellent introduction is on 83–86.

[47] *Iratok az igazságszolgáltatás történetéhez* [Documents on the history of the administration of justice], 4 vols. (Budapest: Közgazdasági és Jogi Könyvkiadó, 1993), vol. 1, 448.

[48] See the report prepared after the collapse of communism of the so-called Fact-Finding Commission, *Törvénytelen szocializmus* [Lawless socialism] (Budapest: Zrinyi Kiadó / Új Magyarország, 1991), 154. For additional facts and figures, see also the four-volume *Iratok az igazságszolgáltatás történetéhez*.

[49] Numbers do not adequately describe the atmosphere of terror that permeated all aspects of everyday life in totalitarian Hungary. Poetry comes closer. In his memorable "One Sentence on Tyranny," written in 1950 but hidden by the author and published during the 1956 revolution, Gyula Illyés wrote that tyranny was present "Not only in the gun barrel, / Not only in the prison cell, / Not only in the torture rooms, / Not only in the nights, / In the voice of the shouting guard"; it also affected the way acquaintances avoided each other, the way friends discussed only apolitical topics, the way parents feared to reveal their private beliefs to the their own children. More than anything else, the totalitarian era in Hungarian history was marked by an immense gap between popular hatred of the Communist regime and professed solidarity with it and between conditions of anxiety and the officially proclaimed euphoria about the new world order. To quote another brief excerpt by Illyés: "Where there is tyranny / Everyone is a link in the chain; / It stinks and pours out of you, / You are tyranny itself." I apologize to the brilliant translator of this brilliant poem, but my English-language copy does not mention his or her name and I have not been able to locate it.

inist paranoia, he was an obvious candidate to demonstrate that Tito, Stalin's archenemy, was working hard to overthrow the postwar Communist regimes. Yet, while Nagy was closely watched by the Hungarian secret police—with their reports regularly forwarded to General Fyodor Belkin, the Vienna-based East European supervisor of Soviet intelligence—his name apparently never came up during the course of top-secret radio contact between Rákosi and Soviet authorities regarding forthcoming arrests and show trials.[50] Why was Rákosi reluctant even to bring up Nagy's name? It seems that Nagy was only demoted rather than purged for three reasons. First, he still had special ties to Soviet authorities. Second, the Kremlin tried not to prosecute Muscovites, lest the West believe it took decades for the Kremlin to find out about successful "enemy" penetration of the Soviet Union in the 1930s. Third, Nagy, given his tendency to fall in line, was an irritant rather than a serious problem for the diehards who ruled the Hungarian party.

Indeed, while Nagy's views on agriculture were different, he did not press hard for their adoption. Under pressure, he withdrew them and as minister for food collection even helped implement the majority's decisions. On the critical issue of the purges, he was silent. He was present when the Politburo discussed the arrest of this or that official, but he is not known to have stood up for any of them. In April 1951, when Rákosi informed the Politburo of the "urgent arrest" of a large group of home Communists—including Kádár, Géza Losonczy, Ferenc Donáth, Gyula Kállai, and others—apparently no one, Nagy included, objected. Moreover, as head of the party's Administrative Department, he played a role in supervising "party work" at such key power ministries as Internal Affairs, Defense, and a few other organs of the government as well.

In 1951–52, as Malenkov, back in Moscow from his Siberian and Central Asian "exile," was being groomed to be Stalin's heir, Nagy—even before Stalin's death—was moving up too. Already a deputy prime min-

---

[50] Rainer, *Nagy Imre*, 432. According to Nagy, however, the Hungarian secret police chief, Gábor Péter, on instructions from the party, was told to prepare materials for his arrest in 1949. As related by Nagy, Rákosi called him in to tell him there was enough evidence to prove that Nagy had provided "theoretical justification" for Rajk's Titoist conspiracy. Rákosi acknowledged that he had a conversation with Nagy but denied Nagy's description of what took place. See T. György Varga, "Nagy Imre politikai levelei 1954, Dec. 14–1956 okt. 9" [Imre Nagy's political letters, Dec. 14, 1954–Oct. 9, 1956], *Új Fórum*, no. 4, 1989, 11–39.

ister, he was selected in November 1952 to be the main speaker at the thirty-fifth anniversary celebration of the Bolshevik Revolution, which gave him visibility and marked him for further promotion. Speaking at the ceremony held at the opera house in Budapest before the party faithful, Nagy, sparing no superlatives, extolled the historic significance of the October Revolution, and praised the "Great Stalin" as well as Mátyás Rákosi, "Stalin's best Hungarian pupil," as he was called.[51]

A brief conversation Nagy allegedly had at the opera with Gábor Péter, head of the Hungarian secret police just before his arrest, strongly hinted at Nagy's continuing ties with high-ranking Soviet officials. According to Péter's subsequent statement, it was Volodya (spelled phonetically in Hungarian as Vologya) who told him then that General Belkin, Péter's Soviet supervisor, had just been arrested in Moscow.[52] How did Nagy know that? What was striking about the conversation was not only that (1) Péter knew Nagy's code name of Volodya from the 1930s but also that (2) Nagy had apparently learned of Belkin's arrest ahead of Rákosi and the whole Hungarian leadership. Hence the answer is that Péter, Hungary's secret police czar, knew of Nagy's old NKVD ties, including his code name, and that Nagy was still so well connected in 1952 as to pick up such an important little piece of Soviet political news ahead of its publication and even ahead of everyone else in the Hungarian political elite, including Péter. It is not entirely mysterious, then, why the Kremlin would soon pick Nagy as Hungary's new prime minister.

· 5 ·

As prime minister, Imre Nagy wanted to make socialism succeed in the country he loved—an elusive task no one before or since could successfully accomplish. His vast experience in the world of Communist intrigue since the 1930s was helpful but not decisive. Though he served in such key jobs as minister of agriculture, minister of internal affairs,

---

[51] *Szabad Nép*, November 7, 1952.

[52] Thanks to Tibor Zinner, chief historian of the Hungarian Supreme Court, a copy of Péter's handwritten confession dated April 20, 1953, in which he relates this encounter with Nagy on November 6, 1952, is in my files. A typed version appears in *Iratok az igazságszolgáltatás történetéhez*, vol. 3, 337–40.

minister for food collection, chief of the party's administrative section, member of the Politburo, and since 1952 as deputy prime minister, he did not become a cunning politician. He was smart; he was not shrewd. He was intelligent; he was not sly. Especially in comparison with the wily Rákosi, he had only modest political skills.

For this reason, too, and from the beginning, his position as prime minister was tenuous. Though he could single-handedly spark an immensely enthusiastic response from his country's *intellectual* elite, his influence at the top echelons of the party and even the government he headed was minimal. Whether he could be an effective leader able to mobilize the *political* elite was always in doubt. The integrity he projected, the commitment to make things better that was a key to his profile, and the willingness to take on Rákosi and his hated acolytes combined to make him a folk hero—a Good Bolshevik in an anticommunist country—but he was not a political heavyweight. An idealistic Communist ready to alter the system, Nagy was certainly not a tough and shrewd leader like Yugoslavia's Tito or Poland's Gomułka in 1956. As Tibor Déry, the prominent writer and strong Nagy supporter who was jailed after 1956, would tell his interrogators, Nagy was a "very honorable, brave, and gutsy man . . . but [not] a genuine [*vérbeli*] politician."[53]

As agreed in Moscow in June 1953, Nagy became head of the government, which was supposed to be the No. 1 job after Stalin's death, but Rákosi remained in charge of the Hungarian Workers' Party (as the Communist Party was called), and the party apparatus supported him, not Nagy. Meanwhile, the Kremlin, reflecting its own internal free-for-all after Stalin's death, put Nagy on a political roller coaster: up one week, down the next. He was called to appear in Moscow to face his Soviet overlords who once instructed him to stay the course and then told him to slow down.

The Hungarian party's Central Committee (called "Central Leadership" at the time) met on June 27, 1953, and dutifully approved the changes ordered by the Soviet leadership. Members of the committee

---

[53] Written testimony submitted to his interrogators on May 3, 1957, in Állambiztonsági Szolgálatok Történeti Levéltára [Historical Archive of the State Security Organs], with many of the same documents deposited previously at Történeti Hivatal [Historical Office], and before that at the Belügyminisztérium Irattára [Archive of the Hungarian Ministry of Internal Affairs, [hereafter cited as AHMIA], V-150.393/6.

and invited special guests listened in stunned silence[54] as Rákosi exercised self-criticism and admitted responsibility for the country's economic woes. He even accepted some blame for the purges and promised to observe "socialist legality." When it was his turn, Nagy blamed Rákosi for the rise of the Hungarian "police state"—a term previously applied to a fascist or a Nazi, never a Communist, country—and called for free debates in the party.[55] In a secret resolution, the Central Committee condemned the Stalinist foursome—Rákosi, Gerő, Farkas, and Révai—for bringing Hungary to the brink of disaster,[56] but no one raised the two questions that should have been asked: Who made the decision to elevate Nagy? If Rákosi and his colleagues had indeed done as much harm to Hungary as the party resolution stated, why were they allowed to continue to hold all the key positions but one? Members of the Central Committee must have suspected, but did not discuss, the ambiguity inherent in Moscow's decision to promote Nagy and to limit his authority by letting the Old Guard retain leading positions.

Even hard-line members of the Central Committee knew that *something* had to be done. In Plzeò and elsewhere, neighboring Czechoslovakia had experienced serious strikes and work stoppages, and on June 15, 1953, major riots broke out in East Berlin and elsewhere in East Germany (the so-called German Democratic Republic).[57] Mistakenly, as it turned out, Nagy believed that citing growing signs of instability elsewhere in the Soviet domain would help him advance the cause of his "New Course." He warned his Politburo comrades of a "catastrophe" if they failed to support "profound changes . . . made through a 'New Course.'"[58] But his warnings of the dangers ahead had a mixed impact

---

[54] Sándor Gáspár was present at the meeting. Interview, October 3, 1991.

[55] Nagy's speech appeared in print more than three decades later, in 1984, in the samizdat journal *Beszélő.* In 1992, after the collapse of communism, all issues of this informative and thoughtful publication were issued in *Beszélő Összkiadás, 1981–1989* [The Complete Edition of Beszélő, 1981–1989] (Budapest: A-B Beszélő Kiadó, 1992). Nagy's 1953 speech is in vol. 1, 628–41.

[56] Sándor Balogh, ed., *Nehéz esztendők krónikája 1949–1953: Dokumentumok* [Chronicle of difficult years 1949–1953: Documents] (Budapest: Gondolat, 1986), 496–510. For long excerpts from the Central Committee resolution in English, translated by András Bocz, see *1956 Revolution*, ed. Békés, Byrne, and Rainer, 24–33.

[57] Cf. Christian F. Ostermann, ed., *Uprising in East Germany 1953: The Cold War, the German Question, and the First Major Upheaval behind the Iron Curtain* (Budapest: Central European University Press, 2001).

[58] For his views and his opponents', see Imre Nagy, *On Communism*, esp. chap. 5 ("Significance of the June 1953 Party Resolution and Its Effect on Our Party"), 66–74.

on his Stalinist colleagues. Yes, something must be done. But they used Nagy's facts to convince themselves that because the concessions he was proposing went too far, they encouraged popular pressure for changes the party could not control.

What was being played out partly behind closed doors and partly in the open was more than the usual factional struggle for power that had always characterized the Communist movement. This time, uniquely in the history of the Soviet bloc, Hungary had two institutionalized centers of power. Nagy, heading the government apparatus in 1953–55, implemented changes in agriculture and in the justice system, and appealed to the nonparty attentive public for support. Meanwhile, Rákosi, in charge of the party apparatus, managed to undermine much of what Nagy had been instructed to do both by the Kremlin and the Hungarian party's (then unpublished) June 27, 1953, resolution.

The message Rákosi conveyed to members of the elite was that they should not side with Nagy because he, Rákosi, was still in charge of the party and it was only a matter of time before he would reassert his full authority. In fact, Rákosi signaled to the party faithful almost immediately that, his self-criticism notwithstanding, he did not really approve of Nagy's program. By making use of Beria's arrest on June 26, 1953, (coincidentally with the adoption of the Hungarians' June 27 resolution) and of the Hungarian bureaucracy's fear of losing control, and by dropping hints that Nagy's measures destabilized the country and polarized the party, Rákosi sought to tip the balance of power in the leadership in his favor.[59]

In a few days, encouraged by the fall of Beria, who was his harshest critic in Moscow, Rákosi went on the offensive at a Budapest party *ak-*

---

[59] For an incisive analysis of new evidence on the Soviet-Hungarian linkage, and the role of Beria, see Kramer, "Early Post-Stalin Succession Struggle." Well before Kramer's discovery of significant archival sources, specialists studying the Soviet leadership often relied on "Kremlinology," i.e., speculation about the struggle for power in Moscow. It was an exercise hazardous to pursue—and hazardous to dismiss. The case of Beria, as described by Daniel Bell, is pertinent here: "While open to easy satire, it is the supercilious who mock it at their peril, as the *New York Post* once learned [in mid-June 1953] when it scoffed at the speculations arising from the fact that all the Bolshevik leaders *but* Beria had appeared on masse at the Bolshoi Ballet. 'Perhaps Beria doesn't like ballet,' said the *Post* archly. Perhaps he didn't, but we never had the opportunity to find out, for two days later [on June 27, 1953] came the announcement that Beria had been arrested as a traitor." Daniel Bell, "Ten Theories in Search of Reality: The Prediction of Soviet Behavior in the Social Sciences," in *Soviet Conduct in World Affairs: A Selection of Readings*, comp. Alexander Dallin (New York: Columbia University Press, 1960), 12.

tiv to counter Nagy's message.[60] Broadcast live, the country could hear not only his rigid speech but also the party loyalists' rhythmic applause after Rákosi indirectly rebutted Nagy's positions. Neither the party's well-tested objectives nor its slogans would change, Rákosi asserted, as he called for renewed "vigilance"—a word from Stalin's lexicon—against those he regarded as Hungary's foreign and domestic enemies. He even humored his audience by reaffirming the party's decision to abandon the practice of blacklisting kulaks, so that, after a well-timed pause, he could add: "But a kulak remains a kulak, with or without a list." General laughter and applause followed.[61]

Nagy fought back. Both the substance and the style of what he said on July 4, in his first speech as prime minister to the Hungarian Parliament, differed from the usual sermonlike, celebratory rhetoric people had been accustomed to hearing in Communist Hungary.[62] He drew on the specifics of the June resolution regarding agriculture and "socialist legality," but he also developed new themes as he promised patience toward religious beliefs and respect for intellectuals. No doubt infuriating Rákosi, Nagy deflated Communist rhetoric about the country's "historic" achievements. "Let's not build castles in the air," he declared.[63]

This forerunner to the Prague Spring of 1968 and Mikhail S. Gorbachev's perestroika, Nagy's New Course was experiencing considerable resistance even before it could get off the ground—but it was still moving ahead. With some political help coming from such unlikely sources as Gerő, Rákosi's trusted lieutenant with excellent Soviet ties,

---

[60] *Szabad Nép*, July 12, 1953.

[61] Ibid.

[62] *Szabad Nép*, July 5, 1953.

[63] U.S. reaction to Nagy's speech was skeptical. The leading, and authoritative, foreign policy columnist of the day, C. L. Sulzberger of the *New York Times* commented in the paper's July 7, 1953, issue: "We have to wonder what is meant by the current change in Hungarian dogmas that Prime Minister Imre Nagy has proclaimed: just another NEP [New Economic Policy] or a tactical break, and not a strategic change?" In its news account published the day before, the same paper reported, however, that "Nagy's promise of a better life has made a deep impression on the man in the street." As described in more detail in chapter 3 below official Washington was indifferent toward Nagy. In his comprehensive and important study, Bennett Kovrig noted that "the State Department gave no official indication that Imre Nagy represented a more liberal, quasi-Titoist brand of communism and therefore deserved treatment different from that accorded to Rákosi; Hungary and the other satellites continued to be viewed as undifferentiated appendages of the Soviet Union." Kovrig, *The Myth of Liberation: East-Central Europe in U.S. Diplomacy and Politics since 1941* (Baltimore: Johns Hopkins University Press, 1973), 146.

and from Farkas, too, Nagy began to implement the government's program. Within a year and a half, more than 700 unprofitable, unproductive, and unpopular collective farms folded (from 5,100 to 4,381); the number of its members fell from 370,000 to 230,000, which was a 39 percent drop.[64] Using central directives, the government lowered investments in heavy industry by an extraordinary 40 percent in 1954, compared with 1953; at the same time, living standards rose by about 15 percent. Modest wage increases benefited 928,000 people or about 10 percent of the population. The government began to issue permits and extended small loans to tailors, plumbers, electricians, and others to open and operate private shops—so long as they hired fewer than three employees.

Nagy's measures aimed mainly at increased consumption to appease the population; he did not introduce any structural changes in property relations that would have reduced the role of the state in the economy which—notably industry, trade, and even the repair sectors—continued to function on the basis of central planning. As Nagy succeeded in introducing some limited incentives for productive collective farms and individual peasants, too, he appeared to emulate Lenin's—and Bukharin's—New Economic Policy of the 1920s. Though these economic measures were popular, the country's economic bureaucracy resisted their full implementation.[65]

Politically, Nagy was not successful in elevating like-minded comrades into leading party positions. Only in early 1954 was he able to promote two old Muscovites, Zoltán Vas and Zoltán Szántó, who had been slighted or felt slighted by Rákosi in recent years. Vas worked on economic issues at the Council of Ministers, while Szántó took charge of relations with the press. They sided with Nagy less because they supported the New Course than because Rákosi and the faction around him had not sufficiently appreciated them.[66] Still, despite the lack of

---

[64] See Ignác Romsics, *Magyarország története a XX. században* [Hungary's history in the 20th century] (Budapest: Osiris, 1999), 378.

[65] For an early if altogether too brief assessment of Nagy's economic policy, see Nicolas Spulber, *The Economics of Communist Eastern Europe* (Cambridge, Mass.: MIT Press, 1957), passim.

[66] After the 1956 revolution's defeat, both Vas and Szántó were kidnapped, together with Nagy and others, and taken to Snagov, a party resort outside of Bucharest in Romania, where they remained under house arrest till 1958. There, Vas dissociated himself from some of Nagy's activities while Szántó—

political allies, Nagy managed to declare a partial amnesty that was to free 748,000 people (mainly small-time criminals), and he made some headway in curtailing the activities of the secret police. By the fall of 1953, several notorious internment and hard labor camps as well as one for middle-class deportees in Hortobágy, in eastern Hungary, were closed down. By November, 15,761 people were released and about 1,170 foreign prisoners, many of whom were held for unauthorized border crossing, were freed and about to be expelled to Western countries. The police were ordered to stop surveillance of some 4,500 people,[67] although the number of secret police informers did not significantly decline.[68]

The rehabilitation of prominent Hungarians began in 1954. The release of anticommunists and noncommunists from prison, such as Anna Kéthly of the Social Democratic Party, occurred soon after with the discharge of Communists jailed in the late 1940s and early 1950s on trumped-up charges as Titoists, imperialist agents, or traitors of the working class. Though the main Communist victim of these show trials, László Rajk, was dead, others almost literally rising from the dead after years of torture had high-ranking friends in the party. Their reappearance on the streets of Budapest was something of a sensation. What would happen to those, notably Rákosi himself, who had sent them to jail? Would their rehabilitation entail a process leading to their readmittance to the party? Would they get their old jobs back? Would such formerly leading figures of the party as Kádár, Losonczy, Donáth, and Gyula Kállai—once all Central Committee members and in Kádár's case also a Politburo and Secretariat member—emerge from years of imprisonment as Communists? If so, would these four, in particular, join Imre Nagy in his struggle against the Stalinist apparatus? Would their political presence further divide the party and perhaps the security

---

a "friend" from the time they were both in Moscow in the 1930s—altogether betrayed Nagy and in 1957–58 formally testified against him.

[67] *Iratok az igazságszolgáltatás történetéhez*, vol. 2, 586–95.

[68] The number of informers was as follows: 1951: 34,626; 1952: 40,842; 1953: 45,521; 1954: 35,900; January 1955: 37,174; January 1956: 35,793. Interestingly, all the informers were Hungarian citizens. The secret police could not find a single foreigner then working at a Western embassy in Budapest to spy for the Hungarians. Erzsébet Kajári, "Az egységesített belügyminisztérium államvédelmi tevékenysége, 1953–1956" [State Security Activity of the Unified Ministry of Internal Affairs, 1953–1956], in *Államvédelem a Rákosi-korszakban* [State security in the Rákosi era], ed. György Gyarmati (Budapest: Történeti Hivatal, 2000), 166–67.

forces as well? The attentive public in Budapest was buzzing with stories, rumors, and speculation.

Trying to deflect attention from his own role, Rákosi had earlier removed and jailed Gábor Péter, the secret police chief, but that in itself did not fully satisfy the newly rehabilitated Communists; after all, the party was still led by the Stalinist Old Guard. Nonetheless, when offered a chance, almost all rejoined the party and continued to believe in the virtues of a socialist society and in the prospect of changing the system from within. Some had serious reservations, some joined up with Nagy, some were too ill to accept a new job—and most, like Kádár, positioned themselves between Nagy and Rákosi. Even though they presently owed their rehabilitation and freedom to Nagy and his New Course, they remembered that at the time of their arrest between 1949 and 1951 Nagy had not raised his voice on their behalf.[69] For this reason, and because they neither trusted nor felt comfortable in the company of pro-Nagy intellectuals, Kádár and Kállai, for example, did not automatically reject Rákosi's various overtures.[70] After his release, Kádár corresponded with Rákosi and then met him in person too on several occasions. However, during one of their encounters, almost certainly on May 14, 1955, Rákosi, devious as ever, built up Kádár's ego by telling him that only he could unite the party's warring factions, but then asked him to sign a statement that he, Kádár, was responsible for his own arrest and imprisonment. Outraged by the offer, Kádár is said to have marched out of Rákosi's office, shouting incredible, unusually vulgar obscenities.[71] Yet, after Nagy's loss of his positions in early 1955,

---

[69] What was left of a five-man committee dealing with issues of state security decided the arrest of Kádár and Kállai on April 20, 1951. Of its five original members, Árpád Szakasits was in jail under a life sentence while Kádár, about to be arrested, was of course "absent" from the meeting. The three remaining members—Rákosi, Gerő, and Farkas, together with József Révai, another Muscovite—made the decision that was submitted to the Politburo the next morning. While Imre Nagy was not in the Politburo from September 1949 through February 1951, he was a full member when Kádár, Losonczy, and Kállai were arrested and sentenced and when Donáth was sentenced. He was presumably also present when the Politburo approved Kádár's and Kállai's arrest. Rákosi immediately cabled Suslov in Moscow about the Politburo's consent, claiming it was "unanimous." The relevant archival documents about this complicated and indeed convoluted "case" against Kádár and the other home Communists—a 700-page account that reads like a courtroom drama featuring a bunch of psychopaths—are cited, explained, and reprinted in *Kádár János bírái előtt: Egyszer fent, egyszer lent, 1949–1956* [János Kádár before his judges: Once up, once down, 1949–1956] (Budapest: Osiris, 2001) ed., with an introductory study, by László Varga.

[70] Interview with Kállai on May 9, 1991.

[71] Many Hungarians claim their language is second only to Yiddish in the richness and variety of its

both Kádár and Kállai accepted positions in the party and the government, respectively, thanks to arrangements made by Rákosi.

Others reacted differently.

Donáth, who left jail full of suspicion toward everyone, initially did not side with Nagy, Rákosi, or Kádár.[72] Because he used to head Rákosi's secretariat, he could not forgive his old boss for sending him to jail and subjecting him to years of cruel imprisonment. Nor could he warm up to Nagy (with whom he met at Nagy's initiative in the fall of 1954 and agreed on the need for more party democracy), because their fights behind closed doors in the late 1940s about agrarian policy were still

---

curses. In this case, Kádár's curse—"*A kopasz kurva anyádat*"—combined Rákosi's baldness with his mother as a whore, or, perhaps, referred to Rákosi's mother as a bald whore. (For more nuanced interpretations, curious readers are advised to consult a Hungarian-speaking friend who is not easily embarrassed.) My source for the story is Lieutenant General József Szalma, then head of the Department of Investigation at the secret police, who was in charge of Kádár's rehabilitation and who escorted his client to party headquarters where this meeting with Rákosi took place; interview with Szalma on July 10, 1991, in the southern Hungarian city of Makó (where, having abandoned his Budapest apartment, he lived practically in hiding after the collapse of communism). I thank Tibor Zinner for arranging this interview and accompanying me to see General Szalma. There is indirect confirmation of Szalma's account in Kádár's letter to the Hungarian Politburo, dated May 16, 1955, in which Kádár referred to a meeting he had had with Rákosi two days earlier. In the letter, Kádár complained about his treatment since his release in 1954—even threatening to become a physical worker again—and added this: "The Politburo must believe that I did not wish, I did not make the 'Kádár affair.' It is hard for me to understand why . . . I must suffer even today detrimental discrimination for an affair in which, as everyone knows, I was assigned the role of a suffering victim [*szenvedö alany*]." In other words, Kádár refused to take responsibility for his own victimization. For the text of this letter, see *Kádár János bírái elött*, ed. Varga, 651–52.

[72] Lack of sleep in barely lit cells and lack of food, combined with years of isolation and torture, made all of the released fearful and suspicious. Donáth was only more so than others. I first met him, in the summer of 1977, in his apartment in the Buda hills. What I recall is how circumspect he was, how little he said. His suspiciousness was very much in evidence; not only had he checked me out very carefully prior to our meeting but during the conversation we sat in an almost completely dark room, with the shutters closed and the curtains drawn. He said his eyes were still sensitive to light. I remember wondering if he was trying to recreate some of the conditions of his old, often dark prison cell. I learned from his wife that he never talked to her about his experiences in jail. He told her to talk to others about anything she wanted to talk about—so long as she never criticized the Soviet Union. He kept repeating to her that which was so obvious to all except a fanatical true believer that he once was: "Just remember we're living in occupied territory [*megszállt ország*]." Interview with Éva Bozóky, Donáth's widow, on May 14, 1991. The following year, I was visited in New York by one of their sons, László Donáth, a Protestant minister turned Socialist politician after the collapse of communism (and a member of the Hungarian Parliament as of 2005). When I told him I was having trouble reconciling his father's role as a dogmatic, hard-line aide to Rákosi in the late 1940s with his subsequent role as the leader of the so-called democratic opposition in the 1980s, Donáth bravely told me not to worry too much: "Those who knew him in the 1980s as the fine democrat he became should also know of his early life when he was duped and deluded." When I told him I was also having trouble taking his father, Imre Nagy, and others off the pedestal by writing candidly about their earlier, and awful, misdeeds and not just about their subsequent heroic deeds, the young Donáth, speaking like a minister rather than a politician, urged me to tell the whole truth. I was, and remain, grateful to this brave and wise man for his encouragement.

haunting the relationship. Nor could Donáth identify with Kádár, his close friend from the days of the small anti-Nazi resistance. In this case, it was apparently a personal grudge rather than ideology that kept them apart.[73] In early 1956, Donáth finally did make up his mind, as he became a key political tactician in the Nagy camp.

Only Losonczy of these four newly rehabilitated, once-prominent Communists stood solidly with Nagy from the beginning. The two had met on November 22, 1954, at a government resort in Mátraháza, and they hit it off very well. Losonczy was too ill to return to his old job at the Ministry of Culture or to take up any other position; he needed rest. He was being treated at a sanatorium for serious physical ailments and psychological disorders developed in jail. Only in 1955, after Nagy's ouster, did Losonczy feel well enough to become an active leader of that informal circle of disappointed Communists devoted to Nagy's return to power. Much later, during the last days of the revolution, Nagy asked him to serve as minister of state, or one of his two deputies, in the cabinet.[74]

Because Nagy could not count either on the party apparatus or the government bureaucracies, or even the newly released Communists, he reached out to two other constituencies. One was an unusually large group of writers, journalists, and university students who joined his cause on their own and early on. The other source of support was the

---

[73] In 1944, when Kádár was on the run and feared arrest as a Communist, Donáth gave him shelter and saved his life, but Kádár, according to Donáth, did not sufficiently appreciate the gesture. It should be added, however, that years later, in 1958, when Kádár was Hungary's new leader and Donáth was tried with Imre Nagy for counterrevolutionary activities in 1956, Donáth was sent to a Communist jail "only" for twelve years instead of being hanged with Nagy—almost certainly because of Kádár's personal intervention on his behalf.

[74] The extraordinary drama and tragedy of Losonczy's life and death is beyond the scope of this book. Suffice it to say that he was in a Communist jail first from 1951 to 1954, and then again, after the revolution, until his death in December 1957. The second time around, having lost not only his faith as a true believer but his mind as well, he volunteered to confess to unimaginable and totally untrue charges against himself and also harmed himself seriously and systematically whenever he was left alone in his cell. For weeks he refused to eat; he had to be force-fed. The prison authorities did not hospitalize him. If they did not kill him, they appeared to be pleased to let him die. The written evidence of what he wrote, drew, said, and—especially—did to himself, which is the single most gruesome account of Communist Hell I have ever encountered, surfaced immediately after 1989 from the archives of the operative division of the secret police. Losonczy's files—the Operative Documents, in some sixteen volumes—are in AHMIA, V-150.000. For a comprehensive account of Losonczy's life that delicately sidesteps the details of his self-mortifying acts committed under the watchful eyes of his jailors in 1957, see György Kövér, *Losonczy Géza 1917–1957* [Géza Losonczy 1917–1957] (Budapest: 1956-os Intézet, 1998).

long-dormant Patriotic People's Front, which Nagy tried to bring to life in the fall of 1954.

As for the dissenting writers, the primary vehicle for their outcry against the Stalinist past and the Rákosi crowd was *Irodalmi Újság* (Literary Gazette), the official weekly of the Writers' Association. Most of the writers were not only party members but also loyal true believers; they now sought, and called for, "socialist renewal." They had joined the party after World War II out of conviction rather than opportunism. Some did not know of the wave of terror that had swept the Soviet Union, others seemed not to want to believe it, and still others managed to tell themselves that the Hungarian version of socialism would be different. That is why so many found it possible to idolize Stalin and revere Rákosi.

Stalin's death and Nagy's rise made a difference—and opened many eyes. "Up until now I had lived on the topmost heights, and from there everything I saw seemed good and bright, and my favoring fortune [*kedvező sorsom*] drew a curtain across my eyes, hiding harsher reality." That was how a young poet, Sándor Csoóri, revealed his inner reaction to Nagy's New Course in August 1953. A few months later, publishing his commentary in the same weekly, István Örkény went further. Defiantly, he wrote: "It was not our intention to write books that offer only a distorted picture of the world, books as hollow as an empty nut. . . . Yet we have written such books. . . . And what should the mission of the writer mean now? . . . that the writer, and no one else, has responsibility for what he writes. That he may experiment and stop being a mere illustrator."[75]

Because their faith had been so blind, the writers turned into angry and unrelenting opponents of Communist orthodoxy. They blamed themselves for having been deceived by Stalinism, and they blamed the party leaders—except Nagy—for having misled them. Initially, their support for Nagy's program was cautious. Then, by 1954 and especially after Nagy's dismissal in 1955 (see chapter 4), they began to ask more pointed questions and make more critical points. *Irodalmi Újság*, in par-

---

[75] Both quotations are from György Litván, "Mítoszok és legendák 1956-ról" [Myths and Legends about 1956], in *Évkönyv 2000* [Yearbook 2000] (Budapest: 1956 Institute, 2001), 29. Kenneth McRobbie translated the Csoóri poem.

ticular, was rapidly turning into a forum for a pro-Nagy platform, so much so that the authorities fired one editor after another. The atmosphere was changing so much and so fast that, as yesterday's loyalists turned into today's dissidents, no competent editor could be found who was sufficiently responsive to the party's diktat.[76]

As Nagy became the writers' banner, the Patriotic People's Front was to offer political space primarily to nonparty people, especially in the countryside. It was to be an institution working within the one-party system and yet at the same time pose an alternative to the party. By the time its congress opened on October 23, 1954—exactly two years to the day before the 1956 revolution would begin—Nagy had fought hard to make it possible for individuals to be allowed to sign up as members, but the Politburo rejected his plan; it was to be a meeting place for existing and thus party-controlled social organizations. Reverting to his old views about gradualism and about the need to build a socialist society with broad support, Nagy had argued, in vain, that "intellectual, petit-bourgeois and non-proletarian strata have a part in the building of socialism . . . [that] cannot be built without their cooperation." He added that "even the slightest possibilities must be utilized to win over a mass of allies, no matter whether they are provisional, undecided, uncertain, or unreliable."[77] The Old Guard in the Politburo did not endorse this view. Nor could Nagy staff the Front with his people, although Ferenc Jánosi, his son-in-law, was eventually chosen as the

---

[76] Almost all the Communist intellectuals who shed their faith did so in 1953, after Stalin's death, and some even as late as February 1956, the time of the Twentieth Congress of the Soviet Communist Party that unveiled Stalin's crimes and debunked the Stalin myth. In Hungary, one of the few who had begun to develop doubts about the Communist system earlier was Miklós Vásárhelyi, one of Nagy's four or five closest advisers. *"Itt valami nem stimmel"* [Something doesn't add up here] was one of his favorite expressions then and later too. In that era of terror, he shared his doubts with only one or two friends he knew from his youth in Debrecen. I discussed his own awakening and many other issues with him on dozens of occasions, starting in 1982 in New York (when and where he wrote the initial version of his memoirs in an office we shared at Columbia University) and throughout the 1990s in Budapest. I am grateful to him for our friendship and for his unparalleled insights, and I cherish his memory. The similarity of our views on many issues notwithstanding, I do not presume to assume his agreement with some of my interpretations, notably my portrayal of Imre Nagy's political skills (of which he had a somewhat more positive opinion). Regarding Vásárhelyi's early realization of the "Communist God" that failed, see György Radó's testimony in prison on May 23, 1957, in AHMIA, V-150.009. For a collection of Vásárhelyi's autobiographical interviews and essays, see his *Ellenzékben* [In opposition] (Budapest: Szabad Tér Kiadó, 1989).

[77] As quoted in Ferenc A. Váli, *Rift and Revolt in Hungary: Nationalism versus Communism* (Cambridge, Mass.: Harvard University Press, 1961), 125.

Front's secretary general. And he was able to make *Magyar Nemzet* the Front's official daily with a strong pro-Nagy orientation.

Still, the congress itself turned into a momentous and indeed fateful event for one reason and one reason alone, and that was Nagy's speech. He spoke about the "common heartbeat" of 9.5 million Hungarians, not about the class struggle. He spoke about the Front being the nation's conscience, not the party. He spoke about the people, not the proletariat, being in charge of the country. True, he did attack Hungary's foreign and domestic enemies, and he did mention the party's important role. But he addressed his audience as if he were running for office in a competitive political system, soliciting the delegates' support and employing clever rhetoric in the process: "I ask: Will the Patriotic People's Front, will you, honored delegates, extend the government the kind of support and confidence that is necessary for overcoming the hardships, for the consistent implementation of the [New Course]?"

As the auditorium exploded with a resounding YES, Nagy added that such an "uplifting expression" of support is going to multiply his government's determination "to fight with the people and for the people—through thick and thin."[78] Broadcast live on radio, the speech appeared to have an electrifying impact. Nothing like this had been heard in years. Instead of using party jargon and reciting the empty slogans usually voiced on such occasions, Nagy found the right tone to speak as one Hungarian to another; he was serious and inspiring, even inspirational. He projected idealism and hope for a better Hungarian future. He felt so relieved and happy after the speech that he even broke into a dance of *csárdás* with a delegate, which did not go unnoticed because Communist leaders seldom if ever allowed themselves to do anything spontaneously. His confident patriotism roused both his spirit, and his audience's, as well.

By reaching out to the public at large, Nagy showed himself to be a genuine and effective leader—a quality he had seldom shown before (or later, for that matter). Out of calculation or desperation, or both, he wanted the Front's congress to give his New Course a new lease on life. As it happened, the congress was Nagy's last hurrah. Even though his

---

[78] The speech is reprinted in *In Memoriam Nagy Imre* ed. Áron Tóbiás (Budapest: Szabad Tér Kiadó, 1989), 62–72.

speech had been apparently approved by the Politburo, which might have been a trap, Rákosi and his acolytes managed to find fault with his emphasis on the common needs and common cause of 9.5 million Hungarians. Nagy did not stress the "leading role" of the proletariat or of the Soviet Union, the importance of the class struggle and the five-year plan, and he even failed to relate the achievements of the people's democracy. In his critics' view, Nagy's unabashed patriotism was but a dangerous exploitation of nationalist sentiments.

As on several previous occasions in his political career, Nagy was seen, again, as a right-wing deviationist. By the end of November 1954 the hardliners began to make the point publicly that the New Course had gone too far. In his diary, Yuri Andropov, the Soviet ambassador to Hungary, recorded his concern about deep divisions and chaotic circumstances in the Hungarian leadership.[79] In January 1955, the Soviet Politburo was ready to demote Nagy (rather than oust him)—if he were willing to admit his faults. The Kremlin asked him to follow the example of Malenkov, Nagy's main patron, and accept a lesser position. Nagy declined (for details, see chapter 4). It took Rákosi and the Soviet Politburo three months to consummate Nagy's dismissal as head of the government.

His dismissal was a function of changes in the Soviet leadership, which included attacks on Malenkov's priorities that resembled Nagy's New Course and Khrushchev's victory over Malenkov. Rákosi, who had persisted against Nagy even when Moscow still favored the prime minister, finally out maneuvered his nemesis. But then why did Nagy not accept the job of deputy prime minister as Malenkov did in the Soviet Union? If he had done so, could he have lasted longer and made a difference?

Nagy himself never answered these questions directly in any of the twenty-five hard-hitting essays he drafted during the summer of 1955[80] or in his two lengthy studies written while under Romanian house arrest in the winter of 1956–57.[81] Nor, in conversations with his sup-

---

[79] Magdolna Baráth, ed., *Szovjet nagyköveti iratok Magyarországról 1953–1956: Kiseljov és Andropov titkos jelentései* [Soviet ambassadors' documents about Hungary 1953–1956: Kiselyov's and Andropov's secret reports] (Budapest: Napvilág Kiadó, 2002).

[80] Nagy, *On Communism.*

[81] One of the manuscripts completed in Romanian exile in Snagov in early 1957 amounts to an autobiography that ends before his encounter with communism in World War I. Nothing proves more con-

porters in 1955 or 1956, did Nagy raise the possibility that he should have accepted a lesser position in January 1955 to remain politically viable. Given his stubborn streak and hatred toward the Stalinist diehards in the Hungarian Politburo, especially Rákosi himself, his choice was hardly surprising. What was surprising was that, for the first time in his political life, Nagy failed to exercise self-criticism. If this was mainly or exclusively a rational choice, that means that he was anticipating post-Stalin changes in the Soviet Union and in the Soviet bloc to accelerate, in which case—he might have thought—the Kremlin would have to turn to him once again. After all, who else could save the "cause of socialism" in Hungary for the Soviet Union? If, on the other hand, his choice was rooted in emotions, then he must have reached the boiling point in his relations with his comrades not only in Budapest but to a lesser extent in Moscow, too, where the struggle for power trumped all serious consideration of what to do about revitalizing the "cause of socialism" at home and abroad.

The testimony of his powerful and polemical essays in *On Communism*, and of his two studies written during Romanian house arrest, suggests that he had only contempt toward Hungary's unreconstructed Stalinists; but he did not give up completely on the Soviet leaders and he did not think that they had given up on him. He correctly assessed the political situation in Moscow as fluid and still changeable, believing that the Kremlin would keep him in reserve and very possibly turn to him one day. For this reason, he decided to turn down the Kremlin's offer—he could not serve as *deputy* prime minister in a government dominated by Rákosi—but he also declined to organize the intellectuals' growing anti-Stalinist campaign. If anything, he tried to restrain them.

---

clusively that Nagy knew the end was near than the subtitle: "1896-195 . . . ?" For a remarkably beautiful edition of this work, see Imre Nagy, *Viharos emberöltő, 1896–195 . . . ?* [Stormy generation, 1896–195 . . . ?] (Budapest: Nagy Imre Alapítvány, 2002). The other manuscript from his Snagov exile circulated in Budapest after the collapse of communism in 1989, but it has not been published; Nagy's daughter has not allowed its publication. (A Hungarian edition is finally scheduled for publication in 2006.) Having read the long manuscript, which occasionally resembles Nagy's various essays published in English in 1957 under the title *On Communism*, my impression is that Nagy's daughter did not wish readers to see that her father remained true to Marxism-Leninism even after the Kremlin had crushed the 1956 revolution. A slightly abbreviated text—together with his numerous letters and appeals as well as the record of his conversations and other activities in Snagov as recorded by the notorious Securitate, the Romanian secret service—has become available in Romanian as *Nagy Imre, Însemnări de la Snagov: Corespondenţă, rapoarte, convorbiri* [Imre Nagy, Notes from Snagov: Correspondence, reports, conversations], ed. Ileana Ioanid (Bucharest: Polirom, 2004).

He often told his more pro-Western allies, such as Miklós Gimes, not to favor "bourgeois" views.[82] Though Nagy's convictions did not at all reflect the party's hard line, of course, his behavior did reflect a true Leninist's political mentality.

Yet Nagy saw that the alternative to reform is not Stalinism but an anticommunist revolution. In an essay written in December 1955, which he addressed to the leaders of both the Hungarian and the Soviet parties and shared with a few of his closest supporters (also quoted at the beginning of this chapter), Nagy wrote prophetically about where Hungary was heading—toward a multiparty system if not toward a revolution:

> Today, probably a return to the policy of the New Course and the application of the June [1953] principles to the economic, political, and social life of the nation could still check the growing crisis and avert catastrophe. But it is doubtful whether a return to the June principles would suffice as a solution tomorrow . . . there is a danger that the masses, having lost their faith, will reject both the June way and the Communist Party, and *it will become necessary to make a much greater retreat in order to keep the situation under control.*[83]

At that time, neither the Hungarian nor the Soviet leaders agreed with Nagy's analysis. They certainly did not heed his advice. They failed to appreciate Nagy's wisdom, and they failed to recognize the centrality of his position in and out of power—and they kept making one critical error after another. The Kremlin's first mistake was to install Nagy in June 1953, without compelling the Hungarian party to back him. The Kremlin's second mistake was to dismiss Nagy in early 1955 and return power to a group of Stalinists that offered no remedies for this increasingly unsteady and tense country's growing problems. The Kremlin's third mistake was to leave him free in 1955–56 and let him be seen, and thus make him appear to be, an alternative to Rákosi and his acolytes.

---

[82] There is a striking resemblance between Nagy's attitude in the mid-1950s toward Gimes and others flirting with Western-style democracy on the one hand and Michael S. Gorbachev's attitude in the middle and late 1980s toward Alexander Yakovlev and Eduard Shevardnadze. I thank Mark Kramer for calling my attention to this point.

[83] Nagy, *On Communism*, 49; italics added. To Nagy, having to make "a much greater retreat" meant the adoption of Western-style political and economic pluralism.

By supporting and then dropping Nagy, the Soviet leaders awakened Hungary's intellectual elite and united it against Stalinism, paving the way for a furious challenge to the Soviet empire. *By stifling within-system reform, the Kremlin made revolution all but inevitable; by removing Nagy from power, the Kremlin made him the coming revolt's only conceivable, if altogether unlikely, inadvertent, and—sad to say—ill-equipped leader.*

3

Washington and Budapest before the Explosion

> The Vice President commented that it wouldn't be
> an unmixed evil, from the point of view of U.S.
> interest, if the Soviet iron fist were to come down
> again on the Soviet bloc, though on balance it
> would be more desirable, of course, if the present
> liberalizing trend in relations between the Soviet
> Union and its satellites continued.
>
> —*Richard Nixon, at a top-secret National Security Council meeting,*
> *July 12, 1956*

· 1 ·

Reading White House, Department of State, or Central Intelligence Agency (CIA) documents once classified as secret or top secret, it is easy to mistake intention with implementation and impact. All postwar documents containing decisions about what to do in or toward Central and Eastern Europe suggest that American policy was dynamic and confrontational. They indicate that, years before Republicans called for the liberation of Eastern Europe and the rollback of Soviet power, the Harry Truman administration had also made far-reaching plans for freeing the

Soviet satellites by employing a variety of overt and covert means short of open warfare.

Yet the plans, detailed and carefully considered, did not translate into practice. No more did the intentions reflected in these documents reveal actual policy than do most New Year's resolutions identify results. Under Truman and even more under Dwight Eisenhower, what American officials intended to do was one thing; what they did and what they accomplished was something else. Contrary to the popular imagination, they were doing far less than they planned or claimed to be doing. This was particularly so with respect to Hungary.

Aside from such isolated acts and measures as the attempted (and failed) invasion of Albania in 1949, conceived and led jointly by the United Kingdom and the United States, and very extensive and very significant broadcasting in several languages into Eastern Europe via Radio Free Europe, the United States did not, because it could not, implement most of its plans. There was a gap not only between what the politicians publicly said and what they in fact did—between proclamations of a grand crusade against communism, on the one hand, and the reality of little or no follow-up, on the other. There was also a gap between a series of once top-secret National Security Council (NSC) policy guidelines aimed at undermining Soviet power and the reality of putting them into practice. The "first gap"—between official sloganeering and meager deeds—is well known and well documented.[1] Far less well known and less appreciated is the "second gap": that while the NSC adopted detailed directives in great secrecy about penetrating the Iron Curtain, the operatives in the field could not implement them.

To understand what happened, it is helpful to view U.S. foreign policy toward Eastern Europe in general and Hungary in particular through three prisms: what the United States *said*, what it *decided*, and what it *did*.[2] First, public statements, particularly during the Eisenhower

---

[1] By far the best study prior to the opening of the archives is Bennett Kovrig, *The Myth of Liberation: East-Central Europe in U.S. Diplomacy and Politics since 1941* (Baltimore: Johns Hopkins University Press, 1973). For the first postwar years, see also Geir Lundestad, *The American Non-Policy towards Eastern Europe 1943–1947* (New York: Humanities Press, 1975). Both titles are telling. For other sources, see the footnotes in this chapter and this book's selected bibliography.

[2] There is, of course, a fourth prism and that is the *impact of policy* on the target country or countries. With the opening of once-secret archives, including Hungary's, it is now possible to study this aspect as well.

administration, portrayed optimistic prospects for the rollback of communism. They meant to highlight a very serious national security concern—Soviet aggression in Europe—and a moral concern—the denial of freedom to the peoples of Eastern Europe—in order to mobilize the American public in simple and morally appealing terms for the difficult tasks ahead. Second, there were secret NSC decisions, gradually declassified since the 1970s, which—taken together—showed extensive plans about the nature and scope of American assistance for the peaceful liberation of Eastern Europe. The third part of policy entailed neither words openly uttered nor decisions secretly made, but actions: what the United States did in fact do in Eastern Europe during the postwar decade, and specifically in and toward Hungary before the 1956 revolt, to realize its professed goals.

Classified information about U.S. actions, released at my request from the CIA's operational files, prompts the surprising conclusion that the United States often resembled a Big Bad Wolf huffing and puffing rather than a serious superpower depleting its Communist enemy's strength. Clearly, official Washington espoused a tall tale during the first decade of the Cold War: that the United States was effectively engaged in a massive effort to change the status quo in Soviet-dominated Eastern Europe. Democrats promoted this tale not only because of national security concerns stemming from Joseph Stalin's policies but also because of the need to counter Republican charges about their alleged inability to understand the gravity of the Soviet challenge. They wanted to show that they understood the Communist threat and had dealt with it. The Republicans, to prove their superior resolve, outbid the Democrats from the beginning, especially after 1952, by advancing publicly the "doctrine" of liberation; it was to demonstrate that they knew better what to do in the face of Communist aggression.[3] Meanwhile,

---

[3] "Liberation" was a frequently used part of the 1952 Republican presidential campaign. John Foster Dulles, earlier a foreign policy adviser in the Truman administration, declared in 1952 that liberation would succeed if the United States made it "publicly known that it wants and expects liberation to occur." He advanced "liberation" as a "dynamic" alternative to the Truman administration's "static" and "defensive" policy of containment. John Foster Dulles, "A New Foreign Policy: A Policy of Boldness," *Life,* May 19, 1952, 146–48. Arguably, at least one of the goals of these statements was to gain political advantage, especially among voters of Eastern European background. (My colleague, Stephen Szabo of Johns Hopkins University's Paul H. Nitze School of Advanced International Studies, who was born and raised in Cleveland in a Hungarian neighborhood, recalls that "Dulles was the hero of Hungarian ethnics" in the 1950s.) In an important study based on extensive research of intelligence sources

the Soviet Union and its East European acolytes happily corroborated Washington's tale of aggressive U.S. conduct in order to blame American foreign policy—"capitalist encirclement"—for their huge military expenditures, harsh policies, and miserable conditions at home.

In fact, however, America was absent when anticommunist disturbances took place in East Germany[4] and in Czechoslovakia in 1953, and it was also absent in 1956—in Poznan, Warsaw, and Budapest—when Poles and Hungarians took up the cause of freedom. This is not to say that the United States did not matter or that it was a paper tiger. The United States mattered, not because of what Washington did but because of what it assured the East Europeans and others it was doing (but was not). Combining the best techniques of Hollywood with those of Madison Avenue, the United States was offering a product—liberation—it could not deliver. The advertising was misleading, but it convinced the oppressed peoples of Eastern Europe that their cause was America's cause, and it reinforced their Soviet oppressors' belief that in America they had an implacable enemy.

The message emanating from Washington damaged U.S. interests. It helped neither the possible liberation of Eastern Europe nor a possible opening with the Soviet Union after Stalin's death.

Hungary, even more so than other Soviet satellites and the Soviet Union itself, felt the effect of misleading signals because, as noted in this

---

in the Eisenhower administration, Jim Marchio concludes that while the Eisenhower-Dulles policy toward Eastern Europe was flawed, it "went beyond the ethnic ballot box and the 1952 and 1956 presidential elections." See his "Resistance Potential and Rollback: U.S. Intelligence and the Eisenhower Administration's Policies toward Eastern Europe, 1953–56," *Intelligence and National Security,* April 1995, 219–41; the quotation appears on 235. For far more details, see the same author's comprehensive and very-well-documented Ph.D. dissertation, "Rhetoric and Reality: The Eisenhower Administration and Unrest in Eastern Europe, 1953–1959" (American University, 1990). For a critical and systematic study that makes good use of declassified documents about decisionmaking in both the Truman and the Eisenhower administrations, see Gregory Mitrovich, *Undermining the Kremlin: America's Strategy to Subvert the Soviet Bloc, 1947–1956* (Ithaca, N.Y.: Cornell University Press, 2000).

[4] In the aftermath of the June 1953 East German uprising, the U.S. government distributed significant amounts of food to East German citizens. Although the local authorities did their best to make it difficult for anyone to pick up the food packages, more than 5.5 million of them had been distributed by October, when the program ended. See Mark Kramer, "The Early Post-Stalin Succession Struggle and Upheavals in East-Central Europe: Internal-External Linkages in Soviet Policy Making (Part 3)," *Journal of Cold War Studies* 1, no. 3 (Fall 1999): 3–66. Kramer also reports that the Kremlin issued a statement calling the program a "clumsy propaganda maneuver." Cf. Christian F. Ostermann, "Keeping the Post Simmering: The United States and the East German Uprising of 1953," *German Studies Review* 15, no. 2 (Spring 1996): 61–89; and Christian F. Ostermann, ed., *Uprising in East Germany 1953: The Cold War, the German Question, and the First Major Upheaval behind the Iron Curtain* (Budapest: Central European University Press, 2001).

book's introduction, "along with the Balkan satellites, [it] had the lowest priority" for Washington of the states of Central and Eastern Europe.[5] Though the United States kept alive the Hungarians' hopes for freedom and independence, the records show no serious effort to make these hopes come true. Before its full absorption by the CIA in 1952, the innocuously named Office of Policy Coordination (OPC) that was in existence from 1948 to 1952 conducted no covert action operations in Hungary.[6] In 1952 the CIA's Office of Special Operations "had no regularly reporting resident agents inside" Hungary.[7] In the same year, the CIA spoke about several "failed" or "aborted" cross-border missions, noting that "capable agents for such missions were hard to locate." Referring to a few couriers who were apparently or theoretically available, the CIA report ruefully recorded that "their training was too poor to warrant sending them on a sweep mission, requiring a long trip to different points in Hungary."[8] In 1953, as indeed in all other years including 1956, "all [CIA] efforts to obtain and maintain contact with reporting sources in Hungary were unsuccessful."[9]

Hungary's low priority, aside from the country's relative strategic insignificance, was largely due to its location; it was harder to reach than East Germany or Czechoslovakia. Until 1955, the part of Austria that bordered on Hungary was under Soviet military occupation. After 1955,

---

[5] CIA, *Clandestine Service Historical Series (CSHP 323)*, May 1972; parts declassified as MORI DocID: 1161462 in March 2005, Hungary, vol. II: External Operations 1946–1965, 82.

[6] Information from James McCargar, who headed the OPC's Southeast European division, which included Hungary; interview in Washington on June 17, 2005. Information confirmed by Frank Lindsay, who as OPC's assistant director was in charge of all Soviet bloc operations; telephone interview on August 18, 2005.

[7] CIA, *CSHP 323* (see fn. 5 above), vol. 2, 51.

[8] Ibid., 52.

[9] Ibid., 74. Geza Katona, the only CIA official in Budapest from 1952 to 1957 (see chap. 1, fn. 4), recalls that supposedly there were three agents operating in Hungary in the 1953–56 period. He sent them money and forwarded headquarters' instructions to them, but he never met them. Katona did not receive any reports from them either. By 1952 and early 1953, there were such serious doubts about the feasibility of engaging in useful intelligence activities anywhere in the Soviet bloc, and not just in Hungary, that Frank Lindsay (see fn. 6 above) quietly resigned. In an interview with the CIA's Oral History Program on July 26, 2000, Lindsay's 1952 memo was quoted to have warned that the plan for a rollback "of Communists in Eastern Europe wasn't going to work too well." (Parts of the interview were declassified at my request in December 2004 as MORI DocID: 1161457.) Somewhat later, in 1954, the intelligence community's analytical staff issued several National Intelligence Estimates that stressed the futility of trying to support anticommunist resistance groups. For more on Lindsay, see Peter Grose's groundbreaking work, *Operation Rollback: America's Secret War behind the Iron Curtain* (Boston: Houghton Mifflin, 2000), passim.

neutral Austria, which took its treaty commitments seriously, did not welcome American intelligence or paramilitary agents on its soil.[10] Furthermore, few Hungarian exiles hired or encouraged by the United States to enter Hungary via Austria or Yugoslavia in the late 1940s and early 1950s returned to tell what they learned—they just disappeared behind the Iron Curtain. Others, due to Soviet and Hungarian penetration of American military intelligence services, became double agents (though they were often caught and dismissed by U.S. officials).

Unable as it was to rely on either diplomacy or on economic means to accomplish its goals, Washington made intelligence agencies central to its policies; however, these agencies did not consider Hungary a prime target, and in any case their modest efforts turned out to be futile. Radio Free Europe, established in 1951 and financed by the CIA, was the only influential tool of U.S. policy; it made itself present throughout the Soviet bloc, including Hungary. Despite jamming, Radio Free Europe's message of hope was widely heard and widely believed.

This chapter deals with what the United States did in or toward Hungary from the end of World War II to the 1956 revolt. There is little discussion here of Washington's rhetoric, and there is only minimal discussion of policymaking (i.e., directives adopted by the National Security Council and others). Instead, the chapter's primary focus is on what the United States was actually doing in the field.

Section 2 deals with what was probably the only successful U.S. operation in Hungary. It involved James McCargar, who in 1946-47 represented a small and mysterious American intelligence organization in Budapest, nicknamed "The Pond." Section 3, after summarizing key NSC decisions affecting Eastern Europe, notably Hungary, highlights the activities of the Office of Policy Coordination (the CIA's predecessor) and the CIA itself. Section 4 deals with Radio Free Europe and its Hungarian broadcasts and balloon actions in the first half of the 1950s. Section 5 offers a brief analysis of the position of the United States on the eve of the revolt.

---

[10] Austrian officials often closed their eyes to allied use of their territory or airspace. See Michael Gehler, "From Non-Alignment to Neutrality? Austria's Transformation during the First East-West Détente, 1953–1958," *Journal of Cold War Studies* 7, no. 4 (Fall 2005): 104–36.

• 2 •

When James McCargar arrived in Budapest in April 1946 to take up his new position as the U.S. Legation's political officer, Washington had not yet developed a concept of how to deal with Hungary. The fact that he was assigned to go to Budapest was revealing, however. McCargar, who had spent much of World War II in Vladivostok, spoke Russian, a language deemed useful in a country—Hungary—that was occupied by the Red Army and controlled by the Allied Control Commission with Marshal Kliment Voroshilov as its chairman. Yet McCargar also knew that, despite the Soviet occupation, Hungary's future was not fully settled. The free elections of 1945, for example, had produced a government in which Communists—even if secret party members and cooperating noncommunists were added to the list—constituted a minority.

McCargar's job was to reach out to all political players in and out of the government, collect as much information as possible, and submit his reports to the Department of State in Washington. Naturally, those he seemed to cultivate were strongly opposed to the Communists and their unscrupulous modus operandi. Some, such as Zoltán Pfeiffer, a fiercely independent Smallholder politician, were members of the coalition government (he resigned his post as state secretary in the Ministry of Justice on December 31, 1946); others, such as Károly Peyer, a veteran Social Democrat despised by the Communists and by his own party's left-leaning comrades, belonged to the opposition. McCargar also met, and knew well, members of the prewar aristocracy who remained in Hungary after the war and who hoped that a noncommunist Hungary would emerge once a peace treaty was signed (as it was in early 1947) and the Red Army withdrawn (which did not happen).

Three months after his arrival, McCargar assumed a second identity at the request of Leslie Squires, the legation's departing political officer, who was being transferred to South Africa. McCargar took over Squires's covert portfolio as Budapest representative of the Secret Intelligence Branch, known by the initiated few as The Pond, one of several small spy agencies operating during World War II and apparently for a time after the war as well.[11] As Naval Intelligence had trained him

---

[11] Cf. Mark Stout, "The Pond: Running Agents for State, War, and the CIA," *Studies in Intelligence* 48, no. 3 (2004): 69–82.

during the war, McCargar was not a novice—as his penetrating book on the tradecraft of intelligence and on his Hungarian experiences would reveal.[12] At the U.S. Legation, only the man in charge with the rank of minister knew that McCargar wore two hats.

The information McCargar gathered was timely and valuable. He inherited eight "assets" from his predecessor, mostly old aristocrats from the interwar Miklós Horthy regime. As the struggle for power intensified, however, more and more people wanted to share information with the United States in the hope that Washington would speak up and do something for Hungary's endangered anticommunists. By early 1947, they were indeed endangered, but they were also numerous. Four out of five voters had backed noncommunists the last time votes were counted (in late 1945), and yet, supported actively by the Kremlin, the Communists acted as if they owned the country. When it came to staffing the political police, for example, they ignored the coalition formula that prevailed in most departments of the government. Their "coalition partners"—the Smallholders, the Social Democrats, and the National Peasant Party—each delegated only a few representatives to serve at the headquarters of Államvédelmi Osztály (ÁVO, Department

---

[12] His *A Short Course in the Secret War* was first published in 1973; its author was identified with the pseudonym "Christopher Felix." Part 1 of the book, as the *New York Times Book Review* put it, is "the thinking man's spy book," while part 2 deals with McCargar's Hungarian experiences. In the introduction to the second edition (1988), "Felix" revealed his real name; this is the edition I cite, below (New York: Dell, 1988). For the sake of full disclosure, I need to mention that I have known McCargar since 1978, when I sent an inquiry to Doubleday, which published the book's first edition, regarding Christopher Felix's whereabouts. About three months later, when I was not thinking of Felix, my phone rang at Columbia University. A man with a deep voice identified himself as James McCargar, asking what he could do for me. Somewhat irritated by the strange caller, I asked what I could do for him. He continued to tease me by responding that I had written to him and now he was on the line. I said I did not remember writing to a McCargar. Oh, he said, your letter must have been addressed to Christopher Felix, but there is no Christopher Felix because Christopher Felix is James McCargar. Though I did not appreciate his sense of humor at that particular moment, I have since come to appreciate Jim's acute intelligence and integrity. He has also helped me understand a little more about the world of intelligence, of which I knew nothing, and I am grateful to him for his continued interest and help. The next chapter in our dialogue occurred in 1980, when he called me with some good news. The background to this call was his unwillingness up to that point in time to tell me the name of the intelligence organization for which he had worked in Hungary. He told me it was not the CIG (Central Intelligence Group), the CIA, or military intelligence, but he did not tell me what it was, saying its very name was still highly classified. When he called in 1980, he instructed me to go to a bookstore and buy *The Great Inquisitor* by John V. Grombach. I did. The book's back cover identified Grombach as the head of "the Secret Intelligence Branch of the War and State Departments." As Grombach thus revealed the name of the Secret Intelligence Branch, McCargar felt free finally to tell me that he worked for the Secret Intelligence Branch and that Grombach was his boss. For more, including McCargar's summary of my subsequent meeting with Colonel Grombach, see McCargar, *Short Course,* 168–70.

of State Security), in the counties, or in the several Budapest districts, but the Communists in charge gave them insignificant assignments.

One of them, a young social democrat McCargar would later identify in his book as "Edmund," had, like Peyer, developed deep-seated hostility toward the Communists and their far-left socialist alies. Having fought the Nazis in World War II, Edmund believed that pro-Soviet totalitarianism should not be allowed to replace Hungary's pro-German, authoritarian regime, which had ruled the country in the interwar era. In November 1945, with Peyer's concurrence, Edmund joined the postwar political police (which became the notorious ÁVO a year later). As a lieutenant, he headed a small force in a Budapest suburb, using his position to take extensive notes on what he saw and heard. When Edmund took it all to the U.S. Legation, he was welcomed as a volunteer, a pleasant surprise, a "walk-in," who did not know that McCargar was a part-time intelligence officer; all he knew was that McCargar worked for the legation's political section.

Neither Edmund nor any of McCargar's other informants asked for or received any money. They were helpful because they hoped that the United States would support their cause. They pressed McCargar for information on American intentions. They sought to assist the United States in the emerging Cold War, and they sought assistance against the local Communists and their Soviet patrons. Because McCargar himself did not know what to expect from Washington or indeed the West in general, his answers tended to be evasive.

Edmund delivered the legation a goldmine of information. On 160 handwritten pages, he provided McCargar with a detailed floor plan of every nook and cranny of ÁVO's headquarters on 60 Andrássy Street, pinpointing the location of each division; giving the names, responsibilities, and tasks of intelligence officials; and listing even the identities of typists in military intelligence.[13] The report included an inventory of

---

[13] Thanks to Edmund, a copy of the report is in my personal files. McCargar recalls that it was "almost certainly" translated into English in Washington. For a summary, see McCargar, *Short Course*, 202–9. The list of names is reproduced in Róbert Gábor, *Az igazi szociáldemokrácia: Küzdelem a fasizmus és a kommunizmus ellen, 1944–1948* [Genuine social democracy: Struggle against fascism and communism, 1944–1948] (Budapest: Századvég, 1998), 373–81. Despite the reference in the subtitle to the years 1944–48, the book offers an extended discussion of the political police that makes use of archival material and carries the story to the mid-1950s; see pp. 159–91.

noncommunists working for the secret police as informers—and described how they were compelled to cooperate.

The most frequently used method, recalling the Mafia's modus operandi, was to threaten the target with retaliation by the Russians. For example, on March 2, 1947, at midnight, the police cornered László Dernői Kocsis, a gray eminence in the Smallholders' Party, near his apartment. On a quiet street, holding pistols to his chest, they seized him and dragged him to police headquarters. Because Dernői Kocsis was an intimate of Hungary's (Smallholder) president, Zoltán Tildy, the ÁVO wanted information on everything Tildy was doing. As it happened, money did not entice Kocsis to enlist, nor did he agree to cooperate when the police tried to blackmail him by bringing up his right-wing political activities during World War II. Only when Kocsis was told he would be handed over to the Soviet Military Police and charged with participation in an anti-Soviet "conspiracy" did he put his signature on the dotted line. Fear of being taken to Siberia did it. Kocsis remained on the ÁVO's payroll for years to come.[14]

Using essentially the same technique, ÁVO successfully "recruited" even a member of the Hungarian Cabinet. In March 1947, officers from the political police visited in his home the minister of information, József Bognár, a prominent Smallholder economist and politician, and told him they had conclusive evidence of his part in a "conspiracy" against "new Hungary." They showed fabricated confessions to this effect by Béla Kovács, the Smallholders' Party's secretary general, who was arrested and taken to the Soviet Union a month earlier as an anti-Soviet "conspirator." When threatened with the same fate, Bognár signed on and became a high-level informer.[15]

The second half of 1947 was particularly difficult for McCargar. According to most historians, it was in 1947 when pluralism in the shadow of Soviet occupation gave way to one-party rule and thus the post-

---

[14] Gábor, *Az igazi szociáldemokrácia*, 165.

[15] Ibid., 168. A gifted man, Bognár stayed on as minister of trade in the Stalinist era, but then he also joined Imre Nagy's cabinet during the 1956 revolt. After the revolution's collapse, János Kádár is said to have offered Bognár a cabinet position. According to Budapest's rumor mill, Bognár called his wife and asked her to get his dark suit ready for the formal swearing-in ceremony. His wife's reply was that after the ceremony he should keep his dark suit on because he would need it at the cemetery for her funeral. In fact, Bognár did not join the Kádár government. Many years later, in the late 1970s and 1980s, I met Bognár on numerous occasions both in Budapest and in New York, but I never felt comfortable enough to ask him if the story was true.

World War II democratic interlude came to an end. The evidence for this view consists of free elections in 1945, followed by candid and passionate parliamentary debates, a thriving private enterprise system, and a largely free press till 1947.[16] Other historians—pointing to the presence and political involvement of the Red Army, Hungary's economic exploitation by the Soviet Union, and the activities of the political police as the not-so-secret arm of the Communist Party—argue that the democratic interlude was but a mirage from the beginning.[17] All agree, however, that by 1947 the pluralist era was over: the Smallholders had splintered, producing the nonommunists' defeat in the tainted elections of August 31 of that year. For McCargar, who had come to identify with the opposition, the issues now were how to save lives: how to assist those who had cooperated with him, and who had to leave now in a hurry. He asked his superiors for permission to help, and they gave him the go-ahead to assist up to twenty-five people to flee. In the end, McCargar reports that he was instrumental in the escape to the West of some sixty-seven prominent Hungarians, all in the last four months of 1947. This was the time when Pfeiffer, who had supplied McCargar the minutes of cabinet meetings, left for Austria and eventually the United States. With the help of coal miners who liked his type of anticommunist social democracy, Peyer managed to reach Austria just one day before the Communists had the Hungarian Parliament lift his immunity, and he too ended up in the United States.[18]

On September 22, 1947, an extraordinary—perhaps unique—request was put to McCargar. President Tildy's son-in-law visited him in his apartment and asked for McCargar's assistance to get Tildy and his

---

[16] Cf. Charles Gati, *Hungary and the Soviet Bloc* (Durham, N.C.: Duke University Press, 1986). The classic work on the subject is Zbigniew Brzezinski, *The Soviet Bloc: Unity and Conflict*, rev. ed. (New York: Praeger, 1961). Brzezinski reports that even as late as 1948 only about half of Hungary's industrial labor force was in the state sector, meaning that the rest was still employed by private enterprise. Ibid., 100.

[17] See, e.g., László Borhi, *Hungary in the Cold War 1945–1956* (Budapest: Central European Press, 2004), passim.

[18] Peyer and Edmund were particularly lucky to have left the country when they did. For almost immediately after they left, one of their interpreters revealed under pressure that Edmund had supplied McCargar detailed information about the Hungarian secret police. Making use of her testimony, the regime tried Peyer and thirteen of his associates in absentia in February 1948. Peyer received eight years, but Edmund was sentenced to death by hanging for betraying the secrets of the ÁVO to the United States. As of late 2005, Edmund lived in a Washington suburb. Peyer died of natural causes in New York on October 25, 1956, which happened to be the third day of the Hungarian revolt. He was seventy-five.

whole family out of Hungary. *The President of the Republic was ready to defect!* The Communists had asked Tildy to testify to the fairness of the elections held the month before. Tildy knew of all the cheating that accompanied the elections. He believed his accommodating approach—what critics called opportunism—had outlived whatever usefulness it might have once had. Publicly, he endorsed the results of the elections, but then he knew there was nothing he could do for his country anymore. His time was up; he was ready to leave. He wanted to tell his story in the West.

McCargar, in turn, was both surprised and torn. He regarded Tildy as weak and much too cautious in the face of Soviet behavior. Yet McCargar understood that Tildy's defection would be a major event in the emerging Cold War. "I felt an instant excitement," he wrote later. "Tildy's role in the past two years could not be easily forgiven or forgotten, but the fact was that he was the President of Hungary. This single gesture [his defection], if it could be pulled off successfully, would compensate for at least some of his errors; its international effects would be tremendous."[19] For once, says McCargar, his superiors immediately agreed that he should help Tildy find his way to the West.

Viktor Csornoky, Tildy's son-in-law, gave McCargar a list of eleven people—Tildy, his wife, and nine relatives, including Csornoky—who would form this group of high-level political refugees. After some consultation with Olivér Harris, code-named "Guy," who was his logistical aide, McCargar concluded that Tildy and his family could not escape from Budapest; the political police were watching him around the clock. Therefore, McCargar urged Csornoky to relocate the whole family to the presidential retreat at Lake Balaton. Then the complications began. Csornoky raised the number of family members Tildy wanted to take along from eleven to fourteen, while McCargar's Hungarian aide concluded that only a group of eight could be picked up and ferried safely in boats to the other side of the lake where cars would wait for them, taking them to safe houses and, at the appropriate moment, to the Austro-Hungarian border.

After discussing the matter with Tildy, Csornoky told McCargar that the president wanted to defect—but he would not leave without his

---

[19] McCargar, *Short Course*, 237.

whole family of fourteen people. McCargar replied that, with the president's surveillance by ÁVO officers tighter than ever, more than eight people would expose President Tildy to unacceptable risks. And so, in the end, Tildy did not defect. He remained Hungary's president until 1948 (when he was placed under house arrest that lasted for eight years). Csornoky was not so lucky. He was tried and hanged in 1948 for currency speculation and for trying to contact a Western intelligence agency in Egypt.

For his part, McCargar returned to the United States.[20] After a short stay in California, the Department of State asked him to work for the newly created Office of Policy Coordination. For several years he was responsible for OPC's Southeast European operations that included Hungary. At the OPC and then as a senior official based in Paris for the National Committee for a Free Europe (which was related to but not identical with Radio Free Europe), McCargar remained interested in Hungary, Hungarians, and Hungarian affairs.[21]

· 3 ·

In Washington, McCargar joined the Office of Policy Coordination in a midlevel position as head of operations in Southeast Europe. OPC, which came into being in June 1948, was assigned the task of weakening Communist authority in Eastern Europe, notably ties with the Soviet Union (while, until their merger in 1952, the Office of Special Operations was in the business of collecting information). Still another agency with considerable interest in the region was the Counter Intel-

---

[20] "The Pond" McCargar represented in Budapest continued to subsist for just a few more years. Its reporting was so poor and unreliable by then that none of its sponsors—the State Department; the Pentagon; and in a minor way, later on, the CIA—wanted to finance it. Colonel Grombach offered his services to Congress and to the FBI, but they turned him down as well. Unable to cope with his forced retirement and bitterly hostile to the CIA, he offered Senator Joseph McCarthy and his allies information about Communists in high positions in the U.S. government, but even McCarthy had no use for him. In 1955, "The Pond" ceased to function as a small intelligence agency. For a review of the last years of "The Pond"—during which McCargar was long gone, and it apparently had nothing to do with Hungary or the rest of Eastern Europe—see Stout, *The Pond*, 75–82.

[21] Cf. "Remarks of James McCargar at the International Conference, 'Hungary and the World, 1956: The New Archival Evidence,' at Budapest, September 1996, to the Radio Free Europe panel." For a retrospective interview with McCargar, see also "Their Man in Budapest: James McCargar and the 1947 Road to Freedom," *Hungarian Quarterly* 42, no. 161 (Spring 2001): 38–62. McCargar received a major decoration in 1992 from the Hungarian government.

ligence Corps, which was the War Department's intelligence outfit. Its initial focus was to hunt down Nazis and fascists after World War II, but soon after the end of the war it was given the added assignment of sending agents behind the Iron Curtain to spy on Soviet and satellite military capabilities.

At first, OPC was an independent agency, established by the National Security Council, which made it subject to supervision in peacetime by the State Department's Policy Planning Staff and in wartime by the Joint Chiefs of Staff. Though its ties to the CIA were poorly defined until 1950, OPC was always located in the same building complex as the CIA; after 1950, policy guidance came solely from the director of central intelligence. Chartered by top-secret NSC Directive 10/2,[22] OPC was, according to that directive, a response to "vicious covert activities of the USSR, its satellite countries and Communist groups to discredit and defeat the aims and activities of the United States and other Western powers." The immense authority assigned to OPC was made clear when Frank Wisner, its founding director, reported to the CIA director, Rear Admiral Roscoe Hillenkoetter, on OPC's "overall program." The program, reproduced here in its entirety, was ambitious beyond belief: [23]

Functional Group I—Psychological Warfare
　　　Program A—Press (periodical and non-periodical)
　　　Program B—Radio
　　　Program C—Miscellaneous (direct mail, poison pen, rumors, etc.)
Functional Group II—Political Warfare
　　　Program A—Support of Resistance (Underground)

---

[22] Michael Warner, ed., *The CIA under Harry Truman* (Washington, D.C.: Center for the Study of Intelligence, 1994), 213–16. The document was considered so secret that the following warning (underlined in the original) was added on its cover page: *"Special security precautions are being taken in the handling of this report. For this reason it is suggested that each member of the Council may wish to return his copy for filing in the office of the Executive Secretary, where it will be held available upon request."* Yet, in less than two months, on August 22, 1948, *Pravda* reported that the United States had set up a special office "for sabotage and terrorism in Eastern Europe." See Grose, *Operation Rollback*, 121. How the Kremlin learned of the founding of the super-secret OPC is no mystery; the likely culprit was Kim Philby, the British agent turned spy for the Soviet Union. Ironically, though at most a couple of dozen Americans could learn of OPC's very existence, the Kremlin knew it all.

[23] "Memorandum from the Assistant Director for Policy Coordination (Wisner) to Director of Central Intelligence Hillenkoetter (October 29, 1948)," in *Foreign Relations of the United States, 1945–1950: Emergence of the Intelligence Establishment* (Washington, D.C.: U.S. Government Printing Office, 1996), 730–31.

Program B—Support of DP's [Displaced Persons] and Refugees
Program C—Support of anti-Communists in Free Countries
Program D—Encouragement of Defection
Functional Group III—Economic Warfare
Program A—Commodity operations (clandestine preclusive
buying, market manipulation and black market operation)
Program B—Fiscal operations (currency speculation, counter-
feiting, etc.)
Functional Group IV—Preventive Direct Action
Program A—Support of Guerillas
Program B—Sabotage, Countersabotage, and Demolition
Program C—Evacuation
Program D—Stay-behind
Functional Group V—Miscellaneous
Program A—Front Organizations
Program B—War Plans
Program C—Administration
Program D—Miscellaneous

Short of sparking World War III, there were few officially stated limitations on what OPC could or could not do. NSC 10/2 stated that
OPC's activities "shall not include armed conflict by recognized military forces, espionage, counter-espionage, and cover and deception for
military operations." Further, NSC directed these activities to be so
"planned and executed . . . that if uncovered the U.S. Government can
plausibly disclaim any responsibility for them."[24]

Although Frank Wisner, a veteran Office of Strategic Services operative in Romania toward the end of World War II, was the new organization's chief executive, George F. Kennan, the veteran Soviet specialist publicly known as the father of containment, was OPC's godfather.
Respected as an advocate of realpolitik vis-à-vis the Soviet Union and
a guiding spirit of the Truman Doctrine that sought to stop Soviet expansion rather than reverse it, behind the scenes Kennan was an early
and strong advocate of the U.S. policy of promoting the rollback of
Soviet power. In the summer of 1948, when U.S. policy was being debated and defined and OPC established, Kennan argued that the first
goal of the United States should be "the emergence of the respective

---

[24] Warner, *CIA under Harry Truman*, 216.

eastern-European countries as independent factors on the international scene." The second goal was the promotion of a federal Baltic Sea region that would "permit a revival of national life." The third goal was to attack Moscow's credibility by psychological warfare and "every other means at our disposal." Finally, the fourth—broadest and most ambitious—goal was to "create situations which will compel the Soviet Government to recognize the practical undesirability of acting on the basis of its present concepts and the necessity of behaving, at least outwardly, as if it were the converse of these concepts that were true."[25]

There was one alternative if complementary approach that Washington—Kennan himself—briefly considered in 1948 (and again in the mid-1950s), and that was the encouragement of nationalist-Communist opposition to Soviet hegemony. The example was Tito's Yugoslavia. Initially, U.S. policymakers had viewed the split between Tito and Stalin as an obscure ideological dispute among Communists that did not have geopolitical significance. However, after the Communist Information Bureau (or Cominform, the Comintern's successor) expelled Yugoslavia from its ranks in June 1948, Washington began to pay attention. The harsh Yugoslav dictatorship was not an appealing model for others in Central and Eastern Europe, but Tito's defiance of the Soviet Union was genuine. Although no one in a position of authority went so far as to claim that "the enemy of my enemy is my friend," the Truman administration began to develop preferential ties to Belgrade and considered assisting similar nationalist-Communist regimes were they to emerge. Insightfully, George Kennan observed that "the aura of mystical omnipotence and infallibility which has surrounded the Kremlin power has been broken." He added: "The possibility of defection from Moscow . . . will from now on be present in one form or another in the mind of every [satellite leader]."[26] By early 1949, Kennan noted that Tito might

---

[25] Kennan's memorandum, entitled "U.S. Objectives toward Russia" and dated August 20, 1948, was prepared for an NSC meeting that day. It is cited and discussed in Mitrovich, *Undermining the Kremlin*, 15–46 (the quotations about the liberation of Eastern Europe and the transformation of the Soviet Union are on 29). See also Grose, *Operation Rollback*, 87–99. The truth of the matter is that Kennan displayed a good deal of ambivalence toward several key issues of the day. As he candidly describes in his memoirs, he approved of the substance but not the tone of the Truman Doctrine. See George F. Kennan, *Memoirs, 1925–1950* (Boston: Atlantic–Little, Brown, 1967), 25–50.

[26] "The Attitude of this Government toward Events in Yugoslavia," PPS/35, dated June 30, 1948, in *State Department Policy Planning Staff Papers* (New York: Garland Press, 1983), vol. 2 (1948), 317–21. At other times, Kennan was skeptical about the prospects for challenging the Soviet Union over its

not have the authority to defy the Kremlin if he were to ease up at home—and that would be most regrettable: "Tito in being is perhaps our most precious asset in the struggle to contain and weaken Russian expansion," he wrote.[27]

Kennan's understanding of the realities of Communist politics had its supporters in high circles in both the Truman and in the Eisenhower administrations—even Secretary of State Dulles flirted with the idea of promoting Titoism—but the United States found no practical way of influencing relations either within or between Communist parties. There is no evidence to suggest that U.S. intelligence officers considered "creating" Titoists or trying to drive a wedge among the leaders of the various Communist parties. Those accused of being Titoists or American agents (or both) in Bulgaria, Hungary, or Czechoslovakia in the late 1940s and early 1950s were in fact loyal, pro-Soviet Communists whose phony trials were meant to warn party members and nonmembers alike against foreign enemies; the "evidence" against them was not planted or concocted by the CIA to split the Communist parties. Only in one case did an ingenious and fateful Western scheme help set up Rudolf Slánský, secretary general of Czechoslovakia's Communist Party, as an anticommunist foreign conspirator, who was then tried and executed in 1952. The scheme that had as its centerpiece a fake document tying Slánský to Western intelligence was carried out a Czechoslovak émigré group called OKAPI working on its own in what was then West Germany.[28] OKAPI's goal was to sow distrust at the top of Czecho-

---

control in Eastern Europe. When a listener raised the issue after one of his lectures at the War College, Kennan candidly if wearily replied: "The fact of the matter is that we do not have the power in Eastern Europe really to do anything but talk. . . . There is no action we can take there except to state our case." Daniel Yergin, *Shattered Peace: The Origins of the Cold War and the National Security State* (Boston: Houghton Mifflin, 1977), 255. For a perceptive account of Kennan's changing perspectives, *see* Wilson D. Miscamble, *George F. Kennan and the Making of American Foreign Policy, 1947–1950* (Princeton, N.J.: Princeton University Press, 1992); chap. 6 deals with "Titoism, Eastern Europe, and Political Warfare."

[27] "Economic Relations between the United States and Yugoslavia," PPS/49, dated February 10, 1949, in *State Department Policy Planning Staff Papers*, vol. 3 (1949), 20–24.

[28] Igor Lukes, "The Rudolf Slánský Affair: New Evidence," *Slavic Review* 58, no. 1 (Spring 1999): 16–187. Lukes reports that U.S. intelligence officers—who learned of OKAPI's "Operation Great Sweeper" that sealed Slánský's fate only after an OKAPI agent had carried an incriminating letter into Czechoslovakia in November 1951—"were very angry." It is not clear from the evidence of Lukes's dramatic account if the Army's Counter Intelligence Corps (CIC) was "angry" because it disapproved of the operation or because it did not know about it in advance. It is clear, however, that CIC canceled its relationship with OKAPI before Slánský's execution. No evidence has been found indicating any ties between OKAPI and the CIA.

slovakia's Communist leadership and thus weaken the regime and its control over society. The operation succeeded beyond OKAPI's wildest expectations.

OPC itself—using the authority granted to it by NSC 10/2 and trying to live up to Wisner's grand plans for what had to be done—initiated (as in Albania) or supported (as in Poland) a number of clandestine operations, of which none turned out well. No similar actions were even attempted in Hungary.

The landing of Albanian exiles in 1949 was the first and only paramilitary intervention—a joint U.S.-British venture London called Operation Valuable—against a Soviet bloc government. The exiles were recruited and trained in Malta, Rome, and Athens mainly by MI6, the British intelligence service, and financed by OPC. The Americans in charge were Wisner, Lindsay, Michael Burke,[29] John Richardson (who would later serve as the top CIA official in Vienna and then in Saigon),[30] and McCargar, all of OPC; McCargar was the de facto case officer who kept in touch with the British through their Washington envoy and Soviet double agent, Kim Philby.[31] If the exiles had succeeded in overthrowing the Albanian regime headed by Enver Hoxha—a particularly sinister Communist boss and a staunch Kremlin ally at the time—similar actions might well have been attempted against other Soviet satellites. Wisner told a colleague that Albania was "a clinical experiment to see whether larger rollback operations would be feasible elsewhere."[32] He assumed that what had worked against the Nazis during World War II would also work against the Communists after World War II.

---

[29] See Michael Burke, *Outrageous Good Fortune* (Boston: Little, Brown, 1984).

[30] Cf. John H. Richardson, *My Father the Spy: An Investigative Memoir* (New York: HarperCollins, 2005).

[31] To my knowledge, the CIA has yet to acknowledge even the existence of the Albanian operation. The most complete account is still Nicholas Bethell, *Betrayed* (New York: Times Books, 1984). See also John Prados, *Presidents' Secret Wars: CIA and Pentagon Covert Operations from World War II through Irancscram* (New York: Quill / William Morrow, 1986), 45–52; Grose, *Operation Rollback*, 154–59; and Michael W. Dravis, "Storming Fortress Albania: American Covert Operations in Microcosm, 1949–54," *Intelligence and National Security* 7, no. 4 (1992): 425–42. Frank Wisner's daughter offers intriguing details and critical insights in Elizabeth W. Hazard, *Cold War Crucible* (Boulder, Colo.: East European Monographs, 1996). For a British perspective that, at times, relies on unexplained or questionable sources, see Stephen Dorril, *MI6: Inside the Covert World of Her Majesty's Secret Intelligence Service* (New York: Simon & Schuster / Touchstone, 2002), 355–403. I have also benefited from several conversations with James McCargar, who was labeled by Bethell the Albanian plan's "American commander."

[32] As quoted in Prados, *Presidents' Secret Wars*, 46.

As it happened, the Albanian operation, which lasted five years, turned into an embarrassing fiasco. Whatever contribution Philby made to the operation's failure,[33] there were deeper, systemic problems that doomed direct interventions; they were far-fetched if not hopeless from the beginning. The prominent British specialist on the Balkans, Reginald Hibbert, observed more than three decades later that "it was a forlorn hope to suppose that exiled followers of the nationalists who had failed in 1944 would . . . be able to raise a following against the iron rule of the Communist Party of Albania after six years of draconian social engineering. The scheme was thought up and implemented by men who had failed to understand the revolutionary forces which enabled Hoxha and the CPA [Communist Party of Albania] to come to power in 1944." Along the same lines, another prominent British writer on defense, John Keegan, wrote: "It is a gruesome story, made all the more so by the perception, apparently denied by the masterminds of subversion, that the Albanian communists, like the Yugoslavs, were far more adept at deciding the future of their country than a bunch of romantic meddlers with a public school education and a free supply of plastic explosives."[34]

The OPC/CIA—OPC formally became part of the CIA, with Wisner as head of operations, in August 1952—undertook one other major act of subversion against the Soviet bloc. It entailed extensive financial support for what OPC believed was the Polish underground that continued to resist Soviet rule. Initially supported by the British, the Freedom and Independence movement (known by its Polish initials as WiN), which grew out of the Polish Home Army in 1945 and claimed 500 activists, 20,000 sympathizers, and some 100,000 potential sup-

---

[33] Despite Philby's own publications and a good number of studies written about him, it is unclear what his Soviet masters had tasked him to do and whether Stalin had any confidence in the accuracy of his reports. It is even possible that Philby did not report in detail on the Albanian operation. It should be noted here as well that, contrary to accounts offered over the years in various books—notably William R. Carson's *The Armies of Ignorance: The Rise of the American Intelligence Empire* (New York: Dial Press, 1977)—the OPC's or the CIA's Operation RedSox program (also identified as RedSox/RedCap) was not involved in Albania or elsewhere in Eastern Europe. There is no evidence for Carson's claim (on p. 369) that "Hungarian revolutionaries [were] aided and abetted by RedSox/RedCap forces." Active from 1949 to 1959, RedSox was a program of illegal border crossings, and it was aimed only at the Soviet Union. Of the eighty-five such man-missions attempted, sixty-two were lost, killed, arrested, or reported missing. CIA, *Clandestine Service Historical Series (CSHP 98)*, July 1971; parts declassified as MORI DocID: 1161460 in December 2004, The Illegal Border-Crossing Program 1946–1959, appendix B.

[34] Both quotes in Dorril, *MI6*, 402.

porters, was gradually infiltrated and liquidated by the Communist authorities; by 1952 it was but a ruse. There was no WiN by then. The pictures passed on to an OPC agent in London showing successful examples of sabotage, such as burnt-out tanks and military barracks, were fakes. The Polish secret police pocketed the OPC's $1 million in gold. In December 1952, Radio Warsaw delightedly broadcast the story of "Western intelligence and WiN"—not only protesting American intervention but also making fun of American naiveté. The Poles kept the story alive for weeks, adding to Washington's embarrassment. Public disclosure that OPC had been led by the nose for almost four years by Polish intelligence was all the more painful because—as Evan Thomas pointed out—it came "on the heels of one of the great betrayals of the Cold War, the perfidy of Kim Philby."[35] (Less than two years later, the CIA had reason to celebrate. It received, debriefed, and made excellent use of Lieutenant Colonel Józef Światło, the first high-level defector from the Polish secret police, who broadcast via Radio Free Europe all he knew to his Polish audience.)

It is unclear whether Frank Wisner understood what happened to his plans and operations either in Albania or in Poland. On the one hand, he believed deeply and sincerely—as did most Americans—that the United States had to play a special role saving the world from the Communists; he had an abiding interest, stemming from his Office of Strategic Services experiences in Romania at the end of World War II, in the future of Eastern Europe; and he also had a bureaucratic stake in clandestine activity. His budget—most of which, during and after the Korean War, was spent on the Far East and not on Eastern Europe—had grown from $4.7 million in 1949 to almost $82 million in 1952; and his payroll grew from 302 in 1949 to 2,182 in 1952 (plus 3,142 people under contract abroad).[36]

On the other hand, Wisner was a serious anticommunist and not some sort of primitive, McCarthy-like crackpot. In Georgetown, where he lived with his family, Wisner surrounded himself with such distin-

---

[35] Evan Thomas, *The Very Best Men: Four Who Dared—The Early Years of the CIA* (New York: Simon & Schuster / Touchstone, 1995), 68.

[36] Warner, *CIA under Harry Truman*, xxv.

guished friends as Charles (Chip) Bohlen; the Alsop brothers; Philip Graham and his family, owners of the *Washington Post;* and others like them—all part of a foreign policy elite preoccupied with the Soviet threat.[37] At the same time, the Georgetown group was contemptuous of the Joseph McCarthy wing of the Republican Party that looked for domestic scapegoats instead; as they saw it, McCarthy could easier catch a cold than a Communist spy.[38]

Apparently torn between a desire to persist and yet avoid another Albania or Poland, Wisner did what Washington bureaucrats do: He canceled "about a third of the eastern European operations" in 1952.[39] He understood that the Kremlin's domination over its satellites was so complete as to leave him with few opportunities for the kinds of ag-

---

[37] For a penetrating and eminently readable profile of Wisner and his environment, see Thomas, *Very Best Men.* I have also learned a good deal about the atmosphere prevailing in the Georgetown salons at that time from one of Wisner's sons, Ellis Wisner (interview, March 25, 2005) and Bohlen's daughter, Ambassador Avis Bohlen (interview, June 20, 2005).

[38] I recall, with considerable embarrassment, an example of how my image of U.S. politicians was formed. In the early 1950s, as I was finishing high school, the Hungarian papers were full of vitriolic attacks on Senator Joseph McCarthy for his "hysterical" anticommunism. Because these propagandists were so strongly against him, I tended to be for him, assuming—as much as I gave it any thought— that McCarthy was a great guy. I figured that he was being attacked so much because he was doing something right. Years later—after I had settled in the United States and caught up with America's recent past— I lost my childish infatuation with this hypocrite and impostor who built his political reputation on people's very genuine fear of communism. My case shows not only that readers behind the Iron Curtain could not believe what they read in the Communist press but also that they should not have necessarily believed the opposite of what they read in the Communist press either. (I am grateful to Julius Varallyay for this insight.) It took me years to begin to assess politicians in the United States and elsewhere not on the basis of the emotional satisfaction and pleasure their slogans might bring me but on the basis of what I could reasonably expect them to do for the common good. Relatedly, I still find it hard to believe that it took years to diminish the impact of the McCarthy phenomenon. The atmosphere of moral degradation and fear was still pervasive when I began to teach in the early 1960s. People of decency and rational judgment did not yet enjoy then the luxury of rejecting McCarthyite insinuations; they had to steer a "responsible course" between defiance and compliance. As James Hershberg, his biographer, notes, James B. Conant, Harvard's president at the time, "personified the crisis of liberal educators who struggled to balance the competing imperatives of academic freedom and Cold War orthodoxy." For an extraordinary case history, see James G. Hershberg, *James B. Conant: Harvard to Hiroshima and the Making of the Nuclear Age* (New York: Alfred A. Knopf, 1993), esp. chap. 31, "McCarthyism and the Crisis of the Liberal Educator 1950–1953."

[39] Dorril, *MI6,* 400. A summary of how Walter Smith, director of the CIA, explained (or explained away) these setbacks to the agency's top brass put it this way: "The Director, mentioning that the Agency had recently experienced some difficulties in various parts of the world, remarked that these difficulties stemmed, by and large, from the use of improperly trained or inferior officers. He stated that until CIA could build a reserve of well-trained people, it would have to hold its activities to the limited number of operations that it could do well rather than to attempt to cover a broad field with poor performance." "Minutes of Meeting [on] Monday, 27 October 1952," in *CIA under Harry Truman,* ed. Warner, 469–70.

gressive measures he had outlined in his ambitious October 29, 1948, memorandum—reproduced above—to the director of central intelligence. His heart was probably still in reversing Communist gains in Europe, notably in Romania, but his attention shifted to the Far East— at a time when Republicans were engaged in a public campaign of stentorian rhetoric about the liberation of Eastern Europe. In fact, and contrary to widespread public perceptions then and since, under Truman there were more U.S. intelligence operations in Eastern Europe than there were under Eisenhower. As noted in chapter 1, the main purpose of the Republicans' rhetoric thus seemed to be the rollback of Democrats from Washington (at which they succeeded) rather than the removal of the Soviet Union from Eastern Europe (at which they failed).

Frank Lindsay, Wisner's deputy, drew more extensive lessons from the failed Albanian and Polish operations. Having played a major role in U.S. clandestine activities during and after World War II, he left the CIA in 1953 for an executive position with the Ford Foundation. As he resigned, he sought to leave behind a long memorandum addressed to Wisner and Allen Dulles, who was by then the CIA's deputy director, "warning that the plan for a rollback of 'Communists in Eastern Europe wasn't going to work well.'"[40]

"Frank, you can't say that" was Dulles's response as he pleaded with Lindsay to modify the text.[41] Modified or otherwise, the final, nine-page memo was still a stinging repudiation of even the *possibility* of bringing about systemic change in the Soviet bloc: "The instruments currently advocated to reduce Soviet power, either directly or by attrition, are both inadequate and ineffective against the Soviet political system," Lindsay wrote. "The consolidated Communist state, through police and political controls, propaganda and provocation, has made virtually impossible the existence of organized clandestine resistance ca-

---

[40] Lindsay's interview for the CIA's Oral History Program; see fn. 9 above. In a telephone interview with me (August 18, 2005), Lindsay confirmed the accuracy of that summary. As reported by Evan Thomas, and verified by Lindsay during the same interview, Lindsay also recalled that, "I began to have real doubts about rolling back the Iron Curtain. It was peacetime, not wartime. The stuff that worked against the Germans did not work against the Russians, who seemed impervious. It was time to back off and think this business through." Thomas, *Very Best Men,* 71.

[41] Peter Grose, *Gentleman Spy: The Life of Allen Dulles* (Boston: Houghton Mifflin / Richard Todd, 1994), 356.

pable within the foreseeable future of appreciably weakening the power of the state."[42] This was not what Allen Dulles, and especially John Foster Dulles, the aspiring Republican secretary of state and the major exponent of liberation, wanted to hear.

As far as Hungary was concerned, the OPC/CIA did develop more modest goals and applied few means to advance American interests there. A review of the agency's operative records covering the years 1946 to 1965 shows few attempts and no success in the major covert activities that Wisner had envisaged using against the satellites when OPC was fully integrated into the CIA in 1952.

The agency's goals were based on a sound assessment of possibilities. Listed among favorable factors was the Hungarians' antipathy toward communism, as well as signs of "discontent, disillusionment, and opportunism" in the Communist Party.[43] Listed among factors unfavorable to operations were "the virtual control of the country" by the political police and Soviet troops, and "the probability that the Red Army would intervene if an overthrow of the Government appeared imminent."[44] What could be done under the circumstances was "to develop indigenous nationwide opposition based on the Roman Catholic faith and the resistance of peasants to collectivization."[45]

Among early psychological warfare activities were the sending of chain letters, mailed out from Switzerland and Hungary itself, which sought to encourage young Hungarians to leave the country (with the agency review noting that there was "no evidence that the chain letters succeeded in inducing Hungarian youth to leave").[46] Other letters, prepared in the United States, were mailed in Budapest to Communist officials just to create a bit of confusion. In November 1955, Soviet am-

---

[42] Ibid.

[43] CIA, *CSHP 323*, vol. 2, 32.

[44] Ibid.

[45] Ibid., 32–33. Cf. "Anti-Communist Resistance Potential in the Sino-Soviet Bloc" (National Intelligence Estimate 10-55), April 12, 1955, http://www.foia.cia.gov/docs/DOC_0000269420_0003.gif. This important National Intelligence Estimate observed that in Hungary "passive resistance . . . by industrial and agricultural workers is impeding the regime's efforts to build a strong and viable economy." It is true that, given old habits and pitiful wages, Hungarians did not work as hard the regime had insisted they should.

[46] CIA, *CSHP 323*, vol. 2, 36.

bassador Yuri V. Andropov reported to his superiors in Moscow that Rákosi had been receiving a series of signed and unsigned letters with "compromising materials" about his colleagues and himself. Rákosi said that "hostile elements" would be happy to see him removed as head of the party.[47]

The CIA also produced four publications mailed from abroad: the anticommunist *Búzakereszt* (Shock of Wheat), a six-page monthly; *Magyar Kommunista* (Hungarian Communist), a publication with a Titoist slant; *Toborzó* (Recruiter), which aimed at the peasantry with a nationalist tilt; and *Magyar Jövő* (Hungarian Future), whose 150 copies were so doctored as to make it appear they were approved by Hungarian authorities.[48] When the Communist press, including *Szabad Nép*, printed strong official protests, the CIA welcomed the protests as a sign that its program was working. Whether it was or was not is unclear because all mail from the West was checked by censors employed in the country's main post office. *Szabad Nép* might have known that these publications were never delivered but used the occasion to call for "vigilance" against foreign enemies.

As for paramilitary activities, there were plans to make use of the Hungarian National Committee, an émigré organization of prominent exile politicians set up in 1951 by the Free Europe Committee (and financed by the CIA). The agency had considerable respect for Béla Varga, the committee's chairman. There were plans to establish a "Hungarian labor service unit" that would be used initially to guard U.S. military supply depots in Germany, but at some point in the future could be used—as a CIA review paper delicately put it—"for other types of operations directed against" the Communist regime in Hungary.[49] With the unit comprising only four to six people, this was to be a small operation that was nonetheless designed to be "potentially capable of de-

---

[47] Katona interview; see chap. 1, fn. 4, and chap. 3, fn. 9, above. As the Hungarian political police closely followed him, Katona sneaked out of his apartment house at night and then—when he was sure he was not being followed—dropped the letters at mailboxes in different parts of Budapest. Whether Rákosi referred to these letters in his conversation with Andropov is possible but not certain. Andropov's report is in *Szovjet nagyköveti iratok Magyarországról 1953–1956: Kiszeljov és Andropov titkos jelentései* [Soviet ambassadors' documents about Hungary 1953–1956: Kiselyov's and Andropov's Secret Reports], ed. Magdolna Baráth (Budapest: Napvilág Kiadó, 2002), 260–64.

[48] CIA, *CSHP 323*, vol. 2, 37–38.

[49] Ibid., 45.

veloping and directing the Hungarian resistance movement."[50] There is no evidence that even these modest plans were ever put into effect.

In the realm of intelligence collection, agency reviews made available to me do not identify by name the CIA officer operating for the United States in Budapest. But, as Geza Katona affirms, he was the only resident agent there in the 1950s, disguised as a U.S. official;[51] what CIA files indicate is that "Headquarters enjoined him from becoming involved in operations and he was directed to concentrate on supporting" tasks, such as purchasing stamps and stationery, mailing letters, and generally helping to look after matters of security.[52] Others being dispatched from the West to gather information in Hungary seldom got there; several attempts failed or had to be aborted. In one case, after guards at the Austro-Hungarian border trapped an agent as he crossed the frontier, he managed to free himself, swim across a river, and pass through a minefield—only to lose his managers' confidence. His story of escape was too fanciful to be believed. He was terminated, though in the absence of proof against him he was allowed to resettle in the West.[53]

How did the CIA obtain any information at all? It seems that much of it came through the resources of Radio Free Europe in Munich (see section 4 below). Another source was diplomatic reporting by the U.S. Legation, which was based initially on Hungarian press reports; however, after Stalin's death and during Imre Nagy's first premiership, Legation personnel did find access to members of the country's reformist opposition and others as well. By then, notably by late 1954, the agency also obtained promises of cooperation from Hungarian diplomats serving in Athens, Munich, and Berlin, but they delivered "little or nothing."[54] In 1953, there was a useful "walk-in" in Vienna, a former official from the Hungarian political police (ÁVH) who presumably updated some of the information about his agency that James McCargar had obtained from "Edmund" in 1947. Increasingly, the agency relied

---

[50] Ibid., 46.

[51] Katona interview; see chap. 1, fn. 4, and chap. 3, fn. 9.

[52] CIA, *CSHP 323*, vol. 1, 66.

[53] CIA, *CSHP 323*, vol. 2, 54. For Katona's own account of some of his activities, see also "Nagy mulasztást kővettünk el" [We committed a major omission], in *Doku 56: Őt portré a forradalomból* [Docu 56: Five profiles from the revolution], ed. Zsolt Csalog (Budapest: Unió Kiadó, 1990), 54–96.

[54] Ibid., 74.

on Western press reports and on Hungarian travelers to gain information or impressions.

Even as the Nagy regime eased up at home, the Austro-Hungarian border became more dangerous and more difficult to penetrate. One of the CIA's reviews reports: "Although prospective agents continued to be sought out, assessed, and recruited, not many panned out. For example, [*name excised*] was dropped for fabrication; [*name excised*] was dropped as a security risk following his arrest for stealing a bicycle; [*name excised*] was dropped after failing a polygraph test and doing poorly under assessment."[55] Growing difficulties facing the border-crossing program coincided with Washington's decreasing interest in East European and especially Hungarian operations. In 1953 the CIA closed its Western European training facilities and terminated its whole border-crossing project.[56] The small Hungarian Operation Unit that remained active at a European location had but "three staff officers and one stenographer," while at headquarters "the Hungarian Branch [consisted of] six intelligence officers and two clerk typists."[57] Although re-

---

[55] Ibid., 67.

[56] After the Twentieth Congress of the Soviet Communist Party in February 1956, and specifically after Khrushchev's extraordinarily important speech denouncing Stalin, the CIA reportedly reopened a training facility in West Germany. Some CIA officials did not want to publish and broadcast to Eastern Europe Khrushchev's so-called secret speech until these paramilitary units were "ready," believing that they would be and could be used if the speech were to spark instability in the region. See David Binder, "'56 East Europe Plan of C.I.A. is Described," *New York Times*, November 30, 1976. The files of the CIA I was allowed to see make no reference to the reopening of a training facility in 1956. Even if one such facility was actually reopened, it does not mean there were Hungarians among the trainees.

[57] CIA, *CSHP 323*, vol. 2, 70. Mention should be made here of military intelligence as well. Operating in Austria and Germany after World War II, the CIC sought to obtain information about Soviet and Hungarian military objects and capabilities. Its records largely declassified, some at my request in 2004, CIC was particularly active right after World War II and again after the Hungarian revolt. After World War II, CIC engaged in efforts to locate war criminals and yet it also made extensive use of them, including members of the pro-Nazi Arrow Cross Party who left Hungary with the retreating Germans and other similar exile groups of dubious background and goals. CIC developed ties with Major-General András Zákó of the far-right Hungarian Veterans' Association, although the latter had closer ties with French intelligence. CIC's 430th Detachment covered Hungarian affairs. Relatively few of the CIC-dispatched agents who entered Hungary managed to return, and their information was of minimal value about the Soviet and the Hungarian military, such as license plates observed on military trucks. Dozens were caught by Soviet and Hungarian counterintelligence, some were tried, others became double agents, and many simply disappeared. For pitiful tidbits of untrustworthy information, CIC paid the high price of association with agents of whom too many were illiterate, pro-Nazi hooligans. For tens of thousands of pages on CIC and its dealings with Hungary and Hungarian exiles, see especially Record Group 319 (Record of the U.S. Army Intelligence Command) at the National Archives and Records Administration (College Park, Md.). For the account of one Hungarian who was caught and then, largely from memory, reconstructed various trials by Communist kangaroo courts as well inhuman conditions in Hungary's gulags, see István Fehérváry, *Börtönvilág Mag-*

liable comparative numbers cannot be found, it appears that there were many more Hungarian agents in Western Europe than American agents in Hungary.

In any case, except for Radio Free Europe (RFE) and its programs of information and propaganda, the CIA did not have any serious Hungarian operations on the eve of the 1956 revolt. In the absence of a "stay behind" or "sleeper" program, it could not call on anyone for assistance. It had trained a few Hungarian exiles before 1953 to be used in case of internal or international emergency, but the trainees were let go; if a few new ones were trained in 1956, which cannot be ascertained, they were not ready for assignments. As for information, the agency and indeed other departments of the U.S. government followed developments as best they could from Western Europe, relying on RFE resources and press reports. According to a Hungarian intelligence review, an apparent exception was when the U.S. Legation in Budapest obtained secret information in 1949–50 and in 1952 about the yearly budget of the Ministry of Defense and the political police.[58]

During the 1956 revolt (see chapter 5), the CIA did not have a single Hungarian-speaking agent in a nearby Western European capital and only one in Budapest.[59] It certainly did not have a fighting unit ready to enter Hungary and assist the revolutionaries. Moreover, if the CIA had chosen to transfer arms or ammunition to Hungarian insurgents at

---

yarországon [The world of prisons in Hungary] (Center Square, Pa.: Alpha Publications, 1978). For two very different perspectives, see Ian Sayer and Douglas Botting, *America's Secret Army: The Untold Story of the Counter Intelligence Corps* (New York: Franklin Watts, 1989); and Christopher Simpson, *Blowback: The First Full Account of America's Recruitment of Nazis, and Its Disastrous Effect on Our Domestic and Foreign Policy* (New York: Weidenfeld & Nicholson, 1988). Unfortunately, all three books contain factual errors. For an wide-ranging summary by Communist researchers in the Hungarian Ministry of Internal Affairs of CIC agents caught and tried, see *Az állam biztonsága ellen kifejtett tevékenység és az ellene folytatott harc* [Activity against the security of the state and the struggle against it], Archive of the Hungarian Ministry of Internal Affairs, A-1364/2. See also Ildikó Zsitnyányi, "Egy 'titkos háború' természete: A Magyar Harcosok Bajtársi Közössége tagjaival szemben lefolytatott internálási és büntetőeljárási gyakorlat, 1948–1950" [The nature of a secret war: The practice of internment and criminal procedure against members of the Hungarian Veterans' Association 1948–1950] *Hadtörténelmi Közlemények*, 2002/4, 1086–1101. After the Soviet intervention in Hungary in 1956, CIC agents became active again, interviewing hundreds of Hungarian refugees in Austria and Germany about military objects and military research as well as about individuals associated with the Communist regime.

[58] *Az állam biztonsága*, 122–23. This review of Hungarian intelligence activities reports, apologetically, that Hungarian counterintelligence was unable to locate the source that passed on this classified budget information to someone at the U.S. Legation. The review claims, however, that the Hungarians managed to penetrate the Legation, possibly by picking up carbon copies of reports.

[59] See chap. 1, fn. 3 and fn. 4 above.

that time, which headquarters on October 29 specifically and formally refused to permit, the transfer could not have taken place because—incredibly—the CIA did not know "the exact location and nature" of weapons that might be available to it in Western Europe. It seems that the weapons were located in early December 1956, about one month after the Soviet Union had crushed the revolt.[60]

· 4 ·

If it were not for Radio Free Europe, the United States would not have been present in Hungary; for most Hungarians, RFE was the United States and the United States was RFE.[61] There was little diplomatic or economic intercourse between the two countries in the 1950s. By sharp contrast, although most Hungarians in the countryside did not have shortwave radios capable of picking up foreign stations' signals, RFE's broadcasts had a steady, growing, and receptive audience in Budapest and other cities. Its advantage over the BBC, which was respected by intellectuals for its objectivity; over the Voice of America; and over Deutsche Welle had to do with RFE's extensive programming: It was on the air (almost) around the clock. Also, with its persistent attacks on communism and hopeful message about the future, RFE made its listeners *feel* good. True, it was not easy to hear. Hungary's Communist proprietors of power, fearful of competition, jammed the station so that words conflated with static, making it impossible not only to distinguish between news and commentary—that was altogether impossible—but even to hear very much at all. Yet that which was heard helped keep the Hungarians' hopes alive.

---

[60] CIA, *Clandestine Service Historical Series (CSHP 6)*, January 1958; parts declassified as MORI DocID: 1203072 in March 2005, The Hungarian Revolution and Planning for the Future, 23 October–4 November 1956, vol. 1, 92.

[61] I wish to acknowledge my indebtedness to A. Ross Johnson, who is completing an authoritative history of Radio Free Europe. He has shared with me his immense knowledge of how RFE policy was made in Washington at the CIA and the Department of State, in New York at the National Committee for a Free Europe, and in Munich, and he has also passed on to me such documents from his files that are relevant to my study. Given the quality of his previous scholarship on Central and Eastern Europe, his experience first as RFE's director of research and then as RFE's president at the end of the Cold War, as well as his unparalleled access to a great variety of documents others have not yet seen before, Johnson's study promises to shed new light not only on the difficult times in the 1950s that my book briefly reviews but also on the long and productive period after 1956 when RFE was no longer burdened by Washington's empty rhetoric on liberation and rollback.

The inspiration for the establishment of RFE came in 1949 from George Kennan, then head of the State Department's Policy Planning Staff. He thought it would provide useful employment to anticommunist refugees from Eastern Europe, who could broadcast in their languages to their own people about the outside world and about what was happening in the Soviet bloc. Such distinguished Americans as Dwight Eisenhower, Allen Dulles, Lucius Clay, and others led the nominally private National Committee for a Free Europe, incorporated in 1949. From the beginning, the Committee was financed almost exclusively by the CIA, although RFE's own fund-raising arm, the so-called Crusade for Freedom, managed to get private contributions as well. The Crusade was but a front to cover up CIA's secret role in funding and supervising RFE's operations.

The radio's influential broadcasts to Eastern Europe began in 1951 and ended four decades later. Those who took the Cold War and thus America's competitive relationship with the Communist world seriously—that is, those who appreciated the gravity of the Soviet challenge—favored RFE as an important instrument of U.S. foreign policy. In the United States, it was backed by a large bipartisan coalition; in Western Europe, support was far more qualified. By 1953–54 diplomats in both the United States and in Western Europe often thought their work would be made easier if RFE did not exist or if it became less confrontational. The old axiom about bureaucratic behavior—"where you sit is where you stand"—generally applied: Those engaged in or favoring psychological warfare against the Soviet Union believed RFE would make life more difficult for the Communists and therefore it was a good idea, while Western diplomats who dealt with Communist governments on a daily basis found that RFE's unsparing attacks on those governments made the task of diplomacy more difficult; they felt RFE should be less inciting and more informative.[62]

After Stalin's death in 1953, the radio faced, and had to find ways to resolve, serious complications in developing a coherent policy toward the target countries in Eastern Europe. The main difficulty involved the uneasy coexistence of three discrete "dimensions" in U.S. policy toward

---

[62] See, e.g., "Summary Minutes of the Chiefs of Mission Meeting at Vienna, September 22–24, 1953," in *Foreign Relations of the United States, 1945–1950*, vol. 8, 86–102.

the Soviet bloc. One dimension was *confrontation:* the willingness to take on the Soviet Union at every opportunity and in every way, short of war. Though the ultimate goal of confrontation was liberation, the immediate goal was to weaken Moscow's ability to subvert Western interests. The second dimension was *competition:* the willingness to contend for the support of uncommitted countries and peoples and also struggle for the allegiance of left-leaning and indeed all other Europeans. The goal of competition was to undermine the Communists' appeal and allow the West to gain the upper hand in world affairs. The third dimension was *cooperation* or *détente:* the willingness to negotiate agreements and reduce tension with the Kremlin in the hope that time will work in favor of the West.

As far as Eastern Europe was concerned, these three components of policy, when viewed in isolation from one another, amounted to conflicting goals—*confrontation* signified efforts to obtain freedom for the region; *competition* signified efforts to encourage the rise of national Communist or Titoist regimes; and *cooperation* signified interest in reform and long-term evolution within the confines of the Soviet bloc. Taken individually, each had something to recommend it. Freedom for the region via liberation—offering geopolitical gain and emotional satisfaction, though no short-term prospect of attainment—would have improved America's strategic position in the world and fulfilled the East Europeans' desire for national existence. The rise of Titoist regimes would have split the Soviet bloc, deflating Moscow's pretensions as the self-appointed leader in the international Communist movement; however, as a limited and morally unappealing (if far more realistic) objective, Titoism would have satisfied neither the Eastern Europeans' hope for systemic change nor the Americans' illusion of omnipotence. Finally, reformist evolution via détente would have held out the promise of peaceful change in Eastern Europe toward the then-popular goal of socialism with a more human (or less Stalinist) face, but neither the United States nor the Soviet Union could easily absorb the domestic political consequences such changes would have entailed.

Taken together, however, a U.S. policy that embraced liberation, Titoism, and Communist reform at the same time was as complicated as it was confusing, and as a whole it defied implementation.

By the mid-1950s if not earlier, many diplomats and ex-diplomats, notably George Kennan, sought to leave the confrontational component in limbo and focus instead only on the competitive and coopera-tive dimensions of U.S. policy. Witnessing the just-emerging Soviet "thaw," they hoped to work for reduced tensions with the Kremlin—even if that meant paying less attention for now to Moscow's domina-tion of Eastern Europe. President Eisenhower supported a more prag-matic outlook; after all, he held a groundbreaking summit in Geneva in 1955, trying to find a modicum of common ground with the new Soviet leaders. Behind the scenes, Vice President Richard Nixon was strongly opposed. In July 1956, he criticized those who thought that "the exis-tence of a lot of neat little independent Communist states throughout the world would help to solve the security problem of the United States." Ever the politician mindful of elections in November 1956, Nixon added that he could think "of nothing which would, from the point of view of domestic politics or of our international relations, be worse than the occurrence of a leak tending to indicate that we at the highest levels were agreeing on a policy for national Communism un-der any circumstances."[63]

Eisenhower could not fully impose his less confrontational outlook on his own government, mainly because he was not sure the Kremlin was really ready to change but partly because any compromise with Moscow risked a furious response from the still-powerful hard-line wing of the Republican Party.[64] In this atmosphere, there was no way to reconcile the appearance of sacrificing the vision of a free Eastern Europe on the altar of either détente or Titoism with attendance at self-

---

[63] For the stunningly candid "Minutes of the 290th NSC Meeting, July 12, 1956," see Csaba Békés, Malcolm Byrne, and János M. Rainer, eds., *The 1956 Hungarian Revolution: A History in Documents—A National Security Archive Cold War Reader* (Budapest: Central European University Press, 2002), 129–35. As Nixon held out for maximalist if unattainable goals—i.e., liberation—he said that "it would not be an unmixed evil, from the point of view of U.S. interest, if the Soviet iron fist were to come down again on the Soviet bloc, though on balance it would be more desirable, of course, if the pres-ent liberalizing trend in relations between the Soviet Union and its satellites continued." With respect to spreading Titoism Secretary of State Dulles, despite his public advocacy of liberation, thought Tito-ism might be a useful step toward independence. Behind the scenes, Dulles kept changing his mind on this issue.

[64] Of the many examples showing President Eisenhower's reluctance to push the "liberation line," and his interest in finding common ground with Moscow, particularly telling was his discussion with Sec-retary of State Dulles in February 1956. Even before Khrushchev's de-Stalinization speech in Moscow, Eisenhower—referring to RFE's ongoing program of launching balloons over Eastern Europe, which released propaganda materials in the air—told Dulles he "doubted the results [of the balloon program] would justify the inconvenience involved." He "thought the operation should now be suspended." (Im-portant to note: The balloon program that started in August 1951 was suspended only after the Hun-garian revolt was crushed in November 1956.) While saying that he agreed with the president, Dulles also told him that "we should handle it so it would not look as though we had been caught with jam

satisfying prayer breakfasts devoted to the enslaved peoples of Eastern Europe. The dimension of confrontation or at least the rhetoric of confrontation had to remain the central part of the policy mix that the United States presented both to its own people and to the world.

As the United States thus navigated the muddy waters of confrontation, competition, and cooperation after Stalin's death, the leaders and staff of RFE undoubtedly *listened* to all of Washington's signals but *heard* only those it wanted to hear—the calls for confrontation. Though the inclination of U.S. diplomats and Western European allies was to play down the confrontational component of U.S. policy, RFE tended to play it up. Seeking to subvert the Soviet bloc that was its mandate, RFE was putting Moscow on the defensive by encouraging the Eastern Europeans to believe that one day, somehow, they would become free. What else should RFE have done? By its very nature, it was in the business of subverting and transforming the Communist world rather than reforming it. How could a radio station created by the United States government to sustain the ideal of a free Europe promote either the Titoist model (which signified foreign-policy independence but domestic repression) or accommodation with the Kremlin (which signified at least partial acceptance of the prevailing status quo)? The simple answer to these rhetorical questions is that RFE had no choice but to stress the confrontational dimension of U.S. policy, but it should have also reported the new complexities of the post-Stalin era in Washington's approach to the Soviet bloc.

Aside from such RFE officials and reporters as Jan Nowak, of the Polish Desk, or Hungarians like Imre Kovács and Gyula Borbándi, almost no one in Washington or at RFE's offices in New York and Munich even contemplated the question of how the United States might or would achieve liberation. *How will it happen?* Among wise outsiders, *The Economist* warned: "To encourage in any way, even by accident, the belief that the West is preparing to go to war for the liberation of Poland, Czechoslovakia and the rest is to mislead millions of gallant people." Seeing the discrepancy between what was publicly said—by RFE,

---

on our fingers." See John Foster Dulles, "Memorandum of Conversation with the President," February 6, 1956, as quoted in Johanna C. Granville, *The First Domino: International Decision Making during the Hungarian Crisis of 1956* (College Station: Texas A&M University Press, 2004), 169.

among others—and what was being done or not done, the prominent British weekly also noted that "what is dangerous is that an unofficial and covert policy of 'actively supporting passive resistance' should run parallel with an official policy of doing next to nothing about Eastern Europe."[65] At RFE, Jan Nowak, who had headed Polish Desk from 1952 to 1976, candidly recalled a few years later that "in the years 1952–1956 I had major difficulty in interpreting and explaining to listeners the true meaning of the liberation policy launched by the Eisenhower-Dulles administration. It was not clear if by 'liberation' the United States meant a rollback of the Soviets by war or by threat of war or if Americans intended to encourage self-liberation by insurgency."[66] Under Nowak's sober and strong leadership, by the way, the Voice of Free Poland was less emotional and confrontational than its Czechoslovak and Hungarian counterparts.

Like everyone else at RFE, members of the Hungarian Desk were fervent anticommunists, of course. The majority subscribed to right-wing but not necessarily radical or far-right views; some of the staffers (using today's idiom) were centrists; one broadcaster was known to have embraced far-left ideas in his youth; and one or two had had ties to extremist right-wing Hungarian parties before or during World War II.[67] Those in the West who referred to the editors and the reporters as "fascists" were wrong.[68] As is customary among political exiles, members of the staff regularly denounced each other, prompting William E.

---

[65] *The Economist*, April 26, 1952, 203–4.

[66] Jan Nowak, "Poles and Hungarians in 1956" (paper prepared for the international conference "Hungary and the World, 1956: The New Archival Evidence," Budapest, September 26–29, 1996), 1.

[67] For a comprehensive, readable, and exceptionally informative account of the vicissitudes of the Hungarian Desk that is unfortunately unavailable in English, see Gyula Borbándi, *Magyarok az Angol Kertben: A Szabad Európa Rádió története* [Hungarians at the English Garden: A History of Radio Free Europe] (Budapest: Európa, 1996), passim. Cf. Arch Puddington, *Broadcasting Freedom: The Cold War Triumph of Radio Free Europe and Radio Liberty* (Lexington: University Press of Kentucky, 2000), 95. Despite its congratulatory subtitle, this is a balanced, judicious book based on the author's interviews with key participants, his intimate knowledge of how the radios worked, and his extensive research in RFE's archives. For the years discussed in this book, particularly valuable is Puddington's chapter on Hungary ("Revolution in Hungary and Crisis at Radio Free Europe"), 89–114, and his important chapter on right-wing attacks on RFE in the 1950s ("Right-Wingers and Revanchists"), 73–88.

[68] In what was otherwise a lively and informative first-hand account by an American reporter, Leslie B. Bain—born in the United States but fluent in Hungarian—reported that "in the opinion of the freedom fighters," many RFE staffers were "discredited fascists and war criminals." See his *The Reluctant Satellites: An Eyewitness Report on East Europe and the Hungarian Revolution* (New York: Macmillan, 1960), 202. Bain also published many articles on Hungary in the influential biweekly magazine *The Reporter*, edited by the legendary Max Ascoli.

Griffith, the station's political adviser and de facto chief for broadcast content, to say—during the course of one of our many conversations years later—that "the Hungarians were likable but difficult."

However, at least until 1956, there was no noticeable disparity between U.S. guidelines and the programs produced and broadcast by the Hungarian Desk. The tone was often passionate, even fiery, and almost always self-righteous; but the substance reflected American instructions. Accordingly, the broadcasts, based on skillful dissection of the Hungarian press and on Western press reports, included news of the kind that interested Hungarian listeners, such as items about happenings behind the Iron Curtain. There were frequent attacks on Communist officials in Budapest, Moscow, and elsewhere. Drawing on an occasional postcard from listeners, which somehow reached the editors in Munich, the Hungarian program at times even identified particularly aggressive or shady local officials by name, letting them know that they were being watched. Soviet economic exploitation was another popular topic. Because Hungary produced some uranium at the time, RFE catered to the popular belief that Hungary had a lot of uranium, which was not true, and that Moscow did not pay enough for this important commodity, which was true. RFE stressed Moscow's domination of the satellites, making it clear that someday Hungary and its neighbors would be free and independent.[69]

As RFE's founders had hoped, the Voice of Free Hungary became an integral part of the domestic political scene. It was the invisible but audible voice of a suppressed people desperate for news and for hope. As a result, RFE's popularity in Hungary—judging by the proportion of listeners choosing RFE over the Voice of America, BBC, or any other station—was phenomenal.[70] Its audience heard what it wanted to hear. Yet, from the beginning, RFE faced a variety of dilemmas and difficulties.

The first problem was the impossibility of reconciling what RFE's

---

[69] Tapes and texts of these broadcasts can be found at the Hoover Institution's not-yet-cataloged RFE archive in Stanford, Calif., and the Hungarian National Archives in Budapest. A special department for the country's top political leadership prepared a particularly useful summary of broadcasts by all "enemy stations," including RFE. Marked "top secret," it is saved on microfilms at the Hungarian National Archives.

[70] Puddington, *Broadcasting Freedom*, 95. RFE's surveys, based on interviews with Hungarian visitors to Austria and Germany, must be carefully evaluated; they might have played down the influence of competing Western stations. On the whole, however, they appear to be accurate.

guidelines formally stated as the radios' basic purpose—"to keep up the hopes of the enslaved people of Eastern and Central Europe"—with another "basic responsibility," which was to refrain from stimulating, encouraging or precipitating "suicidal action based on hopes of armed liberation from the outside."[71] While the broadcasters may have understood the distinction, it is doubtful that Hungarian listeners—who, because of widespread jamming, did not even hear everything—could tell the difference between the United States offering hope but no help; in reality, the fine print was a distinction without a difference. Of course, many if not most listeners, captivated by American salesmanship, preferred to ignore the point that they were not getting what they thought they were being promised.[72]

The second and related problem was RFE's tendency to exaggerate. A seemingly minor but revealing example was the discussion about the proper subtitle for leaflets prepared by RFE Press in New York and in Munich and either mailed to Hungarian addresses or released from balloons over Hungary. Without debate, the title of the publication was set as *Szabad Magyarország* (Free Hungary). But there were two suggestions for a subtitle: *A Nemzeti Ellenállási Mozgalom Lapja* (Journal of the National Resistance Movement) or *A Nemzeti Ellenzéki Mozgalom Lapja* (Journal of the National Opposition Movement).[73] In each case the acronym was *NEM*, a word meaning *no* in Hungarian. The decision was to use *resistance*, not *opposition*, even though there was no resistance and certainly no resistance movement in Hungary in the 1950s.[74]

---

[71] Undated statement—probably issued sometime in 1956—titled "The Evolution of RFE's Policy," RFE archives, Hoover Institution. This statement, referring to the 1952 presidential campaign when the "liberation of the captive peoples was raised," repeats RFE's "Special Guidance for Broadcasters on Liberation," dated September 2, 1952, as follows: "We of RFE . . . cannot comment upon these statements with unqualified optimism, for to do so would be to deceive our listeners by inspiring in them exaggerated hope of Western intervention." Note that this guidance barred "comment" rather than reporting on the topic of liberation, and prohibited only "unqualified" optimism. The very name of the station, broadcast at the beginning and at the end of each program and thus dozens of times a day, contradicted the intention of this guideline. Pronouncing every syllable for special effect, the announcer proclaimed: "This is Radio Free Europe, the Voice of a Free Hungary."

[72] Quite typical was a comment made by a Hungarian refugee—a young textile worker—to RFE interviewers in Vienna on October 22, 1954: "Everyone is happy to know someone stands behind us. It would be good if the Americans were to occupy Hungary so that we might live a life worthy of human beings." Untitled report, RFE archives, Hoover Institution.

[73] Information from Róbert Gábor, who worked on these leaflets in New York for RFE Press (interview, July 25, 2005).

[74] See the immensely important conclusions of a secret study prepared under contract to the U.S. De-

Of course, propaganda is like advertisement: It has to exaggerate to be effective—but exaggerations could also backfire. In this case, the invention of a resistance movement tended to strengthen the often-heard case by hard-line Communist elements for "vigilance" against all enemies, foreign and domestic, and renewed suspicion toward everyone. Sadly, RFE's wish for resistance blinded it to the fact of its nonexistence.

The third problem was that RFE's managers, advisers, editors, and especially staffers on the Hungarian Desk did not take sufficient note of new circumstances after Stalin's death. Like most policymakers in Washington itself at that time, they did not understand the seriousness and implications of the on-again/off-again processes of de-Stalinization in the Soviet Union; they did not take seriously the Titoist—or national Communist—challenge to Moscow's domination of international communism; and they did not recognize the significance of Imre Nagy, Hungary's reformist prime minister from 1953 to 1955. They continued to put forth maximalist demands, refusing to make distinctions among Stalinists and anti-Stalinists, Titoists, revisionists and dogmatists, Maoists, whatever. Given Nagy's record as prime minister from 1953 to 1955, members of RFE's Hungarian section should have been the first to understand that all Communists were not alike.

Especially for these three reasons, RFE's managers did not contemplate the possibility of trying to achieve partial gains; they were mesmerized by fantasies of a slam-dunk. Exemplifying its all-or-nothing mindset was a cartoon RFE printed, together with a brief leaflet, in early 1955, which was then dropped by balloons over Hungary. The cartoon called "Double Funeral" portrayed the recently demoted Soviet leader Georgi Malenkov in one casket, with Imre Nagy, just removed from power, lying next to him in a smaller one. Referring to Nagy, the accompanying commentary (entitled "Moscow's Lackeys") said, sarcasti-

---

partment of the Army, dated January 5, 1956, titled "Hungary: Resistance Activities and Potentials." The conclusions state: "If one were to believe the claims of émigré organizations and the reports of the Communist press, there has been considerable organized resistance of the covert variety in Hungary. However, an analysis of the available information leads to the conclusion that there is really no organized underground movement at the present time. . . . Further, there is evidence that the Communist regime itself was either the sponsor of some of the organizations reported or invented them for the purpose of building up a case against individuals whose removal from positions of public influence was desirable." The full text is deposited at the National Security Archive in Washington in its "Soviet Flashpoints" collection. For a long excerpt, see Békés, Byrne, and M. Rainer, *1956 Hungarian Revolution*, 86–105.

cally, that "another 'great leader' is gone," and "it does not matter which 'comrade' is in charge, Rákosi, Nagy, or [Nagy's Stalinist successor, András] Hegedüs, for as long as traitors and Soviet lackeys continue in power more of the products of our labor and more of our wealth will be squandered at the orders of their masters in Moscow."[75] For Hungarians who were allowed to leave the hated collective farms or were released from prison or internment camps under Nagy's prime ministership, this was not only untrue but offensive. Which comrade was in charge *did* make a difference; to them Nagy's ouster *was* a serious setback.[76]

RFE's maximalist outlook also revealed itself in commentaries on the 1955 Geneva summit between President Eisenhower and Soviet leaders. Leaflets, as well as broadcasts, dealing with the "spirit of Geneva" played down the "detail" that for the first time in the postwar era the two sides actually met face to face at the highest level. Instead, a typical commentary discussed the Kremlin's insincerity, which was true enough, stressing that no concessions were made on Eastern Europe, which was also true.[77] Missing was appreciation for the step the president of the United States did choose to take—rightly or wrongly— to find out the intentions of the Kremlin's new, post-Stalin leaders. The message RFE seemed to convey to its Hungarian readers (and listeners) was that as Moscow did not capitulate on Eastern Europe, there was no point in discussing lesser issues between the two sides. The editorial closely reflected the American management's guidance on how to assess the summit for East European audiences.[78]

Meanwhile, observing, in 1955, the Geneva summit, the Austrian peace treaty, and Nikita Khrushchev's visit with Tito, a few of the more

---

[75] RFE archive, Hoover Institution.

[76] Nagy did not make it easy for RFE to see in him the prospects for even limited change. In his otherwise moving and very important address to the Congress of the Patriotic People's Front on October 24, 1954 (see chapter 2 above), Nagy lashed out against RFE's Hungarian leaflets, referring to its authors as traitors and worse. As intelligent analysts should have recognized, this was a political feint— the price Nagy had to pay to reassert his reformist domestic program.

[77] "Genfi szellem" [Spirit of Geneva], *Szabad Magyarország*, no. 12, n.d., 1. I wish to thank István Deák of Columbia University for making available to me his collection of leaflets from 1955 and 1956. A junior member of Radio Free Europe Press at the time, he has since become the leading American scholar on modern Central European history. I greatly benefited from his description of how RFE Press worked.

[78] Cf. "On the Four Power Conference," Special Guidance 22, June 2, 1955, RFE archives, Hoover Institution.

open-minded editors and writers on the Hungarian Desk began to question America's actual commitment to liberation. Leading the way was Imre Kovács, who during World War II fought the Nazis and afterwards led the anticommunist wing of the small National Peasant Party as its secretary general. After he escaped from Hungary in 1947, he lived in Switzerland and then in New York and eventually joined RFE Press. Having impeccable anticommunist credentials, and writing in his private capacity as a politician in exile, he published an essay in the January-February 1956 issue of the émigré bimonthly *Látóhatár* (Horizon), published in Munich, in which he flatly asserted that the emperor had no clothes: "The West will not start a war," he wrote, "in order to liberate the countries of Eastern Europe." He went on to say that it was time to prepare the Hungarian people for the more realistic possibility that change would be achieved by peaceful means and by reform.[79] He broadly hinted that there was a Titoist dénouement in Hungary's future. Echoing this essay, Gyula Borbándi, the bimonthly's editor and an RFE employee in Munich, followed up in the next issue of the magazine with the pointed argument that the West's interest in the freedom of Eastern Europe was limited, and that statements by Western politicians suggesting otherwise should not be taken at face value.[80]

To no one's surprise, exiled politicians—unwilling to face, let alone accept, new realities in the Cold War—promptly denounced the two authors. The attack came primarily but not exclusively from the right. Undoubtedly under pressure in what was an election year in the United States, management called in the "heretics" and told them their views were "erroneous." In Munich, Griffith, the political adviser, lectured Borbándi at some length in a formal setting on June 21, 1956, about RFE and its role as a propagandist engaged in a vital struggle, noting that employees should not expect to have full freedom to express their views if those views differed significantly from RFE's. Griffith said the proper way would have been to submit these views in a memorandum rather than publish them in a magazine. Whereas neither Kovács nor Borbándi

---

[79] Imre Kovács,"Kijózanult emigráció" [Sober-headed emigration], *Látóhatár,* January-February 1956, 4–11, as quoted in Borbándi, *Magyarok az Angol Kertben,* 195–96.

[80] Gyula Borbándi, "Az emigráns politika új útjai" [New ways for immigrant politics], *Látóhatár,* March-April 1956, 113–18, as quoted in Borbándi, *Magyarok az Angol Kertben,* 196.

backed down, Borbándi promised to publish contributions offering different perspectives in the next issue or issues of his magazine. With that the formal hearing ended, but Griffith called in Borbándi for a private discussion as well. According to Borbándi's account, Griffith told him he would not be dismissed, demoted, or reprimanded, but that he should be careful because his enemies would continue to try to make his life miserable.[81] Not for the first time, Griffith—a liberal democrat with strong anticommunist convictions[82]—protected an employee from far-right attack.[83]

Though the formal proceedings against Kovács and Borbándi were gentle enough, their argument did not fall on fertile soil. In the summer of 1956, as the U.S. presidential campaign heated up and the outbreak of the Hungarian revolt approached, Radio Free Europe and its Hungarian section did not play down, let alone abandon, the empty rhetoric of liberation.[84]

---

[81] Borbándi, *Magyarok az Angol Kertben*, 196–98.

[82] Griffith belonged to that group of American intellectuals who were as committed to liberal values as they were opposed to communism and fascism. Zbigniew Brzezinski, who first met him in 1953 and knew him well, and who concurs with that characterization, calls Griffith a man who was also "truly incisive, extremely knowledgeable, and sincerely dedicated to the cause of freedom in Central and Eastern Europe." (Interview with Brzezinski, September 9, 2005.)

[83] Griffith is also known to have defended members of the Hungarian desk much earlier, in 1951, when a U.S. Embassy official in Lisbon accused two staffers of "Communist association." Puddington, *Broadcasting Freedom*, 82. Puddington's perceptive summary of the context of these attacks is worth quoting: "The radio station's adversaries came almost exclusively from the ranks of ultraconservatives, who were convinced that its message was insufficiently anti-Communist. Given the wrenching divisions that erupted over America's Cold War policies in later years, the fact that ardent right-wingers were RFE's chief detractors might strike many as unusual. In the 1950s, however, the real debate over American foreign policy did not involve a division between Right and Left, but pitted mainstream anti-Communists against ultra-anti-Communists. To some of the ultras, RFE's brand of anticommunism did not measure up." Ibid., 81. RFE staffers—unlike broadcasters for the Voice of America—were largely protected from attacks by the far right, not only because of Griffith and other American advisers at RFE stood up for them but also because of Cord Meyer, head of the CIA's International Organization department that supervised Radio Free Europe (but not the Voice of America). Because Meyer himself had been suspended once when the FBI turned his youthful liberal inclinations into "Communist associations," he took the issue seriously and presumably resisted demands by the radio's far-right critics. For his own dramatic account of what happened, including the text of the FBI's charges against him, see Cord Meyer, *Facing Reality: From World Federalism to the CIA* (New York: Harper & Row, 1980). Ironically, Meyer, after leaving the CIA, became a columnist for an American daily that featured both right-wing and far-right views.

[84] Here, and in chapter 5 below, I offer a critical assessment of RFE's Hungarian broadcasts before and during the revolt. I hasten to add, however, that my view of RFE's subsequent work is very favorable. In the 1980s, I reviewed a whole week of Hungarian broadcasts for the Board for International Broadcasting, RFE's supervisory agency, and I found it all informative and balanced. Unfortunately, many critics of RFE, such as Senator J. W. Fulbright, continued to judge RFE on the basis of early mistakes that were gradually corrected after 1956.

• 5 •

To say the least, the Hungarian revolt took the United States by surprise. No official in Washington, at Radio Free Europe Committee headquarters in New York, or in Munich anticipated what was about to happen. No U.S. government agency had made any plans for such an eventuality. Why not? Why didn't the Policy Planning Staff of the Department of State prepare a diplomatic proposal that could have been dusted off and presented to the secretary of state or the president of the United States? Why didn't the CIA prepare proposals for overt or covert action, or both? Why didn't the managers of RFE prepare plans for serious commentaries to be broadcast that would have advanced both U.S. interests and the Hungarian people's desire for a better life?

The reason, in a nutshell, was *not* the absence of information; it was the lack of interest in partial change.

By early and mid-1956, mainly because Western correspondents had growing access to both official and unofficial sources in several Communist capitals, the United States had plenty of information about the Soviet bloc. Having learned in March that Khrushchev had delivered an unscheduled, secret speech at the Twentieth Party Congress in February denouncing Stalin's crimes, the CIA made it a top priority to get a copy—and it did.[85] The speech was translated into Hungarian, of course, and RFE presented it in its entirety and in summary form as well. It also broadcast quotations from the world press about its meaning and significance; the view most frequently mentioned was that while communism was on the defensive, it was not about to abdicate, and therefore it had to be pushed harder to make genuine concessions. The Khrushchev speech—and anti-Stalinism in general—was welcomed less as a sign of change than as a helpful propaganda tool to be used to castigate and divide the Communist world. Against the background of three critical events in 1955—the Geneva summit, the Austrian peace treaty, and Soviet-Yugoslav rapprochement—it was now Khrushchev's extraordinary address that mattered, setting off considerable excitement about incorporating it into Western efforts showing that even his successors saw Stalin as a monster.

Information about Hungary was also plentiful. Though the United States did not have secret sources in Budapest, Washington analysts had

---

[85] Cf. fn. 56 above.

learned by then how to read between the lines in the Hungarian press. U.S. Legation dispatches revealed growing awareness of political and intellectual ferment in the country. In particular, the Legation conveyed a good deal of learned speculation about the meaning of Rákosi's dismissal in mid-1956, which coincided with a stopover by Soviet leader Anastas Mikoyan in Budapest—on his way from Moscow to Belgrade. Was the Kremlin so eager to appease Tito that it offered Rákosi's head as proof of its good intentions?[86] There were also more frequent visits there by Western correspondents, some of whom—notably the very well-informed Simon Bourgin of *Time* magazine—often showed up in Munich to describe what he had seen.[87]

Although both Washington and Munich were more knowledgeable than they used to be, their understanding of the Communist regimes' vulnerabilities did not reflect changing realities. RFE and U.S. intelligence analysts dealing with Hungary overlooked the possibility that Nagy and his anti-Stalinist followers represented the most serious challenge to the Stalinist regime. They believed it was the Catholic Church and the peasantry that would shape the country's future. That analysis was right about the church as of, say, 1946, but not in 1956. With József Cardinal Mindszenty and dozens of priests in jail, and others terrorized by the Hungarian secret police and forced to inform on their colleagues, the church had lost the influence it had once had. As for the peasantry, it never was—not then, not before—a revolutionary force in Hungarian society; the peasantry tended to submit to the authorities instead.

If Hungary were to change, then, it would have had to come from within the Communist Party and from increasingly distressed, angry, and vocal intellectuals (see chapter 4). RFE analysts knew well that the party was beset by factional struggle, but they did not understand that some of yesterday's Stalinists had become genuine anti-Stalinist reformers. Their broadcasts did not offer even a modicum of encouragement to Nagy and his supporters. To identify Nagy & Company rather than the church as the force most likely to weaken the Communist

---

[86] See, e.g., "Dispatch from the Legation in Hungary to the Department of State," August 30, 1956, in *Foreign Relations of the United States, 1955–1957* (Washington, D.C.: U.S. Government Printing Office, 1985), vol. 25, 231–41.

[87] Thanks to Bourgin, transcripts of three of his lectures at RFE/Munich—dated May 22, 1956, July 5, 1956, and August 31, 1956—are in my personal files. Bourgin was a frequent visitor and a perceptive observer. The title of his July lecture—the only one with a title—was "Intellectual Revolt in Hungary and Petőfi Circle Discussion (From a Recent Visitor to Budapest)."

regime would have required recognition of the usefulness of nonsys-temic change—acceptance of the proposition that the only realistic, practical alternative to communism for the time being was reformed communism rather than capitalism, freedom, and independence. In-deed, Korea aside, the United States did not pursue limited goals, aim-ing as it might have at something less than the complete defeat of com-munism. Seeking partial gains was neither the American nor the Eastern European émigré broadcasters' way, certainly not at a time of justified concern about communism and Soviet aggression. America's Communist enemies were powerful, determined, and hostile, and the Cold War was for real.

In addition, bureaucratic inertia stood in the way of pursuing lim-ited change. Fearful of communism and anxious to protect the United States against its enemies, Washington had set on a course of action in 1946–47 from which there was no easy escape. The CIA's operational division and Radio Free Europe had been set up to do what they could to get rid of communism rather than to reform it and make it only less repressive and aggressive. Though a few officials at the Department of State were on the lookout for attainable goals, they did not constitute an effective countervailing force to initiate a new approach. Besides, Secretary of State Dulles was comfortable with the old policy mix.

Political circumstances did not favor abandonment of the goal of lib-eration either. Both major parties assumed the existence of an "ethnic vote" in such critical states as Illinois, Michigan, Ohio, Pennsylvania, New York, and New Jersey, with Poles, Hungarians, Czechs, and others voting as a bloc on the basis of which of the two parties was *really* com-mitted to liberation. The Republicans led the way, promising "the end of the negative, futile and immoral policy of 'containment' which aban-dons countless human beings to a despotism and godless terrorism."[88] Buttressing such bravado was the fear Senator McCarthy had generated, which all but stifled rational discourse in the U.S. government about communism and how to deal with it. The effect of intimidation was seen in the 1956 Democratic platform that tried to outbid the Repub-licans by condemning the Eisenhower administration "for its heartless record of broken promises to the unfortunate victims of Communism.

---

[88] Republican Party Platform of 1952, at http://www.presidency.ucsb.edu/platform.phb, 55.

... We look forward to the day when the liberties of all captive nations will be restored to them."[89]

Did those who proposed, wrote, and endorsed such inflated rhetoric know that it had no underpinnings in policy? It appears that some did, but most did not. Frank Lindsay had reached a reasonable assessment about the failure of rollback (and left the CIA in early 1953), and Imre Kovács advocated gradual change in his essay printed in the émigré journal *Látóhatár* in early 1956. C. L. Sulzberger, the preeminent foreign affairs columnist of the *New York Times*, wrote frequently and wisely about promoting Titoism in Eastern Europe.[90] Yet for every Lindsay, Kovács, or Sulzberger, there were thousands of officials who chose not to go against the received wisdom of the moment. Fearing to be labeled timid or "soft" on communism, elected politicians, in particular, shied away from embracing such sober advice. Détente with the Kremlin or Titoism as a first step toward freedom did not resonate with their constituents while liberation could and did, especially among the East European ethnic communities of the northeast and the Midwest. Advocating anything short of victory would have been tantamount to appeasement. In an oft-quoted essay, "The Illusion of American Omnipotence," D. W. Brogan observed in 1952 that "probably the only people in the world who now have the historical sense of inevitable victory are the Americans."[91]

Perhaps especially in the 1950s, American political culture did not favor a quest for limited foreign policy goals. Walter Lippmann's classic counsel first published in 1943—"The nation must maintain its objectives and its power in equilibrium, its purposes within means and its means equal to its purposes, its commitments related to its resources and its resources adequate to its commitments"[92]—appealed only to professional students of foreign policy. Such experts as Lippmann, Hans Morgenthau, and Charles Burton Marshall, along with many others, repeatedly commented about the need to bring ends and means into a harmonious relationship—saying the United States should do what it

---

[89] Democratic Party Platform of 1956, at http://www.presidency.ucsb.edu/platform.phb, 66.

[90] "American Policy in Eastern Europe," *New York Times*, April 18, 21, and 23, 1956.

[91] *Harper's Magazine* 205 (December 1952): 21–28. Brogan neglected to mention that Communists had also long believed or at least advocated a "historical sense of inevitable victory."

[92] Walter Lippmann, *U.S. Foreign Policy: Shield of the Republic* (Boston: Little, Brown, 1943), 7.

can rather than what it believes it must—but they were outside kib-itzers with no political constituencies to lose.[93] These experts—I had called them "limitationists" in my first scholarly article[94]—offered an al-ternative that lacked emotional appeal; they wanted, and expected, Americans to be as excited about their team hitting a single as about hitting a home run.

Before the brave days of the Hungarian revolt, Americans wanted to believe that they did not have to settle for a single because a home run was possible. They wanted to believe that the appeal of freedom was so strong that they would not have to use force and yet the oppressed people would rise—and somehow prevail. They wanted to believe that Washington, having offered "hope," would not necessarily have to offer help. In such an atmosphere, few were willing to question how this would all play out. Doubts were stifled by groupthink and the culture of Amer-ican exceptionalism. *In such an atmosphere of triumphalism, a diplomatic strategy that would have focused on the calm pursuit of partial gains fell by the wayside.* This is why Hungarian broadcasters in Munich and their American managers had so few conflicts: The Hungarian editors, re-porters, and commentators did not have any difficulty gaining the go-ahead from their American bosses to egg on their Hungarian listeners.

And this is why American policy toward Hungary, and Eastern Eu-rope in general, was long on words and short on deeds—in place was "NATO" of a different kind: No Action, Talk Only.

---

[93] See, esp., Lippmann *U.S. Foreign Policy*; Hans Morgenthau, *In Defense of the National Interest* (New York: Alfred A. Knopf, 1951); Charles Burton Marshall, *The Limits of Foreign Policy* (New York: Henry Holt, 1954); and J. W. Fulbright, *The Arrogance of Power* (New York: Vintage Books, 1967). Perhaps the clearest explanation of this perspective—that problems abroad should be mitigated because they can-not always be solved—was offered by Charles Burton Marshall in this colorful warning against exces-sive ambitions: "Suppose money grew on trees. Suppose power were for the asking. Suppose time could be expanded and contracted as in the story by H. G. Wells. Suppose Aladdin's lamp, the seven-league boots, and the other fairy tale formulas for complete efficacy were to come true and to be made monopolistically available to Americans. We would then have a situation in which we could do any-thing we wanted. We could then equate our policy with goals. In the world of fact, however, making foreign policy is not like that at all. It is not like cheerleading. It is like quarterbacking. The real work comes not in deciding where you want to go—that is the easiest part of it—but in figuring out how to get there. One could no more describe a nation's foreign policy solely in terms of objectives than one could write a man's biography in terms of his New Year's resolutions. Foreign policy consists of what a nation does in the world—not what it yearns or aspires to. The sphere of doing, as distinguished from the sphere of desire and aspiration, is governed by limits." Charles Burton Marshall, *The Exercise of Sovereignty: Papers on Foreign Policy* (Baltimore: Johns Hopkins University Press, 1965), 41.

[94] Charles Gati, "Another Grand Debate? The Limitationist Critique of American Foreign Policy," *World Politics* 21, no. 1 (October 1968): 133–51.

4

Moscow and Budapest before the Explosion

> As people today refer to the young people of 1848 [who fought for Hungarian independence against Austrian and Russian oppressors], so I wish that history will remember the young people of 1956 who will help our nation in creating a better future.
>
> —*Tibor Déry, a disillusioned Communist writer, speaking at a tumultuous, nine-hour debate of the Petőfi Circle on June 27, 1956*

· 1 ·

Although the Kremlin had plenty of reasons to worry about the shaky state of Hungary's economic and political life, its policies toward Hungary were largely a function of the struggle for power at the top of the Soviet hierarchy following Stalin's death. In particular, as a result of a temporary hard-line alliance between Molotov and Khrushchev at the turn of 1954–55, Malenkov lost out—and so Nagy, Malenkov's protégé, had to go too. Reversing the very policies they had initiated and implemented in June 1953, the Soviet leaders dumped Nagy irrespective of what Mikoyan, Khrushchev, Malenkov, and even Voroshilov (especially when he was drunk) and the otherwise dogmatic but smart Suslov must have known all along, which was that only Nagy and further reforms could save their cause in that troubled country. Masterminding this political and ideological somersault was Khrushchev, who ganged up with Molotov, his former archenemy, against Malenkov, his former ally, in order to undercut Malenkov and end up in the No. 1 position. To achieve this goal, for a few months in 1954–55, Khrushchev adopted several of Molotov's views, including opposition to change in Central and Eastern Europe.

As they undid the 1953 Hungarian de-Stalinization processes, the Soviet leaders acted in response to *their* uncertainties and *their* internal politics, combined with a misguided notion of how to ensure stability in Central and Eastern Europe. In 1953, worried about instability, they promoted Nagy; in 1955, worried about instability, they demoted him. In 1953, they knew they needed Nagy and reform; by early 1955, they failed to remember what they knew in 1953.

Complicating matters was the prevalence of what may be called a "disconnect"—the Hungarians call it *fáziseltolódás* or phase-delay—between Moscow and Budapest in the second half of 1955 (after the short-lived Khrushchev-Molotov coalition began to fall apart at the July 1955 Central Committee plenum) and especially in 1956 (after Khrushchev formally dethroned Stalin at the Twentieth Congress of the Communist Party of the Soviet Union, or CPSU, in February). The Hungarian leaders even failed to take note of the Kremlin's surprisingly, and radically, new approach toward Austria and Yugoslavia in mid-1955. András Hegedüs, who had by then replaced Imre Nagy as Hungary's prime minister, recalled later that he and his colleagues did not draw the proper lessons from the Kremlin's new "peaceful coexistence" line: "Despite the signing of the Warsaw Pact [in May 1955] there was an ongoing thaw in international relations. We did not expect this and we did not prepare for it. We did not draw the appropriate conclusion from two important developments: the Austrian State Treaty and Khrushchev and Bulganin's 'going to Canossa' in Belgrade. We fell behind by a move or two! We did not read the signs on the wall!"[1]

As a result of this "disconnect," the Hungarians exceeded the Krem-

---

[1] András Hegedüs, *A történelem és a hatalom igézetében: Életrajzi elemzések* [Spell-bound by history and power: Autobiographical assessments] (Budapest: Kossuth, 1988), 235.

lin's instructions. Nagy was supposed to have been demoted; instead, he lost all his positions, even his party membership.

The Soviet leaders turned against Nagy in late 1954. Though they did so mostly because of the ongoing domestic struggle for power and advantage, another consideration was growing fear of losing control over the bloc. Serious disturbances in 1953 in East Berlin and in Plzen made them increasingly reluctant to further extend de-Stalinization to their dependencies.[2] The issue was no longer Mátyás Rákosi's blind observance of Stalinist dogma, as it was in June 1953, but the supposedly negative consequences of change under Nagy since then. In Moscow, old, imperial interests and habits had again come to replace the initial hope after Stalin's death that some concessions to the people of Central and Eastern Europe would buy regional stability. In a dramatic encounter in the Kremlin in January 1955 (see section 2 below), Khrushchev & Company degraded Nagy—the very man they had elevated to the top leadership post fewer than two years earlier because he was seen as the man best qualified to temper popular hostility to the Communist system. As it happened, Nagy was now converted—in the eyes of the Soviet leaders—into a right-wing deviationist, an opportunist, a favorite of the class enemy and of the imperialists.

There were other reasons, too, for Moscow's turn against Nagy in late 1954 and early 1955. Aside from intricate infighting in the Kremlin and new fears that Hungary under Nagy was unstable—maybe even more so than before—the decision reflected favorably on Rákosi's political agility. First, while on vacation in the Soviet Union in late 1954, he managed to convince several CPSU Politburo members that Nagy, his nemesis, was a dangerous anti-Soviet nationalist.[3]

---

[2] Cf. Mark Kramer's three-part tour de force, "The Early Post-Stalin Succession Struggle and Upheavals in East-Central Europe: Internal-External Linkages in Soviet Policy Making," *Journal of Cold War Studies* 1, nos. 1, 2, and 3 (1999).

[3] Although records of Rákosi's presumably informal conversations with Soviet leaders have not been found in Russian or Hungarian archives, his own account—when compared with the Soviet leaders' change of heart and Ambassador Andropov's contemporary dispatches to the Kremlin—seems quite accurate. See Mátyás Rákosi, *Visszaemlékezések 1940–1956* [Memoirs 1940–1956], 2 vols. (Budapest: Napvilág, 1997), vol. 2, 971–72. Cf. András Hegedüs, *Élet egy eszme árnyékában: Életrajzi interjú* [Life in the shadow of an ideal: Memoir interview] (Vienna: Zoltán Zsille, 1985), 216–17. In the fall of 1954, Hegedüs, a deputy prime minister at the time, visited Rákosi twice in Moscow (where he was convalescing in a sanatorium). Rákosi told him that the Soviet leaders had come to "oppose Imre

Second, with Soviet ambassador Yuri Andropov in his corner, Rákosi had an influential ally who knew how to manipulate the Kremlin. The ambassador's deftly composed dispatches in 1954–56, which have since surfaced from secret Kremlin archives, reveal how he bolstered party leader Rákosi over all other possibilities, notably Nagy.[4] Though appearing impartial and judicious, Andropov played Iago to the Kremlin's Othello by implying that the alternative to Rákosi was chaos, not reform.

Third, by January 1955, Nagy's original advocates in the Kremlin were either dead (Beria) or partly demoted (Malenkov), and Malenkov, to stay on as a player, turned coat, backed the new anti-Nagy consensus, and strongly denounced his former Hungarian protégé. Fourth and finally, the Kremlin's endorsement of Hungary's intransigent Stalinists in 1955–56 may have been also due to a serious geopolitical concern about the rise of a potential mini-alliance made up of Austrians, Yugoslavs, and Hungarians. A cooperative venture along such lines was not far from Tito's or Imre Nagy's mind,[5] and for Moscow it was an implicit threat to its claim to sole leadership of the world Communist movement and even more directly to the newly founded Warsaw Pact.

If the Soviet Union had consistently applied the spirit of its new foreign policy initiatives and its on-again, off-again domestic de-Stalinization campaign to Hungary, it should have fired Rákosi, Ernő Gerő, Mihály Farkas, and their ilk and strengthened Nagy in the Hungarian party's Politburo, Secretariat, and Central Committee. This did not happen, however. On the contrary, the Kremlin reversed Nagy's reform-oriented New Course, and in so doing split the Hungarian party and

---

Nagy's behavior and considered Hungarian conditions as they were developing dangerous." In conversations with Hegedüs, Molotov testified to the accuracy of Rákosi's assessment.

[4] As Andropov advanced his barely hidden agenda, which was to turn Moscow against Nagy, he displayed the skills of a cunning politician that the world would come to face later in his career when he became head of the KGB and, eventually, of the CPSU. Cf. Magdolna Baráth, ed., *Szovjet nagyköveti iratok Magyarországról 1953–1956: Kiszeljov és Andropov titkos jelentései* [Soviet ambassadors' documents about Hungary 1953–1956: Kiselyov's and Andropov's secret dispatches] (Budapest: Napvilág Kiadó, 2002). This excellent volume contains eighty-one secret cables from the Soviet Union's Budapest Embassy to Communist Party, government, and KGB headquarters in Moscow. During an interview in the summer of 2003 in Moscow and in an e-mail message sent to me in early 2005, Alexander Yakovlev kept stressing the significance of Andropov's "sinister activities" in and toward Central and Eastern Europe, particularly Hungary. I am grateful to the late Mr. Yakovlev for taking an interest in my study, shown in his willingness, confirmed in another email message only two months before his untimely death in October 2005, to write the preface to this book's Russian edition.

[5] Cf. Imre Nagy, *On Communism: In Defense of the New Course* (New York: Praeger, 1957), passim.

sparked the intellectuals' powerful movement against the return of the Old Guard. More than anything else, it was political division at the top and the intellectuals' disaffection that created a prerevolutionary mood in the country.

As noted, there was a "disconnect" as well between Moscow and Budapest with respect to two of the Kremlin's foreign policy innovations in the mid-1950s.

One was Soviet-Yugoslav rapprochement. Earlier, notably from 1948 to 1953, Soviet and Hungarian references to the Yugoslav dictator Tito had been unusually hostile; Tito was regularly identified, for example, as the "chained dog of American imperialism." Relations with Belgrade had advanced after Stalin's death but at first, for a couple of years, Moscow preferred to upgrade only state-to-state rather than party-to-party relations, favoring renewed contact but not renewed comradeship. This is why the world was astonished when Khrushchev, received by Tito in his sparklingly white military uniform, landed in Belgrade in May 1955 and began his speech at the airport by addressing the old renegade and arch-enemy with these words: "Dear Comrade Tito!" *Comrade* Tito? There were those in the Soviet leadership, notably Molotov, who had approved upgrading state-to-state relations but not the restoration of comradely relations with a country they continued to regard as nonsocialist. Behind such ideological reservations did they conceal their defense of Stalin's, and Molotov's, excommunication of Tito's Yugoslavia from the Communist camp in 1948, but this time Khrushchev prevailed.[6] The Hungarian party reluctantly followed his lead, but it was not adopting conciliatory measures that Tito was expecting; Rákosi did not want to make up for the venomous insults he had hurled at Yugoslavia and its leaders in the late 1940s and early 1950s.

Nor did Moscow and Budapest share exactly the same perspective with respect to Austria, another of Hungary's next-door neighbors. The

---

[6] In his fine, and wonderfully readable, biography of Khrushchev, William Taubman reports that when Molotov continued to take exception to Khrushchev's policies even after the Belgrade visit, Khrushchev blamed him for uniting and mobilizing the world against the Soviet Union. "Khrushchev pointed to Korea. 'We began the Korean War. Everyone knows we did,' he exclaimed." By "we," Khrushchev meant Molotov. William Taubman, *Khrushchev: The Man and His Era* (New York: W. W. Norton, 2003), 268. In contrast, Khrushchev seemed to be pressing for the doctrine of "peaceful coexistence": Don't make enemies if you don't have to, but stay ready, compete vigorously, and remain vigilant.

Kremlin, after years of saying *nyet*, agreed in May 1955 to the Austrian State Treaty that provided for all foreign troops based in Austria since 1945, including Moscow's, to be withdrawn; in exchange, Austria pledged only to forgo NATO membership in the future. The Austrian deal had a major implication for Hungary (and Romania): It forced Moscow to act promptly to find another legal rationale for stationing its forces in the two countries. The old excuse—that the Soviet military remained there to maintain communications links between Soviet troops in Austria and the Soviet homeland—was suddenly "inoperative." This is why the Kremlin established the Warsaw Pact in May 1955, just one day before the signing of the Austrian State Treaty. An alliance in name only, the Warsaw Pact was an instrument of Moscow's control over its dominion, allowing the Soviet Union to keep its troops "temporarily" in Hungary and protect the Communist regime there. Still, Austria's newly gained independence and neutrality signaled changing times in the Soviet approach to the outside world.

For official Budapest, these two events were disquieting, even ominous. In Rákosi's very neighborhood, and not at some distant land, Soviet foreign policy was on the move. What with the Geneva summit of 1955, too, it appeared that Moscow was making new deals in Europe—some of them near the Hungarian border—that could have an impact on Soviet relations with members of the bloc as well, especially Hungary (because of its proximity to Yugoslavia and Austria). Yet, given all the infighting in the Kremlin and also the ever-changing party line, no one could be sure what Moscow had in mind. Even well-informed insiders were mystified. What did the Soviet expedition to Belgrade, the withdrawal of troops from Austria, and the smiles of Geneva signify? Were they nothing but a modern version of the old Leninist tactic of taking one step backward at a time of Soviet vulnerability (after having taken at least two steps forward), or was Moscow making real concessions in an effort to come to terms with the West?

Rákosi had, or should have had, every reason to worry about the changes taking place in the Soviet Union and in Soviet relations with Austria and especially Yugoslavia. If the Kremlin was indeed experimenting with a new foreign policy course and if it were to apply it to its East European client states, he would have to go. After all, the Kremlin had made it clear to him back in June 1953 that he was responsible for what had gone wrong in *his* Stalinist Hungary (see chapter 2). Since then, Rákosi had not changed; in 1955, he was not even an improved version of his old self. Because no East European leader had attacked Tito more viciously than he did, would Tito now seek revenge? Would he want to humble his arrogant Hungarian foe? Would he try to persuade Moscow to undo Nagy's dismissal? After all, Nagy was far more acceptable to the Yugoslavs. His views also coincided with the Kremlin's new anti-Stalinist idiom.

In the end, the ups and downs of Soviet policy toward the region created a strange paradox. At the helm again, Hungarian Stalinists acted in such a way as to undermine the Communist system *because they remained Stalinists*, while former Stalinists turned pro-Nagy reformers undermined the system *because they became anti-Stalinists*. The battle between dogmatic and disillusioned Communists turned out to be the essential backdrop to what was to happen in the fall of 1956.

Along these lines, focusing on the relationship between Moscow and Budapest, section 2 of this chapter describes a dramatic summit in the Kremlin on January 8, 1955, that returned Rákosi to center stage. Section 3 deals with the rise of growing opposition to the Stalinist diehards in 1955 and especially after the Twentieth CPSU Congress in 1956, which involved mainly Jewish-born intellectuals in a movement that sought Nagy's return to power. Section 4 offers a glimpse of Nagy's role in Soviet-Hungarian relations during the summer of 1956 as intricate maneuvers involving Moscow, Budapest, and Belgrade showed considerable Soviet anxiety about Hungary on the eve of the revolution.

· 2 ·

The Hungarian Politburo delegation that met the Soviet Politburo in the Kremlin for four hours on January 8, 1955, consisted of Rákosi and Nagy as well as Farkas and two younger leaders, Lajos Ács and Béla Szalai. Szalai took detailed notes.[7] With the important exception of Beria,

---

[7] "Notes of Discussion between the CPSU CC Presidium and a HWP Leadership Delegation in Moscow on January 8, 1955," in *The 1956 Hungarian Revolution: A History in Documents*, ed. Csaba Békés, Malcolm Byrne, and János M. Rainer (Budapest: Central European Press, 2002), 60–65. Csaba Farkas translated the document from Hungarian into English. Unfortunately, these notes offer only a

who was by then dead, the Soviet delegation was composed of almost exactly the same leaders who in 1953 anointed Nagy as prime minister and put Rákosi down. Soviet ambassador to Hungary Yuri Andropov was also present, but he took no active part in the discussion. This time, Szalai's notes reveal, the Soviet Politburo took Rákosi's side in the fight between the Hungarians. At one point, Khrushchev even suggested that Nagy could have the same fate as Stalin's victims in the 1930s.

Calling Nagy "conceited and undisciplined," Voroshilov began the proceedings by telling Nagy that he had "to admit his mistakes unconditionally." These mistakes had to do with his neglect of industry, especially heavy industry, and with his excessive interest in agriculture. Contrary to facts known by all, Voroshilov claimed that land was "not nationalized in Hungary," implying it was Nagy's fault. He ended up his harangue with what seems to have bothered the Soviet leaders most: that Nagy had appealed "to the public against certain members of the [Hungarian] Political Committee" [Politburo] and that "border[ed] on treason." Those were strong words.

Molotov came next. "In July 1953," he said, "Comrade Nagy was lobbying in his speech for the peasants to leave the agricultural cooperatives. [Interruption by Comrade Nagy: it was not my idea. We were given advice here. . . .] Indeed, Beria gave you such advice at the time, but after Beria's arrest we warned you to think twice and be careful. Comrade Nagy supported the withdrawal from the cooperatives with much pathos, which aggravates his mistake." Citing Nagy's article of October 20, 1954, in the Hungarian party daily,[8] Molotov went on to crit-

---

few details about what the five Hungarian participants said, except for a few interjections and a statement that "they presented their opinion about the main issues of Hungary's political and economic situation, with special emphasis on the palpable conflicts within the party leadership and their possible causes." A subsequent Hungarian Politburo meeting held in Budapest on January 13, 1955, indirectly but conclusively confirmed the accuracy of Szalai's notes. No Russian record of this meeting has yet been located.

[8] "A Központi Vezetőség ülése után" [After the Central Committee's Meeting], *Szabad Nép*, October 20, 1954. For a first-rate analysis of Nagy's article, see János M. Rainer, *Nagy Imre: Politikai életrajz* [Imre Nagy: Political biography], 2 vols. (Budapest: 1956-os Intézet, 1996 and 1999), vol. 2, 92–93. Rainer correctly points out that Nagy's article was indeed quite "radical" for its time. Nagy argued that before June 1953 (when he took over the prime ministership) the country had not been doing well and the party had lacked "collective leadership"; he praised the "rehabilitation" of innocent political prisoners; and he promised speedy democratization in the future. As the Soviet leaders reminded him, Nagy found nothing good to say about pre-1953 Hungary; of course, the same Soviet leaders had found nothing good to say about pre-1953 Hungary during their June 1953 encounter in the Kremlin. Moreover, in hardly more than a year later, in February 1956, Khrushchev was to denounce Stalin and

icize Nagy for deflating the achievements of Soviet agriculture and other achievements both in the Soviet Union and in Hungary before June 1953—as if all good things in Hungary had begun since Nagy's promotion. "You said that you are unable to work together with Comrade Rákosi," concluded Molotov. "There is no better leadership in Hungary than that of Comrade Rákosi."

Next was Kaganovich: "The Soviet Union liberated Hungary. Why did Comrade Nagy fail to mention that in the article [of October 20, 1954]? You do not write about what happened in the last ten years either. You think that everything [was] wrong. That is not our opinion." Warming up, Kaganovich went on to claim that Nagy's "ideas reflect the opinion of the petit bourgeoisie *and partly that of the enemy.* . . . When you talk about [improving] the standard of living, you support the village bourgeoisie. *The motto of prosperity was the catchword of Bukharin. . . . You simply rehash some ideas that have already been smashed in the Soviet Union*" (italics added). Echoing the Soviet consensus, Kaganovich nevertheless did not urge Nagy's removal from power. "It would be much better," he said, "if you could correct your mistakes and carry on working as before."

This was the formula Malenkov recommended to Nagy: Assume sole responsibility for neglecting investments in heavy industry (even though both Nagy and Malenkov had cut such investments with the full support of the whole Soviet Politburo). When Malenkov spoke, he also referred to Nagy's October article in *Szabad Nép,* which he said he had read "with considerable anxiety. Had Comrade Nagy not signed it, we would have thought that someone alien to the notion of Marxism wrote it. Rotten movements hide behind Comrade Nagy." This erstwhile sponsor of Nagy went on to indicate how Nagy could save his job and his neck: "Comrade Nagy has to write down for himself what kind of mistakes he has made, then he has to submit it to the Political Committee."

In his brief and relatively mild intervention, Mikoyan was apparently the only Politburo member to allude to their previous encounter in

---

assess the Soviet Union's Stalinist past far more harshly than Nagy did in his article with respect to Hungary. Showing, impressively, that he was capable of making independent judgments, Nagy's article had *preceded* Khrushchev's speech by fifteen months. Yet, when all is said and done, it is unclear why the Soviet leaders kept citing this article rather than Nagy's far more widely known speech and appearance at the October 1954 Congress of the Patriotic People's Front; see chap. 2, fn. 76, above.

1953. "When Comrade Rákosi made mistakes, we criticized him and he corrected his mistakes. However, he is a man of principles. . . . [But] Comrade Nagy said: 'I am unable to work with Rákosi.' This is the language of ultimatums. . . . If he cares for the party's interests and for Marxism, he [should] condemn his mistakes."

Khrushchev was the last speaker. Unlike his colleagues, he acknowledged that Nagy's criticism of Rákosi was not without merit and that Rákosi had not yet overcome his mistakes. That said, Khrushchev then mercilessly attacked Nagy—the man he had helped install as prime minister only eighteen months earlier—in every possible way and for every possible error. Nagy was representing "antiparty ideas." He was "weak." He encouraged peasants to withdraw from agricultural cooperatives. He was a vain primadonna: "You are not given the opportunity to realize your program, so you say you are not accountable and resign. Your resignation and reticence are nothing but attacks on the party." He was even responsible for the "rather poor state" of proletarian internationalism in Hungary—witness frequent "outbursts of nationalist feelings" at various sports events.[9]

Rambling on, Khrushchev also noted that Voice of America was hoping Nagy would "become a traitor. They hope that there will be Soviet, Yugoslav, and Hungarian [versions of] socialism. . . . Churchill is rubbing his hands now. . . . (Intervention by Comrade Voroshilov: They hope that Hungary will be the same as Yugoslavia.)" Then Khrushchev

---

[9] It is not clear who or what Khrushchev's target was. In the mid-1950s, when Hungary's national soccer team was arguably the best in the world, and so was its water polo team, Hungarian fans were obviously happy and enthusiastic. I attended a good number of soccer and water polo games in those years, but I do not recall any violence or political insults by the fans. The only exception was in 1954, when Hungary beat all of its opponents in the World Cup but lost the final to West Germany, 3–2. Then the fans demonstrated against the coach of the national team, blaming him for the loss and calling for his resignation. I do remember a water polo game between Hungary and the Soviet Union, probably in 1954, that was won by the Hungarians, and although the fans behaved themselves well the two countries played all of their subsequent games behind closed doors so as not to reveal publicly "Soviet inferiority." Khrushchev's apparent interpretation of the correct meaning of proletarian internationalism—that Hungarian fans should not be rooting for their team—boggles the mind. Much later, after Moscow crushed the Hungarian revolt and certainly after Khrushchev made his remarks, there was a famous (or notorious) water polo game at the 1956 Melbourne Olympics between the two countries. On December 6, during the semifinals, the Hungarians were ahead 4–0 when the game was called in the last minute. The referees sought to prevent angry Hungarian fans reacting to a Soviet player, Valentin Prokopov, who had hit a Hungarian player, Ervin Zádor, in the eyes with his fist. With Zádor and perhaps others bleeding, the water was red. (I have seen a documentary with original footage showing the events just described.) Hungary went on to win the gold medal. Such was the revenge Hungarians took for their country's betrayal and defeat in November 1956.

brought up Churchill again: "You [Nagy] have come under the influence of the masses. People have to be told the truth. The standard of living can only rise if the people themselves are producing more. Even the bourgeoisie know that much; even Churchill is aware of it."

Picking up where Kaganovich had left off, Khrushchev let Nagy know that he was being watched—and that bad behavior would have serious consequences. In an explicit threat Nagy would deeply resent, Khrushchev said that while Nagy was not "without merits . . . Zinoviev and Rykov were not without merits either; perhaps they were more meritorious than you are, and yet we did not hesitate to take firm steps against them when they became a threat to the party." As Nagy knew only too well, Zinoviev, one of Lenin's close allies and head of the Comintern in 1919–26, was shot on Stalin's orders in 1936; Rykov, who was head of the Soviet government in 1924–30, was executed in 1938. As a survivor of Stalin's purges in the 1930s, Nagy had no trouble putting two and two together.

Nagy certainly heard the message, but—almost uniquely in the recent history of the Soviet bloc—he chose not to comply. He was prepared to bend but he was not prepared to break under the pressure of the political lynching that he had just experienced. Returning to Budapest, he defied the Kremlin's demand for capitulation. His stubborn determination to be his own man trumped his devotion to the party and to the Soviet Union. If the Soviet leaders had *asked* him to concede that he made a mistake by publishing that article in the previous October without clearing it with Rákosi (who was on vacation), he might have met their request. If they had *asked* him to increase investments in heavy industry, he might have followed Malenkov's example and changed the budget to reflect modified priorities. But the Soviet leaders turned *everything* upside down, telling him that he had done nothing right even though what he did was what the Soviet leaders had told him in June 1953 to do.

Besides, Nagy was not prepared to retreat to become one of Rákosi's assistants—even if he were to retain the prime minister's title. He was smart enough to know that humbling himself now would guarantee complete defeat later, and he was too proud and too brave to play a part in his own demise. Moreover, and despite what had just happened to Beria, Nagy seems to have understood well that Kaganovich and

Khrushchev were bluffing; they were not going to have him killed. Upsetting as their threats were, they were unconvincing. In this respect, at least, times had changed: After Stalin's death he was far less likely to share Bukharin's or Zinoviev's or Rykov's fate.

During the session, Nagy's feelings were definitely hurt; his illusions were no longer intact.[10] Though he continued to revere the Soviet Union, the homeland of socialism, he was not going to be kicked around by Khrushchev & Company.

His defiance of the Kremlin was born that day—on January 8, 1955.

Five days later, at a meeting of the Hungarian Politburo on January 13, 1955, Nagy did not apologize for his alleged faults.[11] He showed no gratitude for what did *not* happen in Moscow: that he did not have to resign even though the Soviet leaders had supposedly promised Rákosi that he would be dismissed.[12] But the Soviet Politburo wanted Nagy to repent, not to resign. If he were to resign, they thought, Hungary's attentive public—writers and journalists, including many party members—would understand that the party had split and they would rush to Nagy's defense. To circumvent that possibility, the Soviet leaders intended, and expected, Nagy to take up an anti-Nagy position, and then he was to pretend that nothing had changed, that he had not changed his mind. (This is what Malenkov agreed to do, except that he was also relegated to the position of *deputy* prime minister.) Amazingly, for the Muscovite politician that Nagy was, he declined to be Hungary's Malenkov. He cared for his program, not his title.

The Politburo meeting in Budapest was a pathetic affair. All those— every member of the Hungarian Politburo—who had supported Nagy fully or partly in previous months turned against him. Facing a hostile and unanimous Politburo solidly against him, he was all alone. The "debate" itself, which went on for several hours, had little to do with policy; it had to do only with politics and personalities. As if they were all

---

[10] That was the strong impression he conveyed at the Hungarian Politburo's meeting five days later. See fn. 11 below.

[11] For a detailed text of this Politburo session, see György T. Varga, ed., "A Politikai Bizottság 1955. január 13. ülésének jegyzőkönyve" [Minutes of the Meeting of the Political Committee on January 13 1955], in *Jalta és Szuez között: 1956 a világpolitikában* [Between Yalta and Suez: 1956 in World Politics] (Budapest: Tudósítások Kiadó, 1989), 39–86.

[12] In his memoirs, Rákosi claimed the Soviet comrades had promised him to treat Nagy more sternly, and therefore he was "rather disappointed" by the Kremlin's decision to allow Nagy to keep his job as prime minister and remain in the Politburo too. Rákosi, *Visszaemlékezések 1940–1956*, 974.

linguists rather than party hacks, the Politburo members debated at length whether the resolution to be issued should identify their policies under Stalin as "basically" (*alapjában*) or "essentially" (*lényegében*) correct; in Hungarian, as in English, this was a difference without a distinction. Another "issue" that involved language was Nagy's reaction to the Kremlin's censure. Nagy: "I *listened* to the [Soviet] comrades' good advice and I'll *attempt* to correct the mistakes." Rákosi: "In our interpretation, Comrade Nagy did *accept* the criticism and *will do* his best to correct the mistakes" (italics added).

What about Nagy's willingness to work with Rákosi? Nagy said he wanted to take the problem to the party's Central Committee and request it to retire him from both the Politburo and the government, for, according to party rules, Nagy claimed, he had the right to make such a request. Farkas: "How would you justify your resignation? Are you sick? No! Are you tired? [If so] Have a holiday! . . . The ultimate consequence [of resignation] would be the formation of a group around you which would cause huge damage to the party." Nagy: "Well, then, how long should I remain prime minister?" Farkas: "As long as the party wants to keep you there." Nagy: "[You all say] I'm not capable of being prime minister, I'm a very bad Marxist, I don't qualify as an economist." Rákosi: "Can't you correct mistakes? Isn't there such a thing as the admission of one's faults?"

As Nagy asked for more time to consider the "comrades' views," he tried to end the meeting on a somewhat conciliatory note. But Rákosi's summary and the Politburo's formal resolution that he proposed were anything but conciliatory. "We" will write a long article, said Rákosi, which will appear in a few weeks under Nagy's signature in the party daily. A new party document will be circulated stressing that "the party's policy was *basically* correct prior to June 1953 as well." The Politburo also stated that "Comrade Imre Nagy's remarks at this meeting failed to advance the resolution of key issues." The Politburo also authorized Rákosi to dismiss Zoltán Vas, Nagy's chief of staff. To be more precise, Rákosi instructed the Politburo to instruct Rákosi to fire Vas.

Gradually, over the next few months, Nagy was unceremoniously dismissed from all his positions and memberships in the government, the party, and even the Academy of Sciences. This is what Rákosi, but not Moscow, chose to do; Rákosi exceeded his instructions. Nagy was publicly accused in March by his Hungarian comrades of such high

Communist crimes and misdemeanors as "undervaluing the leading role of the party," "right-wing opportunist deviation . . . concerning socialist industrialization" and concerning the peasantry, too, as well as revision of "the Marxist-Leninist doctrine of the dictatorship of the proletariat."[13] Though the Kremlin wanted to keep Nagy in reserve, Rákosi did not. He sought revenge on Nagy for having been humiliated in 1953, but the Kremlin promptly if secretly dispatched Suslov to Budapest to talk directly with Nagy about his future. For his part, Nagy still refused to admit his errors or accept a lesser position; he did not agree to the "Malenkov formula."[14] The Suslov mission failed. In April, Nagy lost his party and government positions. He was not even allowed to teach economics. In November, he was expelled from the party he had helped found in 1918—*that* bothered him the most. The day it happened, he ran into a friend, Tamás Aczél, a writer, and told him: "Look what they've done to me. . . . After so many years as a party militant. . . . These absolute nonentities. . . . But I told them the truth."[15]

Once he was no more than a pensioner, Nagy's appeal and popularity extended to almost all Hungarians. For the silent anticommunist majority, this Muscovite suddenly became "one of us." For the disillusioned, anti-Stalinist elite that admired, even worshipped, him, he became a symbol of what they had once believed socialism was all about and should be again.

· 3 ·

The Hungarian Communist intellectuals' effort to reform the Stalinist system—the "revolt of the mind"—commenced during Nagy's prime

---

[13] *Szabad Nép*, March 9, 1955.

[14] Tamás Aczél and Tibor Méray, *The Revolt of the Mind: A Case History of Intellectual Resistance behind the Iron Curtain* (New York: Praeger, 1959), 324.

[15] Tibor Méray, *Thirteen Days That Shook the Kremlin: Imre Nagy and the Hungarian Revolution* (New York: Praeger, 1959), 41. Published more than three decades before the archives began to open up on events surrounding Nagy and 1956, this book as well as *Revolt of the Mind*, cited in fn. 14, above, remain among the most important and certainly most readable works on the subject. We now know more details, especially about Soviet decisionmaking, but the substance of what we know is not significantly different from that reported in these two superb accounts. If my interpretation of Nagy and the intellectuals around him differs from these two books, it is because I write from the perspective of five decades that has tempered my enthusiasm, and made me examine their limitations together with their dedication and courage.

ministership in 1953–55, before his dismissal. It was then, just after Stalin's death, when most writers, journalists, and various intellectual hangers-on turned away from their Marxist-Leninist god. However, a few of them began to have misgivings about the implementation of communism if not the system itself even earlier, before 1953. For them the processes of gradual disillusionment started during the purges against Communist officials in the early 1950s.

Miklós Vásárhelyi, for example, was on the staff of the Communist daily *Szabad Nép* after World War II. He was a true believer. When in 1949 he learned of the arrest and disappearance of several of his comrades from the wartime underground, including László Rajk, he had a hard time believing they were agents of Tito or of the United States. As he related it in various recollections about his life[16] and in conversations with me, he was initially much too afraid to admit it to himself that the charges against his comrades and friends were false. How could they be *false* when "the party" testified to their truthfulness? And yet how could they be *true* when he knew from firsthand experience how loyal, dedicated, and indeed fanatical Communists these putative "traitors" were?

Once he came close to admitting to himself the possibility that the party was mistaken, he did not know what to do with his discovery. If he were to tell a friend of what he thought, would not that friend be obliged to report him to the political police? Besides, who could he trust with his misgivings? How—and even where—could he unburden himself? Though he felt a strong need to share his growing doubts, he had to think of the need to protect himself and his family. After Rajk's trial in 1949, he began to confide his initial concerns to his friend, Géza Losonczy, a Communist official who happened to be his neighbor.

When Losonczy was arrested in 1951, together with Sándor Haraszti, János Kádár, Gyula Kállai, and others, Vásárhelyi's anxieties grew. Every time a car drove by his apartment house at night, he was listening and waiting for the dreaded knock on the door. But then, after a while, Vásárhelyi chose to unburden himself, this time to József Szilágyi, a childhood friend from Debrecen. Whispering on the balcony

---

[16] Miklós Vásárhelyi, *Ellenzékben* [In Opposition] (Budapest: Szabad Tér Kiadó, 1989), passim. See also chap. 2, fn. 74, above.

of his apartment house where he did not think listening devices were hidden, Vásárhelyi confessed to his friend and comrade that he had doubts—that "something was wrong here" (*itt valami nem stimmel*). As Szilágyi was also baffled by the humiliating public testimonies of purged officials, the two agreed that what some of the accused said did not appear to be true and the way they said it was unlike their way of speaking.[17]

In the early 1950s, Vásárhelyi was transferred from the party daily to a lesser position as editor of a monthly published in Russian and English for foreign consumption. It was an unimportant job and an unimportant publication, but it was there that he met a key future contact to Imre Nagy—Nagy's daughter, known by all as Zsóka, who was an ed-

---

[17] Vásárhelyi made the right choice when he chose to reveal his doubts to Szilágyi. This hero of all heroes of 1956, Szilágyi served as chief of staff to Imre Nagy during the revolt. He was to be tried with Nagy and Vásárhelyi and others in 1958, but in the end he was tried alone in April 1958 (while the others were tried in June) because the secret police simply could not control his behavior. His intransigence against his jailors knew no limits. Yelling and screaming at them, he kept demanding, for example, that the court call in as a witness János Kádár, who betrayed the revolution and ruled Hungary in 1958. Though both he and the rest of the Nagy group were tried by a kangaroo court behind closed doors, Szilágyi's behavior made even a secret trial impossible. His case separated from the others', he was sentenced to death and executed in April. Details of his interrogations and minutes of the trial can be found in the Archive of the Hungarian Ministry of Internal Affairs [hereafter cited as AHMIA], V-150.000/73. For long summaries and a portrait of this Communist idealist who turned into a brave and a furious enemy of Kádár's Hungary, see István Javorniczky, *Eljő az a nagy, szép idő* [Beautiful times are still ahead] (Budapest: A Héttorony Könyvkiadó, n.d. but circa 1991). In the early 1990s, I met Szilágyi's daughter, Júlia, who seemed to have inherited not only her father's courage but also an extraordinary feel for insight, nuance, and distinction. A trained psychoanalyst, Szilágyi raised one of the more agonizing questions about human behavior under the circumstances of her father's imprisonment. On the one hand, she admired her father and cherished his memory without reservations; on the other, however, she asked why he had to be so intransigent as to make this kangaroo court sentence him to death. Did he want to die to make up for the remorse he felt for his Communist past? Was it more important for him to compensate for his feeling of guilt than to come home to his wife, his son, and to her, his daughter? She wondered: *"What could have been more important to him than us?"* (italics added.) Why wasn't his family and even himself more important to him than his cause, she demanded to know, but she knew there could be no reply. See Javorniczky, ibid., 193, for an especially moving section that combines a daughter's deep sorrow about a father who was not there when she needed him with her immense if tormented respect for the choice he made. The contrast between these two old friends—Szilágyi and Vásárhelyi—is also instructive. Under arrest after the 1956 revolution, Vásárhelyi did not shout at the interrogators; he did not question their authority. He told me in 1992: "I never argued with these bastards. What for? I wanted to go home to my family without betraying my friends." From their questions, he figured out what the interrogators knew about him and his activities, and then he confirmed what they already knew. He offered no new information, and he never "sang" on his codefendants. Sentenced to five years in jail, he then returned home to his wife and three children. In the 1970s and 1980s, he became one of the prominent leaders of the so-called democratic opposition that helped bring down the Communist regime in 1989. Readers of this footnote might try to imagine, as I have tried to do for many years, how they would have behaved under the circumstances, and which behavior—Szilágyi's or Vásárhelyi's—they admire or respect more and why.

itor and translator for the magazine's Russian version. At the time, Imre Nagy was a high-ranking member of the party leadership—soon to be prime minister too—while Vásárhelyi was a magazine editor with good if by then somewhat tentative party credentials. After Nagy became prime minister, he brought in Vásárhelyi to keep an eye on the Hungarian press; his job was to inform the editors of the country's leading papers of the correct political line they should pursue (as seen by Nagy) and report to Nagy on what he observed. This was the time when his historian friend, György Litván, began calling Vásárhelyi "MikiPress."[18]

Both while Nagy was prime minister and after he was ousted, too, Vásárhelyi tried to introduce him to the country's writers and other intellectuals intent on reforming the system. This proved to be hard, because Nagy's Muscovite experiences, and instincts, made him reluctant to allow anyone to get close to him; he preferred to deal with everyone only through proper channels. He knew he was being watched, and mainly for this reason he did not reach out to potential supporters. This was the case even after he became a pensioner with nothing to do— except to prepare memorandum after memorandum addressed to Rákosi, the party's Central Committee, and the Soviet leadership, too.[19] As Vásárhelyi continued to provide Nagy with news and rumors about the incipient revolt of the mind, Nagy listened and *very* cautiously encouraged him to stay engaged.

Indicative of Nagy's hopes and orientation after his ouster, he sent copies of his studies and letters not only to the Kremlin but also to Tito via the Yugoslav Embassy in Budapest. Nagy's messenger to the Yugoslavs, aside from Vásárhelyi, was Miklós Gimes, another rebellious ex-editor from *Szabad Nép* and then *Magyar Nemzet*, who as a foreign correspondent observed everyday life in Western Europe—and returned as a changed man increasingly skeptical of and even hostile not only to Stalinist communism but to all other varieties as well. As probably the single most liberal and pro-Western Nagy supporter, Gimes went so far

---

[18] "Miki" is the nickname for Miklós; the expression identified Vásárhelyi as a one-man press operation. He always knew what was going on, and—because he knew the background of just about every official and editor in Budapest—he also knew who should be notified of which piece of information and who should be left in the dark.

[19] Nagy's numerous memoranda explaining and defending his positions on a variety of issues appeared in English as *On Communism*. His letters to the party leadership were published for the first time in 1989 in *Új Fórum*, no. 4 (1989): 11–39.

as to convince skeptical acquaintances that he was no longer a Communist.[20] He was not, and yet he was a leading light in this pro-Nagy, reform-Communist group simply because there was nowhere else for him to go. On account of their past, Gimes and a few others like him—notably Losonczy; János Kornai, who was to become a world-famous economist years later at Harvard; and Vásárhelyi—still belonged to this reform-Communist circle even though they were beginning to doubt that the system could be repaired.

Others—the vast majority around Nagy and especially Nagy himself—remained Marxist-Leninists who believed in the superiority of the Communist model of development and subscribed to the then-fashionable argument that Stalin had diverged from "Leninist norms." In other words, their criticism focused on the Stalinist terror, policies favoring the rapid pace of industrialization, decisionmaking by a small circle around Rákosi and his acolytes, and perhaps especially the narrow limits placed on open debate. Partly out of calculation, mainly because of conviction, they believed that discussion of Hungary's alliance with the Soviet Union as well as the country's one-party system and its "socialist" economic orientation should be off limits. Thus, with a few exceptions, Nagy and his supporters were still within-system Communist reformers. They had shed their Stalinist faith. They found their hero in Imre Nagy. They stayed with Nagy in good times (when he was prime minister) and in bad times (after he was ousted). They renewed their commitment to "socialist legality" after the Twentieth CPSU Congress

---

[20] Sándor Révész, *Egyetlen élet: Gimes Miklós története* [Unique Life: The story of Miklós Gimes] (Budapest: 1956-os Intézet and Sík Kiadó, 1999), 288. In addition to this comprehensive, insightful, and beautifully written biography, see also a particularly moving account of the relationship between Gimes and his loyal, dedicated lover in Aliz Halda, *Magánügy* [Private Matter] (Budapest: Noran, 2002). During the revolt, Gimes published a new, pro-Nagy, and liberal daily called *Magyar Szabadság*. After the revolt, he published an illegal, mimeographed publication against the Soviet-imposed regime. Legend has it that Gimes—apparently still guilt-ridden about his Communist past and ready to court disaster—managed to get hold of Kádár's direct telephone number and called him from a phone booth. In jail, before his trial, Gimes was initially among the most intransigent members of the Nagy group; like Nagy, he refused to answer questions put to him by interrogators. In June 1958, he was tried with Nagy and sentenced to death. By then, he was a broken man, only a shadow of his former self. In the end, he confessed to his "erroneous" ways and apologized repeatedly. Because Gimes did not take part in any serious organizational activity during the revolution, the punishment was particularly harsh and totally unwarranted. His obstinacy, combined with his Jewish past, sealed his fate. In addition, Kádár, who played the key role in determining many sentences in the post-1956 period, must have been especially irritated by Gimes's tenacity. So was Ferenc Vida, the presiding "hanging judge" in his case, who used to know Gimes well when they belonged to the same Communist Party cell. Gimes's file is in AHMIA, V-150.000/3.

in February 1956. If they were still idealists, they were by then idealists without too many illusions. Their articles and poems in *Irodalmi Újság*—a small-circulation weekly sold on the black market for five to ten times its official price—spoke of disappointment and anger and of the need for renewal. By then there were several other publications voicing similar attitudes and themes.

Aside from the Writer's Association, which met behind closed doors, the most important meeting place for the reformers was the Petőfi Circle. This was a forum created, ironically, by the Association of Communist Youth for those seeking incremental change. It was initially approved by Rákosi as a vehicle to co-opt rebellious intellectuals and college-age students, and it began to attract ever-growing audiences and attention after the Twentieth CPSU Congress. The authorities considered closing it down, but only in the aftermath of a tumultuous, nine-hour debate focusing on freedom of the press, or more precisely the lack of it, held on June 27, 1956, did they feel confident enough to initiate a crackdown.[21] What happened was that while most speakers, addressing six thousand people, demanded only the expansion of freedoms, a few hinted at the need for fundamental or systemic political transformation. "I am sincere when I say that I trust our youth," said Tibor Déry, a radical writer. "I am asking these young people, these young Hungarians, to keep in mind the deeds of the young people of 1848 [a reference to Hungary's war of independence against Austrian and Russian oppressors]. *As people today refer to the young people of 1848, so I wish that history will remember the young people of 1956 who will help our nation in creating a better future. [Long, rhythmic applause.]*"[22] (Italics added.)

---

[21] A lively account of the debates in Petőfi Circle in English is John P. C. Matthews, *Tinderbox: East-Central Europe in the Spring, Summer, and Early Fall of 1956* (Tucson: Fenestra Books, 2003), 145–63. See also *Revolt of the Mind*, 398–412. The authoritative history in Hungarian is András B. Hegedüs, ed., with the assistance of János M. Rainer, Mária Ember, and Róbert Bohó, *A Petőfi Kör vitái hiteles jegyzőkönyvek alapján* [The Petőfi Circle's Debates on the Basis of Authentic Transcripts], issued in seven volumes by various publishers in Budapest between 1989 and 1994. Hegedüs, not to be confused with the prime minister of 1955–56 with the same name, was one of the secretaries of the Petőfi Circle.

[22] Matthews, *Tinderbox*, 156–57. Of course Déry's speech was an almost direct call for revolution against the Communist regime, not its reform. An embittered and brave old Communist, Déry was expelled from the party soon after he delivered these remarks. In late 1957, he received a nine-year jail sentence for "counterrevolutionary activities." Prior to the debate at the Petőfi Circle, Déry rehearsed his speech at the Journalist Club for two of Nagy's closest associates, Géza Losonczy and Sándor Haraszti, as well as two of his writer friends, Zoltán Zelk and László Benjámin. See Déry's interrogation of September 1957 in AHMIA, V-150.001/2.

Several of the speakers, notably Losonczy, angrily insisted on taking up the issue of Imre Nagy's expulsion from the Communist Party. It was past midnight when the audience, made up of party members and non-members alike, picked up his words, shouting like one: *"Vissza a pártba!* —literally "Back to the party!"—meaning "Return Nagy to the party!" The atmosphere was charged with political electricity. Just a few months before the popular revolt in October, this crowd, with a few ex-ceptions like Déry, still believed that Hungary's problems could be, and should be, solved by Nagy's readmission to the ranks of a bankrupt party pursuing bankrupt policies. The vast majority of the speakers did not consider putting an end to the system; they sought to reform it. "I don't want freedom for the enemies of the people," said Tibor Méray, for ex-ample. "But I want freedom for the people."[23] The language was old-fashioned and the objective limited, but there was nothing strange or particularly undemocratic about it *at that time* because the one-party state was the framework not only for current activities but for political expectations as well.

Through informal, personal ties, and from behind the scenes, the Nagy group affected these debates. Vásárhelyi, expelled from the party in 1955 for his "antiparty," oppositional activities and employed as a librarian, was regularly in touch with the Petőfi Circle leadership, no-tably its main organizer, Gábor Tánczos.[24] So was Losonczy. Reflecting Nagy's cautious view—his conviction that "provocations" must be avoided at all cost—their advice was to refrain from excessive rhetoric. As Déry's implicit call for revolution showed, the circle's leadership could not always control the substance of what was being said.

The particularly long and often dramatic press debate became the talk of Budapest, and so did Imre Nagy's birthday party on June 7.[25] The reformist group, mainly party members and recently expelled

---

[23] Ibid., 159.

[24] Vásárhelyi, *Ellenzékben*, 138–41.

[25] For a vivid reconstruction of the party held one day after Nagy's actual birthday, see Gábor Murányi, "Születésnap az Orsó utcában: Nagy Imre köszöntése vagy 'politikai demonstráció'?" [Birthday Party at Orsó Street: Greeting Imre Nagy or "Political Demonstration"?], *Magyar Nemzet*, June 6, 1991. This important article, which even presents in facsimile the invoice for food and drinks delivered for the occasion by a catering service, was based, in part, on the confessions of the party's main organizer, Ferenc Jánosi, Nagy's son-in-law, who was extensively interrogated about the party on August 5, 1957. See AHMIA, V-150.000/9.

members—writers, journalists, actors, musicians, university professors, the cream of Hungary's intelligentsia—came to pay homage to the man they all hoped would soon return to power. Several high-ranking party functionaries attended, too, but it was the presence of Zoltán Kodály, the world-famous composer who had pointedly stayed away from politics whenever he could, that made the event so special. About one hundred invited guests showed up, bringing modest gifts to the smiling and visibly happy former prime minister. He was very much at ease, for a change. No speeches were made, but the mood was hopeful, even confident.

Domokos Kosáry, the country's leading noncommunist historian, recalled many years later his own experience that day: "As Imre Nagy stood next to me, I raised my glass and said: 'Mr. Prime Minister, I hope that a year from now we could officially address you this way. To your health!' Imre Nagy turned to me and said: 'Thank you. But why do we need to wait a whole year?'"[26]

As it happened, assimilated, secular Jews played a key role in the revolt of the mind. Their preponderance as guests at the birthday party, as speakers at the Petőfi Circle, and as contributors to various publications favoring Nagy's reinstatement, was quite striking. They were certainly not religious or observant Jews but people born into Jewish families. Often enough, their names or their families' names had been hungaricized. They did not discuss, even among themselves, their common history. They considered themselves Hungarians, not Hungarian Jews or Jewish-Hungarians. In postwar Hungary, the very issue of who was or was not Jewish or born Jewish was largely taboo, except for private references to many Communist leaders' and political police officials' "Jewish" past. For this reason, too, no one knew then or can know today exactly who was or was not "Jewish" among Hungary's leading anti-Stalinists; it is hard to be certain about either the number or the percentage of Jewish-born intellectuals who wrote for opposition papers like *Irodalmi Újság* or took part in the debates. However, having reviewed hundreds of names and biographies, and consulted knowledgeable historians as well as old participants, I estimate that in the mid-1950s close to three-fourths, or 75 percent, of the active anti-Stalinist

---

[26] As quoted in Rainer, *Nagy Imre*, 202.

Hungarian intellectuals had Jewish ancestors. While this might be re-garded as a very high proportion considering that people of Jewish back-ground made up less than 2 percent of the population, it was not quite so high considering two facts of life: the prominent role Jewish-born men of letters always played in Hungary's intellectual life—and their apparent need now to atone for their Stalinist past.

The issue, as complex as it was, remains controversial to this day. Half the story—how Jewish-born Communists had helped to implement Hungary's Sovietization in the 1940s—is still the subject of obsessive debate.[27] Completely unmentioned, meanwhile, has been the "Jewish role" in disassembling the Stalinist regime in the mid-1950s. *If they are to be blamed for bringing communism in, they should surely receive credit for bringing it down.* In fact, however, neither proposition was or is par-ticularly accurate. Most "average" Hungarian Jews, like other Hungari-ans, were wary, afraid, and largely passive throughout this era; "average Jews" contributed little either to the rise or the demise of communism.

The extent to which the "revolt of the mind" reached, or influenced, the country's urban or rural population was another difficult question to assess. At party headquarters, there was widespread concern about the industrial "working class" showing signs of opposition to Hungary's Stalinist Old Guard. Was the concern genuine or only an excuse for a

---

[27] See chapter 2 above. For a critical assessment of charges rooted in anti-Semitism, see also "A Note on Communists and the Jewish Question," in my *Hungary and the Soviet Bloc* (Durham, N.C.: Duke University Press, 1986), 100–7. For a comprehensive and judicious treatment, see István Deák, "Jews and Communism: The Hungarian Case," in *Dark Times, Dire Decisions: Jews and Communism,* ed. Jonathan Frankel, Studies in Contemporary Jewry, Avraham Harman Institute of Contemporary Jewry and Hebrew University of Jerusalem; (Oxford: Oxford University Press, 2004), 38–61. With respect to the historically prominent role of Jews, Deák reports that, "In 1910, for instance, when Jews made up 5 percent of Hungary's population; . . . 42.4 percent of the journalists were Jews by religion. In the Hungarian capital . . . 48.4 percent" [of the journalists] were Jewish. In his authoritative study that deals only in a brief epilogue with the Jewish question after World War II, János Gyurgyák notes that in 1956 there were Jews on "both sides of the barricade." He mentions by name *eleven* who supported the revolt and *two* who did not; the ratio strikes me as accurate. *See* his *A zsidókérdés Magyarországon: Politikai eszmetörténet* [The Jewish question in Hungary: History of political thought] (Budapest: Osiris Kiadó, 2001), 590. Anti-Semites have gone so far as to insist that a "Judeo-Bolshevik" conspiracy was responsible for bringing communism to Hungary in 1919 and in 1945, making pure and poor Hun-garians the victims of their sinister design. The issue, of course, goes beyond the Hungarian case. E.g., Jewish-born Polish intellectuals—in 1956 and again in 1968—played a prominent role in attacking the worst features of the Communist system. For background, see, e.g., G. L. Gluchowski, "The De-fection of Jozef Światło and the Search for Jewish Scapegoats in the Polish United Workers' Party, 1953–54," paper presented at the Fourth Convention of the Association for the Study of the Nation-alities (CAN), held at the Harriman Institute, Columbia University, New York, April 15–17, 1999; www.columbia.edu/cu/sipa/regional/ECE/gluchowski.pdf.

possible crackdown on Nagy and his supporters? When Rákosi heard of people greeting Nagy during his walks, he was beside himself. Some of the prominent writers associated with Nagy reported that strangers somehow recognized and congratulated them for their brave stance. If not during the summer recess, by early September 1956 there was a good deal of favorable reaction on university campuses to the intellectuals' movement for change. There were signs that the normally apolitical technical intelligentsia was also restless. With the regime increasingly on the defensive, there was uncertainty not only about how it would respond to the revolt of the mind but also about what the Kremlin would allow the Hungarians to do.

· 4 ·

In 1956, Moscow's assessment of the Hungarian situation changed once again. Support for Rákosi, so much in evidence in the first half of 1955, began to fade in mid-1955 when Khrushchev, despite Molotov's opposition, made up with Tito's Yugoslavia; support for Rákosi further eroded in the aftermath of the Twentieth CPSU Congress in 1956. The reason for change had to do mainly with Khrushchev's political opportunism. When he needed help from Molotov, Kaganovich, Voroshilov, and others to demote Malenkov and make room for himself, he favored Rákosi; when Khrushchev's need for the Stalinist old timers against Malenkov ceased to be a pressing concern, Rákosi and his acolytes in Budapest mattered far less. The change was gradual. In 1956, as the year progressed, it was becoming increasingly clear that the Kremlin was ready to remove Rákosi and replace him with a "Hungarian," that is, non-Jewish, colleague. Among those under consideration initially were András Hegedüs, the prime minister, and possibly János Kádár, not Imre Nagy.

In the spring and summer of 1956, the Kremlin was responding to two events taking place outside Hungary. One was the reverberations of Khrushchev's secret speech denouncing Stalin and Stalinism, which had leaked to the West and was being broadcast by Western radio stations, and which exacerbated existing tension and confusion within the Communist elites of Central and Eastern Europe, notably those of Hungary and Poland. How could it be that Moscow reinstalled the Stalinist

Rákosi in 1955 while it dethroned Stalin in 1956? Would the Kremlin also dethrone now "Stalin's best pupil," as Rákosi used to be called? The other event very much on the Kremlin's agenda was the outbreak of riots in Poznan, Poland, on June 28, 1956, which was the day after the Petőfi Circle's dramatic "press debate." Poznan—a working-class rebellion rather than some protest by always-dissenting intellectuals—made it imperative for the Kremlin to come to terms with the management of growing instability not only in Poland but also in Hungary and elsewhere in the Soviet bloc as well.[28]

By the end of June and the beginning of July 1956, the Soviet leaders began to take a second look at Rákosi's usefulness.[29] In addition to their fear that something like Poznan could also happen in Hungary—in 1953, after all, there were work stoppages and the like in such major industrial centers as Csepel, Ózd, and Diósgyőr—they were under pressure by Tito, their new-old friend, to replace Rákosi and his cohorts. "These men," Tito had said of Rákosi and his ilk, "have their hands soaked in blood, have staged trials, given false information, sentenced innocent men to death. They have had Yugoslavia mixed up in all these trials, as in the case of the Rajk trial, and they now find it difficult to admit before their own people their mistakes."[30]

When Suslov visited Hungary in June, he did not (yet) act on Tito's concerns; all he recommended to his Kremlin colleagues on his return was the replacement of some "Jewish comrades" with "real Hungarian cadres."[31] Following an insistent, uncompromising cable by Ambassador Andropov on July 9,[32] the Soviet Politburo met on July 12 and—

---

[28] For a comprehensive account based on archival sources and accompanied by an inspired assessment of Soviet policies and dilemmas, see Mark Kramer, "The Soviet Union and the 1956 Crises in Hungary and Poland: Reassessments and New Findings," *Journal of Contemporary History* 33, no. 2 (April 1998): 163–214. For further details, see also Mark Kramer, "New Evidence on Soviet Decision-Making and the 1956 Polish and Hungarian Crises," *Bulletin of the Cold War International History Project*, issues 8–9 (Winter 1996–97): 358–84.

[29] In addition to sources specifically identified, the following paragraphs draw on my earlier account in *Hungary and the Soviet Bloc*, 136–37.

[30] *Documents on International Affairs, 1955* (London: Oxford University Press, 1958), 271.

[31] Suslov's June 13, 1956, message to the Kremlin as cited in Kramer, "Soviet Union and the 1956 Crises," 176–77.

[32] Ibid., 178. The text of Andropov's important cable is reproduced in full in Russian is in *Sovyetskiy Soyuz I Vengerskiy krizis—1956 goda: Dokumenti* [The Soviet Union and the Hungarian crisis in 1956: Documents] (Moscow: Rosspen, 1998), 137–42; for the text in Hungarian, see Baráth, *Szovjet nagyköveti iratok Magyarországról*, 318–24.

concerned about "the imperialists' subversive activities" but unwilling to change the party line yet—decided to dispatch Mikoyan to Budapest to take another look.[33] When Mikoyan—on his way to Belgrade to see Tito—stopped in Budapest, he was not formally authorized to make personnel changes there. Once there, however, Mikoyan, despite Suslov's somewhat sanguine report and his colleagues' disinterest in replacing Hungary's Stalinist diehards, did not like what he saw. On July 13, only one day after his arrival, he told Rákosi to resign.[34] Though he also raised the question of why the Hungarians "were not applying repression and arrests against the chief instigators among the enemy,"[35] Mikoyan still seemed uncertain of what else to do. On July 14, he met privately with János Kádár. At the end of what amounted to a job interview, held in a jovial atmosphere, Kádár remarked: "Lots of people here say that the Soviet comrades often interfere in Hungarian affairs, and it never works out well. Why shouldn't you interfere now? It might work out well this time." According to the note taker, "Comrade Mikoyan replied with laughter," and the two then enjoyed a hearty lunch together.[36]

---

[33] For a very brief and confusing version of this Politburo session in Russian, see *Sovyetskiy*, 149–50; for the text in Hungarian, see Vyacheslav Sereda and Jámos M. Rainer, eds., *Döntés a Kremlben, 1956: A szovjet pártelnökség vitái Magyarországról* [Decision in the Kremlin, 1956: The Soviet Politburo's debates about Hungary] (Budapest; 1956-os Intézet, 1996), 19–21.

[34] According to Prime Minister András Hegedüs, this is not how it happened. In his version of events, he and Rákosi received Mikoyan at the airport. In the car, on the way to the guesthouse, Mikoyan turned to Rákosi: "The [Soviet] Party Presidium [Politburo] thinks that in the given situation, claiming ill health, you must resign, Comrade Rákosi. Comrade Hegedüs must take over the position of the First Secretary." Cognizant of his modest talents, Hegedüs claims that he declined the appointment. See András Hegedüs, *Élet egy eszme árnyékában* [Life in the Shadow of an Ideal] (Vienna: Zoltán Zsille, 1985), 242–45. Although available Russian archives do not support this version of what happened, it is quite probable that Khrushchev and Mikoyan, without Politburo discussion and approval, agreed between themselves in Moscow, before Mikoyan's departure, that Rákosi must go; Kramer's interpretation of the documents is that Mikoyan had a broad mandate from the Soviet Politburo to restore the Hungarian party's unity. He also adds that Rákosi did not expect to be dismissed. On the contrary, he "had been hoping to gain Soviet backing for his proposal to 'smash the Nagy conspiracy' once and for all—a proposal that envisaged the arrest of Nagy and several hundred other 'conspirators' as well as a broader crackdown—and thus he was stunned by Mikoyan's recommendation. Nevertheless, Rákosi had little choice but to accept the Soviet 'advice.'" Kramer, "Soviet Union and the 1956 Crises," 179. Kramer's reference is to an unconfirmed but eminently believable story circulating in Budapest that Rákosi had prepared a list of 400 Nagy supporters to be arrested in the very near future.

[35] Vyacheslav Sereda and Aleksandr Stikhalin, eds., *Hiányzó lapok 1956 történetéből: Dokumentumok a volt SZKP KB levéltárából* [Missing pages from the history of 1956: Documents from the former CPSU Central Committee's archive] (Budapest: Zenit, 1993), 40–48. For Mikoyan's top secret cable of July 14, 1956, in English, as translated by Svetlana Savranskaya, see *1956 Hungarian Revolution*, ed. Békés, Byrne, and Rainer, 143–47.

[36] Ibid., 49–56.

In the end, the top party job went neither to Kádár nor to Hegedüs, and certainly not to Nagy, but to Ernő Gerő, the old Muscovite and one-time Comintern functionary who was, like Rákosi, also Jewish born. With Mikoyan in attendance, the Hungarian party's Central Committee debated the appointment for several days, discussing rather openly Gerő's many faults, too, but after Mikoyan spoke up in favor of Gerő's promotion, the vote was unanimous. For tactical reasons, Gerő himself was reluctant to take on the new assignment; he must have realized that most Hungarians were perceptive enough to see no difference between him and the just-ousted Rákosi.

In his thirty-minute speech to the Central Committee, Mikoyan also spoke at some length about Imre Nagy. He said that much as Nagy deserved the punishment, it was a mistake to expel him from the party in 1955. Despite Nagy's mistakes, Mikoyan said, the door should be open to Nagy's readmission to the party—once he distances himself from the "anti-party group" around him.[37] Most Central Committee members were surprised by what they had just heard. They did not know previously that in 1955 Moscow had approved Nagy's demotion, but that his expulsion from the leadership and even the party was Rákosi's doing. What was news in Mikoyan's message was that, while Nagy should change, the Hungarians should keep him in reserve. In his tendentious memoirs published forty years later, Vladimir Kryuchkov, then press secretary to Ambassador Andropov and decades later the uncompromising head of the KGB, wrote that "Mikoyan trusted Nagy and believed that one could rely on him."[38] That was a huge lie. Mikoyan, this wiliest of the wily men of the Soviet Politburo, did not trust anyone, let alone Nagy, but he grasped better than his more doctrinaire colleagues the urgent need for reform in Soviet–Eastern European relations.

Even Voroshilov, the Politburo's one-time Hungarian expert—who had turned against Nagy, his former protégé, so ferociously in January 1955—appeared to be having second thoughts. Zsigmond Strobl Kisfaludi, the noted Hungarian sculptor, was in Moscow to make a bust of Marshal Voroshilov. After a few drinks, Voroshilov told the maestro: "Things do not go well in your country. . . . Rákosi? A vulgar blackguard.

---

[37] Ibid., 59–65.

[38] Vladimir Kryuchkov, *Lichnoye delo* [Private case] (Moscow: Olimp-Akt, 1996), 54.

. . . And Gerő is just as worthless. . . . There is only one honest man in the whole party leadership. He is Imre Nagy."[39] Voroshilov, of course, was wrong. At that time, Nagy was not a member of the leadership of the Hungarian party, nor even of the party itself.

For now, the Kremlin chose not to reinstate Nagy. Mikoyan visited him on July 21, 1956, during another stopover in Budapest on his way back from Belgrade to Moscow. Though Andropov was still reporting sarcastically about Nagy's "stubbornness,"[40] Mikoyan and Nagy apparently had a good discussion; at their meeting, "Mikoyan overflowed with amiability."[41] Meanwhile, as Mark Kramer reports, the Soviet military command found that its Special Corps "had not yet worked out a secret plan to handle large internal disturbances in Hungary." On July 20, a "Plan of Operations for the Special Corps to Restore Public Order on the Territory of Hungary" was finally signed. Code-named "Volna" or "Wave," it showed "that the Soviet leaders wanted a reliable fall-back option in case their attempts to bolster political stability in Hungary failed."[42]

With the left hand seemingly not knowing, or not wanting to know, what the far-left hand was doing, Moscow's signals were quite confusing—and puzzling too. The messages often changed from one day to the next. Different leaders offered different diagnoses of how to treat the patient. Different parts of the Soviet bureaucracy responded differently to Hungary's time of troubles. According to Nagy's memoirs, written in Romanian captivity in early 1957, a particularly mysterious incident took place sometime in September or in October 1956, on the eve of the revolt. In Nagy's account, the incident was some sort of provocation. If it happened at all, it began with the arrival at Budapest airport of sixty to seventy young Russians. Nagy did not seem to know who they were or exactly when they arrived, but they were not real tourists. They refused to show the content of their suitcases to Hungarian customs officials, though in the end the officials did open them—and found Soviet weapons hidden in each. According to Nagy, the "tourists" then

---

[39] Tibor Méray, *Thirteen Days That Shook the Kremlin: Imre Nagy and the Hungarian Revolution* (New York: Praeger, 1959), 47.

[40] Sereda and Stikhalin, *Hiányzó lapok 1956 történetéből*, 72–74.

[41] Méray, *Thirteen Days*, 55.

[42] Kramer, "Soviet Union and the 1956 Crises," 180.

claimed that the customs officials had smuggled the weapons into their suitcases[43]—an unlikely tale. Was Nagy's information correct? If it was, who were these "tourists"? The answer might be found in the KGB's archives, but they remain closed for research.

As the Soviet leaders both vacillated and worked at cross purposes, too, Nagy remained on the Kremlin's waiting list, the subject of feverish diplomatic activity. In the early fall of 1956, Mikoyan and Suslov held consultations with Gerő and Kádár, who was by then Gerő's deputy, and Khrushchev arranged for Gerő to meet "accidentally" with the "vacationing" Tito in the Crimea.[44] There, on the condition that Nagy would be rehabilitated and as a gesture of goodwill toward the anti-Stalinist Khrushchev, Tito agreed to receive Gerő in Belgrade the following week. Finally, on October 13, Nagy was readmitted to the party.

Before leaving for Belgrade to apologize for the Hungarian Communists' past behavior, Gerő worked out a compromise that called for Nagy's readmission to the party without preconditions. Nagy did not have to recant and the party did not have to admit its error for having ousted him. To his close supporters' dismay, Nagy accepted the formula. Much as he despised Gerő and the other diehards in the party leadership, he wanted to show he was still a disciplined and loyal Communist. He was grateful to his Soviet comrades for letting him come back to the party that had endowed his life with meaning, significance, and a mission for almost forty long years. He returned home, again, but the hour was late, and even he could not save the "cause of socialism" in Hungary.

---

[43] Cf. Imre Nagy's long, unpublished memoirs called *Gondolatok, emlékek* [Thoughts, memories]. In a typed copy I have in my personal files, this passage is on p. 13 of what is either an appendix or the author's afterthoughts. Written in Romanian captivity in early 1957, the memoirs, parts of which appeared in Romanian in 2005, are scheduled to appear in Hungarian in 2006. No information has been found in available Soviet or Hungarian archives that would substantiate Nagy's account about the Soviet "tourists," though such information could surface one day from the KGB's still closely guarded archives. I thank János M. Rainer for confirming the absence of evidence regarding the accuracy of this episode.

[44] Veljko Mićunović, *Moscow Diary* (Garden City, N.Y.: Doubleday, 1980), 116–17.

5

The Revolt That Failed

> I could not sleep [on October 30th]. Budapest was
> like a nail in my head.
>
> —*Nikita Khrushchev, explaining his change of mind about using
> military force to crush the Hungarian revolt*

· 1 ·

It is not self-evident when the 1956 Hungarian revolution began, but it is
clear that Imre Nagy was central to its beginning and to its outcome as well.

The revolution began, perhaps, in the winter of 1944–45, when the
Red Army occupied Hungary, and when over a period of three years the
Hungarian Communists, relying on deception, intimidation, and force,
seized power. It began, perhaps, in June 1953, when Moscow appointed
the reform-minded Nagy as Hungary's new prime minister. It began,
perhaps, in early 1955, when the Kremlin deposed Nagy and returned
to the saddle Mátyás Rákosi, the Stalinist diehard, and when a group of
disillusioned Communist intellectuals continued to back Nagy and
pressed for authentic de-Stalinization in their country. The revolt may
have begun in Moscow, then, where the post-Stalin Soviet leaders kept
changing their policies toward the hapless satellites, fostering the kind
of divisions in the Hungarian hierarchy they meant to curb.

To the extent that it was sparked by events outside Hungary and the Soviet Union, the revolt began, perhaps, in Belgrade in the late 1940s, when Tito's Yugoslavia broke ranks with the Soviet bloc and embarked on a still-totalitarian but anti-Soviet path of national communism. The revolt may have begun in Washington after World War II, when the U.S. government declared the containment of Soviet power and then the liberation of Eastern Europe as its key objectives. The revolt began, perhaps, in Munich in the early 1950s, when Radio Free Europe (RFE) went on the air and kept its audiences' hope for the region's emancipation alive, insinuating that the West was prepared—even anxious—to offer at least nonmilitary help.

Given the two countries' historic ties, the Hungarian revolution may have begun in Poland on June 28, 1956, when the Polish regime brutally crushed the workers' uprising in Poznan, and continued on October 19, 1956, when under popular pressure the Polish party returned its former leader, Władysław Gomułka, to his old position. Gomułka—who had lost his job in 1948, his party membership in 1949, and his freedoms in 1951—was something of a "nationalist" Communist, akin to Nagy. Both Gomułka and Nagy were devoted Communists who found *some* aspects of the Soviet model inappropriate if not irrelevant for their more developed countries.

To put it mildly, the Kremlin did not like what was happening in its front yard. Incensed, in particular, about the Polish Communists' proposed removal of Polish defense minister Konstantin K. Rokossovski—who was a marshal in the Soviet Army but partly of Polish descent—angry Soviet Politburo members took off for Warsaw, arriving uninvited, with a furious Khrushchev demanding to know what was going on: "We shed our blood for this country and now [you're] trying to sell it out to the Americans and the Zionists. But it won't work." Gomułka calmly replied: "If you talk with a revolver on the table you don't have an even-handed discussion. I cannot continue the discussion under these conditions."[1] Amazingly, and despite reports of Soviet troops marching on

---

[1] For a memorable journalistic account that reports Khrushchev's remark, see Flora Lewis, *A Case History of Hope* (Garden City, N.Y.: Doubleday, 1958), 209–10. For Gomułka's account of his own reply, see L. W. Gluchowski, "Poland, 1956: Khrushchev, Gomułka, and the 'Polish October,'" *Cold War International History Project Bulletin*, issue 5 (Spring 1995): 1, 38–49.

Warsaw to induce compliance, Khrushchev backed down. For now, the "Polish October" was victorious.

Could the same thing happen in Hungary?

The fires of the Hungarian revolution were set off on October 21, 1956, by students at the University of Szeged and then at Budapest's Technical University, who defied the authorities by reestablishing—for the first time since 1948—an independent organization called the Association of Hungarian University Students, known by its Hungarian acronym as MEFESZ.[2] Then, on October 23, a beautiful late autumn day, thousands of young Hungarians in Budapest walked to the statue of József Bem, a revered Polish general who fought for Hungarian independence in 1848, to show solidarity with the Poles' struggle for change. Students of the Technical University organized the rally, but soon others joined them as well. After nervous consultations on the phone, leaders of the Petőfi Circle also endorsed the rally. Typical of prevailing chaotic conditions, the Ministry of Internal Affairs first banned the march already in progress, but then—after two enterprising editors at Rádió Kossuth, the state radio, concocted and broadcast a "news" item that claimed an official green light for the event—the ministry lifted its initial ban moments later. . . . Paying little or no attention to the government or the party, thousands walked peacefully in an atmosphere as carefree as it was hopeful. At General Bem's statue, the speakers read patriotic poetry, recalled Bem's courage and contributions, praised the bravery of Hungarians fighting for independence in 1848–49, and held up the example of camaraderie between Hungarians and Poles.

As preparations for the demonstration got under way midmorning, Géza Losonczy—the editor released from Rákosi's jails during Nagy's prime ministership—called on Nagy and their closest friends to meet at his apartment at half past 10 A.M. They got together to figure out what was going on and what to do. Losonczy's own summary of what transpired there, and subsequent accounts by several participants, shows

---

[2] For a brief eyewitness report on the rebirth of MEFESZ in Szeged, see Leslie B. Bain, *The Reluctant Satellites: An Eyewitness Report on East Europe and the Hungarian Revolution* (New York: Macmillan, 1960), 95–96.

that this was a genuine political caucus—the first of its kind for the "Nagy group."[3]

With Nagy, Miklós Vásárhelyi, Sándor Haraszti (Losonczy's father-in-law), Szilárd Ujhelyi, and—arriving late—Miklós Gimes in attendance, as well as Losonczy, of course, the six reformers saw eye to eye on the goal of seeking "a Polish-type dénouement," stressing that "a multiparty system was out of the question." They also agreed on the need to make personnel changes, expecting the Hungarian Politburo to call on Nagy and ask him to join the leadership.[4] With respect to the composition of a new Politburo and a revamped Central Committee, they assumed that Nagy would return to his old post as prime minister while a new Politburo would be made up of reformers, such as Nagy, Haraszti, Losonczy, Ferenc Donáth, and Zoltán Szántó (who subsequently betrayed the others), and a somewhat larger number of centrists led by János Kádár as the party's new first secretary, as well as Ferenc Münnich, Sándor Gáspár, and József Köböl. Lacking enough experienced people committed to Nagy's faction to both run the country and at the same time control the party, the inclusion of centrists was a political necessity. And, particularly important, all agreed that Nagy should join the leadership only if his supporters were also invited to occupy high positions in the party and in the government; the party's Stalinist Old Guard should not be allowed to co-opt Nagy, isolate him, and rule in his name.[5]

---

[3] The only more or less contemporaneous written source for what happened there is Losonczy's summary, prepared a month later in Romanian captivity; it was eventually published in *História*, February 1990, 34. I have also discussed this critical meeting with two participants, Szilárd Ujhelyi (on July 3, 1991) and Miklós Vásárhelyi (on July 19, 1991, and many other occasions). To avoid even the apperance of a "conspiracy," these reformers had never met like this before.

[4] Earlier, on the 22nd, two dissident members of the party's Central Committee had called on Nagy to tell him that, given signs of rising tension at the universities and also among workers in large industrial centers, his help would soon be needed.

[5] Though the Nagy group's leading political tactician was Donáth, Vásárhelyi was the "organization man." The two of them and several others had a common experience in the 1930s when they were students at the University of Debrecen and when they joined Hungary's small, illegal Communist Party. The "Debrecen group" included Donáth (age forty-three years in 1956), Losonczy (thirty-nine), Vásárhelyi (thirty-nine), Ujhelyi (forty-one), and Szilágyi (thirty-nine). In 1937, they formed the so-called March Front with a group of writers known as village explorers or populist writers, such as Imre Kovács, Péter Veres, and Ferenc Erdei. (Veres was the main speaker at the Bem statue on October 23.) These youngsters in Debrecen took the March Front rather seriously; they believed in joint action by the left as ordered by the Comintern in 1935. However, Nagy's probable "favorite" among his supporters was Haraszti (fifty-nine), the outspoken newspaper and magazine editor, who was one year younger than he was (and who was not part of the Debrecen group). Jailed in 1951, Haraszti was on death row for two and a half years. Freed by Nagy, he publicly and frequently referred to Rákosi as a murderer. Nagy and Haraszti saw eye to eye most often, while Haraszti and the increasingly liberal

Losonczy and his friends differed somewhat on what to make of the students' rally and how to use it to advance their reformist cause. All disapproved of the government's initial decision to ban the march, but Nagy and Ujhelyi apparently also suspected that either the march or the ban was a provocation by the party or the secret police—and when the prohibition was lifted, Nagy did not think the government should have caved under pressure. Nagy also declined to attend another student rally that was taking place on the Pest side of the city, because he believed it would be wrong for him to show up there; after all, he was now a party member.[6]

After four hours of discussion, Nagy continued to fret about the demonstration's "serious consequences." He worried that the party leadership, controlled by Ernő Gerő, András Hegedüs, and other members of the old school, would blame him for the students' zeal and assertive mood. He feared the rallies might disrupt or even reverse the process that had just begun with his readmission into the party and continue with his imminent co-optation into the leadership. Nagy also declined to join his friends who went downtown to see for themselves what was going on; he went home instead to attend to his grandchildren and take a nap.

Meanwhile, as some 200,000 people lined up on Kossuth Square in front of the Parliament Building, Nagy began to receive message after message saying he must get ready and address the crowd. He declined on the ground that he was just a private citizen. He waited for "the party" to turn to him. Valéria Benke, head of the radio station, called around 7 P.M. to ask for Nagy's advice: Should she allow the university students to voice their sixteen demands on the air? Nagy took excep-

---

Gimes often disagreed. By the summer of 1956, according to Vásárhelyi (interview, July 19, 1991), Gimes favored completely free elections. Haraszti asked him: What if the people were to elect Cardinal Mindszenty (the archconservative head of the Catholic Church)? Gimes replied that if that was what the people wanted, that was what they should get. Aside from György Fazekas, his closest friend, and a dissident journalist, Pál Lőcsei, no one yet seemed to share Gimes's views on the need for such unlimited pluralism. Despite their disagreements, however, Nagy respected Gimes who—unlike other friends—read Nagy's various studies, appeals, and polemics with great care, and offered the kind of constructive criticism that Nagy greatly appreciated.

[6] Earlier, around midnight on October 22, Nagy declined an invitation to meet with the students at Technical University and advise them on a platform they were debating. His astonishing reply to the emissary reflected his long experience in the Communist movement: "[The students] may ask me a series of questions I would not be able to answer because I am not familiar with the relevant party positions on these issues." Nagy's 1957 testimony as cited in János M. Rainer, *Nagy Imre: Politikai életrajz* [Imre Nagy: Political biography], 2 vols. (Budapest: 1956-os Intézet, 1996 and 1999), vol. 2, 240.

tion to one or two of the demands, and then he replied that while in her place he would broadcast them, she should not follow his "personal advice" but instead let the Politburo decide the matter.[7] After a few additional calls, however, Nagy began to compose a speech. Because it was full of old-fashioned formulations, none of the dozen or so friends present in his house approved of it. The reason for the difference between Nagy and his friends was that earlier in the day the others had witnessed the demonstration—and immersed themselves in the new atmosphere —while Nagy had not. In any case, only when two Politburo members sent an urgent message for Nagy to come right away did he decide to go.

It was around 9 P.M. when Nagy finally arrived in the Parliament Building. He was led to a balcony overlooking the square; when the crowd noticed his presence, the silence was sudden and complete. Although Nagy apparently realized that his prepared talk was inappropriate, he could improvise only at the very end. He was not a good public speaker; all his life he had read his speeches. This time, it was all over after the first word: "Comrades!" The crowd replied: "We're not comrades any more!" They wanted a leader who would say: "My friends, let's go to the radio and make sure our demands are heard!" Or, better yet: *"My friends, let's go to party headquarters across the square and tell the Stalinist 'comrades' there their time is up because our time has come!"*

Nagy was not that kind of a leader. He asked the crowd to be patient, saying that ongoing discussions in the party would lead to a promising dénouement. Had he delivered that speech just a few hours earlier, it might have been a reasonably good one; however, by now its content was obsolete, and the party jargon he used was grating. Both desperate and brilliant, and sensing that he was making a great mistake, he finished his dreadful address—and started to sing the National Anthem. At the last minute, he regained his composure and a bit of goodwill from the crowd as well.

---

[7] Minutes of Nagy's statement to his interrogators on June 14, 1957. Hungarian National Archive, XX-5-h, Vi. 12. d., vol. 1, 73. It is probable that Nagy objected to the first and fifth of the students' demands because the first one called for "the immediate evacuation of all Soviet troops" while the fifth one called for "general elections by universal, secret ballot . . . with all political parties participating." The remaining fourteen demands had to do with the purification of the Communist Party, the selection of Imre Nagy as prime minister, and the reorganization of the country's economic life and judicial system. Thus, aside from the radical demands 1 and 5, the initial student petition amounted to moderate, within-system change and socialist goals, with emphasis on the reinstatement of Imre Nagy and his "New Course" of 1953–55.

Elsewhere in the city, near Heroes Square, the Stalin statue was coming down, but—incredibly—the dictator's boots could not be removed. Students put Hungarian flags in them. They then dragged the rest, in pieces, through the city to near the National Theater. Less than a mile from there was the Rádió Building, where one delegation of university students after another still tried to enter to read their sixteen demands on the air. The doors were locked. Inside, guards wearing the uniform of the secret police—though all or nearly all draftees—received supplementary help so that there were about fifty and soon as many as five hundred poorly equipped guards protecting the building. From the balcony, Benke, the head of the city's two radio stations, called on the students to go home. Addressing them as "comrades," she made the same mistake as Nagy. "We're Hungarians, not comrades," came the reply. The crowd, having heard parts of party leader Gerő's speech broadcast at 8 P.M., got angrier and larger. Rumors spread throughout the city that the dreaded secret police were shooting at the students. Trucks arrived out of nowhere with Hungarian military units bringing light weapons and handing them to the youngsters on the street. No one knew then, or knows now, who started the shooting.

Throughout the city, a vast insurgency was under way. Opinions differed about Gerő's speech: Some thought it was just stupid; others figured it was *meant to* provoke a strong response from Moscow so that Soviet troops would be dispatched promptly to restore order. For sure, it poured oil on the fire. He spoke about the "enemies of our people" who were attempting to "undermine the power of the working class, loosen the worker-peasant alliance, undercut the leading role of the working class in our country, and shake our people's faith in our party." There were those, Gerő said, who were slandering the Soviet Union, trying to "create a contradiction between proletarian internationalism and Hungarian patriotism," and who "endeavor to loosen the relations which link our Party to the glorious Communist Party of the Soviet Union."[8] Gerő seemed to know little of what was going on outside party headquarters, and he did not seem to or want to understand the dy-

---

[8] "Radio Address by Erno Gerő, First Secretary of the Hungarian Workers Party, October 23, 1956," in *National Communism and Popular Revolt in Eastern Europe: A Selection of Documents on Events in Poland and Hungary, February–November 1956*, ed. Paul E. Zinner (New York: Columbia University Press, 1956), 402–7.

namics of events. Following his totally inappropriate address came the announcement that the Central Committee would meet on October 31—eight days from then. Did they think they had eight days to think it over? Soon, the radio issued a correction: The meeting will take place "in a few days." Did they think they had a few days to think it over? Soon, the radio announced still another correction: The Central Committee would meet right away. Conditions were truly chaotic.

At Gerő's request, Nagy, accompanied by his son-in-law, Ferenc Jánosi, showed up at party headquarters at about 10 P.M. When Nagy arrived, Gerő, apparently not for the first time, was on the phone with the Kremlin, discussing the need for Soviet troops already stationed in Hungary to intervene and help restore order. The Kremlin agreed, making those sitting around in Gerő's room heave a sigh of relief.[9] With most of its members absent, the Central Committee met, focusing on personnel issues. Nagy proposed that Kádár replace Gerő, but Kádár declined the offer. Gerő stayed on. The Central Committee dismissed from the Politburo the worst Stalinists from Rákosi's entourage. Nagy, together with Szántó, joined the Politburo; Losonczy became an alternate member; and Donáth was made a party secretary. Losonczy and Donáth, who were not present, refused to serve because Nagy failed to bring in as many reformers as they had agreed at Losonczy's apartment that Nagy would do. As far as they were concerned, what was being done, and what Nagy accepted, was a case of "too little, too late." Meanwhile, all that the "street"—a new notion gaining currency, describing the insurgents—heard was that Gerő was still in charge.

Inside, the party was rearranging the deck chairs on its rapidly sinking ship. But outside, the world's first full-scale anti-Soviet and anti-communist revolution had commenced.

· 2 ·

The Hungarian drama played out in three acts:

- During the first, *confrontation phase* of the revolution, which began the evening of October 23 and lasted through October 27, the "street"

---

[9] Minutes of Nagy's statement to his interrogators on June 8, 1957, Hungarian National Archive, XX-5-h, Vi. 12 d., vol. 1, 75.

and the government worked at cross-purposes. The insurgents received considerable encouragement from the United States via RFE to insist on their demands, while the new Hungarian government led by a disoriented Nagy was under immense pressure from the Kremlin to restore order.

- In the second, *coordination phase* of the revolution—from October 28 to October 30—the Nagy government began to implement the insurgents' demands and the Kremlin moved toward accommodation, while RFE kept "demanding" additional concessions.

- In the third, *cooperation phase* of the revolution, which began on October 31 and ended with the Soviet intervention on November 4, the government and the insurgents approached a modus vivendi, while the Kremlin deceitfully prepared to smash a united Hungary—by then led by a coalition government that had come to enjoy the insurgents' support—and RFE still urged its listeners to be wary of compromise solutions.

▪ 3 ▪

The first phase in Budapest: Imre Nagy and the government.[10] During the first phase of the revolution, Imre Nagy did not seem to understand he was facing an altogether new situation. He was the only potentially credible political leader on the scene, but he allowed himself to become part of the regime he had bravely opposed. He did not yet identify with the insurgents. He was rather passive. Unsurprisingly, given his background, he was unsure both of his loyalties and of himself. When he received delegations led by his reformist supporters, he was more aloof than friendly. His inability to take charge became—for a few critical days—a defining feature of the revolution itself.

Spending the night of October 23 at party headquarters, at times attending an ongoing Central Committee meeting, at times waiting outside in a hallway, Nagy learned only at around 5 A.M. on the 24th that he was designated to be Hungary's new prime minister.[11] For four

---

[10] In this and the following two sections, I discuss the three phases of the revolt by sequentially treating the four key actors: Imre Nagy and the government; the insurgents; the Moscow decisionmakers; and the United States (including the Central Intelligence Agency, CIA, and Radio Free Europe in Munich). Because of the focus of this study on "failed illusions," and also because of limitations of space, I do not discuss important developments outside Budapest and in other foreign capitals.

[11] For what Imre Nagy did that day and night, see Rainer, *Nagy Imre,* 237–52; Tibor Méray, *Thirteen Days That Shook the Kremlin: Imre Nagy and the Hungarian Revolution* (New York: Praeger, 1959),

days, he was not the Imre Nagy people imagined him to be, so much so that rumors spread that he was the "prisoner of the Politburo." His behavior was mysterious. Wasn't he the person who just a year earlier incisively predicted that if the party continued to stifle his reform agenda, "it will become necessary to make a much greater retreat in order to keep the situation under control"?[12] It seemed that Nagy was not prepared for what he had anticipated. Perhaps because he now felt compelled to observe party discipline, or because he did not know what to make of his new role and responsibility, or because he was still troubled by his encounter at Kossuth Square the night before where the huge crowd did not appreciate him, or perhaps as a result of just being very tired, Nagy did not rise to the occasion.

In a sense, Nagy was a prisoner, not of the Politburo so much as of his own Communist past—of a limited ideological perspective and a political mentality shaped by intraparty intrigue—from which he could not escape. For days, he did not raise the two obvious political questions he (and his colleagues) should have asked: *What concessions must they make to the insurgents? And how could they then sell these concessions to the Kremlin?* Before the opening of the archives in 1989 and the publication of new memoirs, it was possible to imagine that Nagy was guided by a sense of realism: that he shied away from supporting the insurgents because he knew his reformist agenda was the limit beyond which the Kremlin would not go. Given the archival evidence, that interpretation can now be dismissed. In fact, the Kremlin sent *conflicting messages* to Nagy, with its chief troublemaker, Anastas Mikoyan, eventually even approving the formation of a multiparty system.

Meanwhile, for four long days, there was an Imre Nagy, the party apparatchik, who believed that a counterrevolution was taking place and it must be stopped. There was an Imre Nagy who was dazed, tired, and out of touch. There was an Imre Nagy who lost his nerve. Much as he hated Gerő, for example, he waited for the Soviet comrades to come and get rid of him. And yet, even then, there was also an Imre Nagy who

65–91; and András Hegedüs, *Élet egy eszme árnyékában: Életrajzi interjú* [Life in the shadow of an ideal: Memoir interview] (Vienna: Zoltán Zsille, 1985), 258–66. He was a "designated" prime minister because, according to constitutional formalities, only the state's Supreme Council—rather than the Communist Party—could select a prime minister.

[12] Imre Nagy, *On Communism: In Defense of the New Course* (New York: Praeger, 1957), 49–50.

was clearly different from those who surrounded him at party head-quarters: *Unlike all others there, Nagy did not approve of Gerő's request for Soviet intervention.* Though he did not rule out the use of force, alone among his colleagues he did not favor the use of foreign, that is, Soviet, forces against the growing insurgency. Nagy also appears to have sensed that Gerő, Hegedüs, and other hardliners wanted to co-opt him in or-der to make him appear to be the man in charge of crushing the rebel-lion—and thus discredit him in the eyes of his supporters. Members of the Old Guard needed Nagy's credibility to accomplish their goal; once that was done, then they could have dispensed with him. In short, the question they asked that night was not how to solve a problem but how to protect their power.

In the morning of the 24th, Rádió Kossuth declared martial law in Nagy's name. When questioned by his interrogators in 1957, Nagy tes-tified that he did not agree to the imposition of martial law. He said that, being only a designated prime minister whose appointment was not yet approved by Hungary's Presidential Council, he lacked authority to sign the necessary document. The radio also announced that the "Hungar-ian government"—that is, Nagy—asked for Soviet military assistance. This was untrue, but the "street" had no way of knowing that. In the event, Nagy refused to back up the request that Gerő, who had no le-gal authority to do so, had made to the Kremlin; in the end it was the outgoing prime minister, András Hegedüs, who—several days later, when he was no longer in office—retroactively put his signature on the document.[13] Because the public did not know what Nagy signed or did not sign, Nagy was identified with these two most unpopular measures. It barely improved Nagy's image that he personally declared in an ad-dress to "the people of Budapest" around midday on the 24th that those who "lay down their arms will be exempted from summary jurisdic-tion."[14] By then, with events changing at an unprecedented speed, his magic appeal, so much in evidence just twenty-four hours earlier, be-fore his speech to the crowd at Kossuth Square, was all but gone.

At party headquarters, meanwhile, personnel issues and intrigues

---

[13] András Hegedüs, *Élet egy eszme árnyékában* [Life in the shadow of an ideal] (Vienna: Zoltán Zsille, 1985), 262–65.

[14] For the full text of Nagy's speech, see *National Communism*, ed. Zinner, 409–11.

dominated the scene. By early morning on the 25th, Kádár finally replaced Gerő; but Gerő stayed on as a member of a small committee of four—with Nagy, Kádár, and Hegedüs—to shape the composition of a new government. Nagy tried to bring in his supporters, but he did not prevail. After several days of talking and bargaining, the government announced on the 27th did not yet reflect Nagy's preferences. There were a few positive signs—such as the appointment of the former Smallholder leader and the country's president in the postwar coalition era, Zoltán Tildy, as minister of state—but the hardliners vetoed the inclusion in the government of the two reform-Communist heavyweights, Losonczy and Donáth.[15]

It was not easy to discern what was going on and especially what to do under such chaotic circumstances. Among the few who saw clearly from the beginning were Losonczy and Donáth—and yet they had a dilemma about how to proceed. On the one hand, they declined to take up the party positions they were offered because they did not want to be part of a leadership dominated by the Old Guard that sought to defeat the insurgency. On the other hand, they did not want to abandon Nagy. When they met him on the 25th, Nagy was apparently not only disappointed but also quite irritated with them; they had deserted him in a moment of need. To resolve the dilemma, the two chose not to serve, but, joined by Vásárhelyi, they remained at party headquarters for now to suggest a passage or two to be inserted into Nagy's radio addresses. One that mattered broke new ground that day. The language was old-fashioned party jargon, but the content was novel. "As Chairman of the Council of Ministers," Nagy declared, "I hereby announce that the Hungarian Government will initiate negotiations concerning the relations between the Hungarian People's Republic and the Soviet Union, among other things about the withdrawal of Soviet forces stationed in Hungary, on the basis of Hungarian-Soviet friendship, proletarian internationalism, equality between Communist Parties and socialist countries, and national independence."[16]

---

[15] For a comprehensive, thorough account, see Zoltán Ripp, "A pártvezetés végnapjai" [The last days of the party leadership], in *Ötvenhat októbere és a hatalom* [October fifty-six and power], ed. Julianna Horváth and Zoltán Ripp (Budapest: Napvilág, 1997), 165–314.

[16] The text of Nagy's speech of October 25, 1956, is reprinted in *National Communism*, ed. Zinner, 416–18.

Because the rest of the speech aimed to satisfy the party leadership and the Kremlin, Donáth and Losonczy still refused to stay on in a formal capacity, although they did attend a Central Committee meeting that evening. There, Losonczy urged the Central Committee to invite a delegation of the insurgents to party headquarters so that all could hear their ideas and demands. Speaking of the "street," Losonczy called for order without bloodshed and suppression. This point and the passage in Nagy's address underlined the two issues facing the leadership: how to find common ground with the insurgents and how to remove the Soviet troops from the country. At this point, however, the Central Committee was not yet willing to proceed toward a peaceful conclusion. Referring to Losonczy and Donáth, Kádár noted that while he did not consider them traitors, the essence of their position was that the party should capitulate. Károly Kiss, a veteran Communist survivor, told Losonczy and Donáth that he "could not live in a bourgeois democracy, only in a people's democracy." In a dramatic demonstration of how far he had come, Losonczy said that he now favored the creation of a multiparty system. The real choice, according to Losonczy, was between saving the cause of socialism on the basis of popular support or with the help of Soviet bayonets. The three early heretics—Losonczy, Donáth, and Vásárhelyi—also submitted a written plea to the party urging an immediate end to atrocities against captured insurgents.[17]

On the 26th, before they were temporarily banished from party headquarters, Losonczy and Donáth arranged a conversation with Nagy who, as Donáth later described the encounter, agreed with their assessment but seemed helpless and unwilling to do anything about it. The calls he received from his wife and his daughter only deepened his sense of isolation and despair. His wife spoke of people who had trusted him and now did not know what to make of his behavior. When his daughter reported that what she was witnessing was a revolution, Nagy replied: "I know it." Hearing that, "he sank into himself, he was silent

---

[17] For a summary, see György Kövér, *Losonczy Géza 1917–1957* [Géza Losonczy 1917–1957] (Budapest: 1956-os Intézet, 1998), 271–82. How Géza Losonczy managed to size up the situation so clearly was the subject I discussed with a number of his friends and colleagues, including his widow (July 3, 1991), often with Miklós Vásárhelyi, and with József Köböl (October 4, 1991). Köböl, who did not always agree with Losonczy, told me: "Rákosi's prisons turned Géza into a passionate, sensitive man. Unlike the others emerging from Stalinist jails, he seemed to know who he was. He was troubled and he was sick, too, but he was also eager to do some good. I found him simply lovable."

and tears ran from his eyes," Donáth later recalled. "He gave the impression of a man who was serving his people, his country, and the cause of socialism, a man full of goodwill and good intentions, [but] a man in a very difficult situation facing events without knowing what to do."[18] The next morning, unable to cope with all the tension of the previous days, Nagy briefly collapsed; Mikhail Suslov, who happened to be there, gave him a pill called Validol that helped Nagy get on his feet. Irony of ironies, Suslov probably saved Nagy's life.

In this phase of the revolt, Nagy and members of the Old Guard who tried to isolate him could hardly be called "leaders" because their "followers" were so few and those few were so ineffective. The press, for example, was not under their control. The dailies did not even appear on the 24th, so as not to have to print Gerő's provocative speech from the night before. On the 25th, *Magyar Nemzet* printed radical demands by the newly formed Revolutionary Council of University Youth. The same day this paper called for full amnesty, the removal of Soviet troops from Hungary, the reintroduction of a multiparty system, and the dissolution of the secret police. The next day, Tibor Méray wrote in *Népszava*, another daily, that he was unwilling to call young people, workers, and soldiers reactionaries, fascists, or counterrevolutionaries just because they sought independence and freedom.

The party lost control over the press and to an extent over the Budapest police as well. The key figure there was the chief of police, Sándor Kopácsi, a man of simple, working-class background, who early on surrounded himself with a group of five or six pro-Nagy intellectuals. They included József Szilágyi, Miklós Gimes, and György Fazekas, of whom Fazekas proved to be particularly influential—because Kopácsi's wife was his wife's cousin.[19] The police refused to side either with the party's Old Guard or with the insurgents, partly because Kopácsi was torn between his oath of office and the guidance he was getting from

---

[18] For the Donáth quote, see Ferenc Donáth, *A Márciusi Fronttól Monorig: Tanulmányok, vázlatok, emlékezések* [From the March Front to Monor: Studies, outlines, recollections] (Budapest: Századvég Kiadó, 1992), 114–15. For the call by Nagy's daughter, see Rainer, *Nagy Imre*, 269.

[19] Cf. Sandor Kopacsi, *In the Name of the Working Class: The Inside Story of the Hungarian Revolution* (New York: Grove Press, 1987). György Fazekas, *Forró ösz Budapesten: Életinterjú* [Hot autumn in Budapest: Memoir interview] (Budapest; Magyar Hirlap, 1989). In an interview with me on June 22, 1991, Kopácsi related an encounter he had with Ivan Serov—head of the KGB who had rushed to Budapest—that took place on or about October 24 at police headquarters on Deák Square. Hardly able

his new advisers—and partly because the police were ill equipped for an emergency. To see what he was supposed to be doing, during the night of the 23rd, Kopácsi apparently opened a sealed envelope with top-secret instructions prepared by his superiors a few months earlier, after the riots in Poznan. The instructions specified how many machine guns and grenades, how much ammunition, and how much food should be available to the police in case of a Poznan-like emergency. But instead of eighty machine guns, there were only four; instead of food for a thousand policemen sufficient to last for six days, they could only find a few apples. The insurgency took the police by surprise—as it did everyone else.[20]

The first phase in Budapest: The insurgents. Who were the insurgents and what did they want?

Hungarian researchers—notably László Eörsi and his colleagues at the Institute for the Study of the 1956 Revolution; László Gyurkó, an independent scholar; and others—have collected vast amounts of information on who the insurgents were, how many of them actually participated in the fighting, where they came from, and what their objectives were.[21] Many of their answers are necessarily tentative or qualified; in some cases, they could not do much better than offer educated guesses.

---

to control himself, Serov could not comprehend why the Budapest police were so totally unprepared for "a confrontation with this fascist mob." Kopácsi told him that because they did not have enough weapons to put down the rebellion, they must seek a political solution to the crisis. I have not been able to find corroborating evidence for this encounter.

[20] Kopacsi, *In the Name of the Working Class,* 115–16. This is how the author described the scene at police headquarters: "It was the moment to open the large red envelope marked on the front: 'PLAN M. Top Secret! Open only in case of ABSOLUTE NECESSITY.' Plan M had been conceived by the Ministry of the Interior at the time of the events in Poznan, Poland, with a view to dealing with a similar situation in Hungary. I called my senior officers, then broke the seals on the envelope, five large and fourteen small ones, and skimmed the text. It started with an exhaustive list of the weapons and ammunition that were supposed to be in the arsenal at police headquarters. I was stupefied to learn that we had '20 heavy machine guns.' In fact, we had only one. As for '80 machine guns,' that was seventy-six more than we actually possessed. And so on: 'ammunition, hand grenades for 72 hours of combat' (we had enough for twelve hours), 'fresh underwear and uniforms, tinned foods, drinks, cigarettes, etc. for 1,000 people, 6 days of combat.' We had none of that except a few uniforms and a few crates of apples. My officers smiled bitterly. . . . The famous Plan M was a fantasy and a fraud. Like so much else the Hungarian bureaucracy put on paper, it bore not the slightest relation to reality."

[21] See, in particular, László Gyurkó, *A bakancsos forradalom* [roughly: Revolution in worn boots] (Budapest: Kossuth, 2001)—a fact-filled and yet readable one-volume history of the revolution that relates both what the insurgents and the government did—and three major studies by László Eörsi, *A Corvinisták 1956: A VIII kerület fegyveres csoportjai* [The Corvinites 1956: Militant groups in the 8th district] (Budapest: 1956-os Intézet, 2001); *A Széna Tériek 1956* [The Széna Square (fighters) 1956]

What emerged from these studies was that the revolt was indeed completely spontaneous. Clearly, it began at Rádió Kossuth during the night of October 23, when student delegations were barred from entering the building and putting on the air their sixteen-point demands. Although the guards surrendered before midnight, the party managed to control broadcasting from another, secret site. As to the outbreak of fighting, it began, partly because of the location of the radio station, in Pest, and that was the part of the city that witnessed the most intensive fighting throughout the revolt. From there, young men spread out in search of trucks and weapons. They had a relatively easy time collecting what they wanted because they encountered little or no resistance at various depots and at nearby army barracks. In four depots, they sequestered some 150 trucks immediately—enough to transport a small army. The crowd, by then dominated by young workers rather than students, drove all around during the night, roaming the city's avenues and streets, some carrying national flags, others just shouting slogans like "Down with Gerő!" When a group of angry people showed up at the Kilián Barracks, not far from the state radio headquarters, some 200 soldiers also joined them. Hospitals began to receive wounded insurgents in the early evening hours; the first report of a rebel killed came at 9:37 P.M.

At one time or another during the revolt, an estimated 15,000 people took part in the armed insurgency.[22] With very few exceptions, they were young; I calculated the average age of one of the largest

---

(Budapest: 1956-os Intézet and Állambiztonsági Szolgálatok Történeti Levéltára, n.d.); and Eörsi, *Mitoszok helyett, 1956* [Instead of myths, 1956] (Budapest; Noran, 2003). Eörsi has also published several other major studies on the subject.

[22] Eörsi, *Mitoszok helyett*, 30. Gyurkó, *A bakancsos forradalom*, 362. Gyurkó (166–67) warned that it was impossible to know precisely how many took active part in the revolt. In each case, the numbers he provides are, and should be seen as, approximations. Gyurkó reported that between October 23 and November 4, about 760 insurgents had died in Budapest as a direct result of the revolt, of whom 30 died on the 23rd, 200 on the 24th, 200 on the 25th, 120 on the 26th, 50 on the 27th, 40 on the 28th, 20 during a cease-fire on the 29th, 40 on the 30th, fewer than 20 on the October 31 and on November 1 together, and fewer than 10 on November 2 and 3 together. (The day when the remaining 30 died apparently could not be established.) *In other words, the fighting all but stopped by October 31, when the Kremlin decided to intervene.* Gyurkó also reports that about 90 percent of those killed died in Pest, and of them almost half died in the 8th and 9th districts that were heavily populated by unskilled workers and their poor families and where the fighting was very heavy. Another, most interesting fact Gyurkó reports is that in five Pest districts where such numbers were collected about one in four of the insurgents killed was less than twenty years old. This is one of the indicators explaining why Hungarians to this day refer to 1956 as "the revolution of the kids of Pest" (*a pesti srácok forradalma*).

groups of fighters at twenty-five.[23] In some places, they occupied buildings and factories without much resistance at all; elsewhere, fierce fighting taking was going on all night. Most of the units were small. For example, in the eighth and ninth districts of Budapest, alone there were thirty-three independent units, including the Corvinites, probably the city's largest single resistance group, that further divided into sixteen additional groupings.[24] In this phase of the revolt, the insurgents did not yet observe any central authority.

The fighters were not only young; they were also—as in all modern revolutions—mostly uneducated and mostly unskilled workers. Though no reliable information is available about the background of all 15,000 (or even most) insurgents, in some units nine in ten had only eight years of education and nine in ten were physical workers.[25] Almost 30 percent of the total number of the Széna Square insurgents whose past could be studied had a criminal record, but a third of those with a record committed "crimes" for illegal border crossing, that is, attempts to escape from Communist Hungary, and similar political offenses against an oppressive state. Thus, while as many as about one in five had run into nonpolitical legal problems prior to 1956, allegations made by the Kremlin to justify the use of force—that the revolt was started by criminals—were nonetheless false. On the whole, the rebels were neither hooligans nor, for sure, upper-class elements trying to return the country to pre-1945 "feudal" or "fascist" conditions. Many may have been fanatics, and many may have been "primitive" in the sense of being uneducated, unrefined, or unsophisticated—but they were not fascists. Of the thousands of fighters identified, for example, only two or three were military officers in the prewar, authoritarian Miklós Horthy regime;[26]

---

[23] I thank Ryan Miller, my research assistant at Johns Hopkins University's Paul H. Nitze School of Advanced International Studies, for doing the math. Drawing on data about fighters in just one large group—the one at Széna Square in Buda—we considered 259 certain participants. The year of birth was available for 202 of them; their average age turned out to be twenty-five years. This corresponds to impressionistic accounts describing the "average" insurgent to have been in his midtwenties. Cf. Eörsi, *A Széna Tériek 1956*, 316–40.

[24] Eörsi, *A Corvinisták 1956*, 22–24. The name of this group comes from the Corvin movie house and the space in front of it that made it directly accessible to József Boulevard and indirectly accessible to the strategically located Üllői Street with its large military barracks.

[25] This paragraph draws on data gathered about the Corvinites in ibid., 12–15 and passim.

[26] Gyurkó, *A bakancsos forradalom*, 168.

indeed, the "street" did not want to "turn the clock back." Their weakness, so understandable under the circumstances, was their youthful disregard for what was or was not possible.

The insurgents were angry, brave, dedicated, and fearless in the face of a despised foreign enemy, and they were ready to die for their country. They started out trying to amend the system, but they ended up trying to transform it; the process of radicalization they experienced was gradual but conspicuous.[27] Having been denied access to the radio so that they could broadcast their demands and having been called "fascists" and "counterrevolutionaries" by Gerő, the insurgents felt cornered. Even then, despite having weapons in their hands and despite years of oppression and exploitation, they engaged in no criminal activities. With the windows of many a storefront in Budapest shattered, there were almost no reports of stolen goods. The insurgents became more radical after the confrontation at the radio station and especially after the massacre by sharpshooters in front of the Parliament Building two days later. Only then did some of them go, look for, and arrest a few secret police members and Stalinist politicians who—with the exception of what would transpire at Republic Square on October 30—were neither tortured nor even kept under arrest for more than a few hours.

Some of the details of what happened at the Parliament Building on October 25 are still unclear. In the morning in a downtown area, a rally began that included young people eager to enjoy a bit of freedom now that the government had suspended the curfew in effect the previous day. The situation was ambiguous. Soviet armed forces that had reached Budapest were trying to restore order, but the Hungarian military did not seem to be with them; as a result, the Soviet forces proceeded on their own, receiving some assistance from elements of the

---

[27] A revealing example of radicalization took place among the Corvinites. Their first leader was László Kovács Iván—Iván was his surname—who identified himself as a "national Communist." Only on November 1 did he lose his position as the group's chief commander; that was when the membership replaced him with the far more radical Gergely Pongrátz (commonly known as "the moustache"). Yet, even Pongrátz reaffirmed his own and his comrades' "socialist" convictions. This is particularly telling because of his subsequent association with right-wing causes both in the United States (where he lived after 1956) and in Hungary (to which he returned in 1991). In his book, he wrote: "In Hungary in 1956 we wanted to turn the Communist social system into a genuinely socialist one" (the quotation appears on p. 25 of the 1982 and all subsequent editions). See Gergely Pongrátz, *Corvin köz 1956* [Corvin passage 1956] (Chicago: author's edition, 1982), reprinted in Budapest in 1985 (samizdat), 1989, and 1992.

secret police (ÁVH, Államvédelmi Hatóság, or State Security Authority). Meanwhile, Colonel Pál Maléter took over command of the Kilián Barracks, near Corvin Passage, and arranged for a ceasefire with the insurgents.

Under these confusing circumstances, some of the demonstrators even approached Russian soldiers in or near their tanks, trying to convince them to come over to their side. Apparently, a few did just that. Then the crowd, its size estimated at 8,000 to 10,000, moved on, in a hopeful atmosphere, to the Parliament Building. There, the guards protecting the Parliament as well as the nearby party headquarters could not figure out who was entering the area (called Kossuth Square). Were the tanks Russian? Did they belong to the Hungarian Army? Suddenly, indiscriminate shooting began. It is still uncertain who started it, the most likely explanation being that a Hungarian ÁVH militia unit positioned at the top of the Ministry of Agrarian Affairs across from the Parliament Building opened fire. What is known is that in the end 60 to 80 protesters were killed and about 100 to 150 were injured. Hungarians tended to blame secret police militias for the massacre.[28]

October 25 thus turned into another critical day. Facing fire, the insurgents felt they had no option but to move on from trying to make improvements to trying to make radical changes. Products of a system that professed to build a new socialist economic, social, and political order, *the insurgents initially rebelled against the failure of that ideal, not the ideal itself; they may have even rebelled against their own failed illusions about the promise of socialism.* It was telling that their key original demand focused on the return to power of Imre Nagy, a man they learned to respect in 1953–55 as a Communist reformer—rather than Admiral Horthy, József Cardinal Mindszenty, or even such leaders of Hungary's democratic interlude of 1945–47 as the Smallholders' Zoltán Tildy. It probably never even occurred to them to raise such issues as the reprivatization of large industry and banks or the return of huge holdings to

---

[28] Endre Marton, a Hungarian-born correspondent for the Associated Press who had spent a year in Communist jails, was at Kossuth Square during the massacre, together with John McCormack of the *New York Times.* Endre Marton, *The Forbidden Sky* (Boston: Little, Brown, 1971), 133–38. My summary is based on Marton's eyewitness account, except that I adjusted the number of people killed and injured to reflect the results of more recent archival research by historians at the Institute for the History of the 1956 Revolution. Cf. John McCormack, "Reporter in Budapest Tells How Protest Grew into War," *New York Times,* October 27, 1956.

large landowners; the country's so-called socialist achievements—at least in the economic realm—were beyond challenge.

The first phase in Moscow. It spoke well for Ambassador Yuri Andropov's frantic reports earlier in 1956—fortified as they that must have been by Soviet intelligence—that not quite everyone in Moscow was totally surprised by the outbreak of violence. As Mark Kramer discovered among declassified documents, the Soviet Ministry of Defense had begun to prepare for large-scale turmoil in Hungary as early as July 1956.[29] Code-named "Wave," the plan called for the restoration of order in less than six hours. It is not known if the Soviet leadership had made similar plans for some or all the countries in the Soviet bloc, or—alternatively—if the Kremlin had particularly superb intelligence about Hungary. In any case, the Soviet Army was ready. More than 30,000 troops were dispatched to—and 6,000 reached—Budapest by the 24th, that is, in less than a day.

The decision to dispatch two divisions from Ukraine and one from Romania, together with the mobilization of Soviet troops stationed in Hungary itself, took place after the outbreak of fighting at the Rádió Building in Pest. The request to the Soviet Embassy and then to Khrushchev was made earlier in the evening, but the Soviet Politburo (called the Presidium at the time), meeting before midnight Moscow time, or at 10 P.M. Budapest time (or 4 P.M. Washington time), did not immediately or automatically approve the request. The useful but very incomplete record of this Politburo meeting—known as the Malin Notes, after Vladimir N. Malin, a senior official in the Soviet party's Central Committee apparatus—showed Mikoyan's opposition to military intervention. He also wanted Nagy to be co-opted into the leadership (which was happening as he spoke) and encourage the Hungarians to restore order. Vyacheslav Molotov led the diehards; he was for intervention and against relying on Nagy. In the end, Khrushchev approved

---

[29] Mark Kramer, "The Soviet Union and the 1956 Crises in Hungary and Poland: Reassessments and New Findings," *Journal of Contemporary History* 33, no. 2 (April 1998): 163–214; the citation here is on 180. See also Mark Kramer, "Hungary and Poland: Khrushchev's CPSU CC Presidium Meeting on East European Crises, 24 October 1956," *Cold War International History Project Bulletin*, issue 5 (Spring 1995): 1, 50–56; and Tibor Hajdú, "Az 1956. október 24-i moszkvai értekezlet" [The October 24, 1956, Moscow meeting] in *Évkönyv 1992* [Yearbook of the Institute for the Study of the 1956 Revolution, 1992] (Budapest: 1956-os Intézet, 1992), 149–56.

the intervention, agreed to Nagy's return to the leadership (but not as prime minister), and sent Mikoyan and Suslov to Budapest.[30]

It is quite likely that when Khrushchev talked to Gerő on the phone in the late evening hours on the 23rd, the two had agreed on co-opting Nagy (without the whole Soviet Politburo's approval). By the time Mikoyan and Suslov arrived in Budapest on the 24th, the Kremlin was definitely hopeful about Nagy. The Soviet news agency TASS mentioned him favorably in its report, and Nagy's declaration of martial law (or state of emergency) that morning made a good impression on the Soviet leaders. At this stage, while everything was up in the air and thus nothing was final, Moscow was looking for a Polish or a Yugoslav outcome. Khrushchev confided in the Yugoslav ambassador later that day that he wanted to find a political solution to the Hungarian crisis, though the ambassador was unconvinced: "[Khrushchev] gave the impression that he had no faith in such a solution."[31]

Despite its impressive firepower and obvious advantage over the insurgents, the achievements of the Soviet Army were limited. By the 25th, the radio was in Soviet hands, but elsewhere the city was not under their control; in several districts, both party and police headquarters were occupied by the rebels, partly because those who were supposed to defend these buildings had defected to their side. The Soviet military intervention, backed by inflammatory Communist rhetoric, only suc-

---

[30] On the Malin Notes and, more generally, the evolution of Soviet decisions with respect to Hungary, see Kramer's translated text and his extensive interpretative notes in his "New Evidence on Soviet Decision-Making and the 1956 Polish and Hungarian Crises," *Cold War International History Project Bulletin*, issues 8–9 (Winter 1966–67): 358–84. Cf. János M. Rainer, "Döntés a Kremlben, 1956: Kísérlet a feljegyzések értelmezésére" [Decision in the Kremlin, 1956: An attempt to interpret the notes], in *Döntés a Kremlben, 1956: A szovjet pártelnökség vitái Magyarországról* [Decision in the Kremlin, 1956: The Soviet Politburo's Debates about Hungary], ed. Vyacheslav Sereda and János M. Rainer (Budapest; 1956-os Intézet, 1996), 111–54; the documents were translated from Russian into Hungarian by Éva Gál. See also Vyacheslav Sereda and Aleksandr Stikhalin, eds., *Hiányzó lapok 1956 történetéből: Dokumentumok a volt SZKP KB levéltárából* [Missing pages from the history of 1956: Documents from the former CPSU Central Committee's archive] (Budapest: Zenit, 1993); the documents were translated from Russian into Hungarian by Tibor Bazsó, Márton Bazsó, Géza Kádas, and András Soproni; Éva Gál, András B. Hegedüs, György Litván, and János M. Rainer, eds., *A "Jelcin Dosszié": Szovjet dokumentumok 1956-ról* [The "Yeltsin Dossier": Soviet Documents about 1956] (Budapest: Századvég Kiadó-56-os Intézet, 1993); the documents translated from Russian into Hungarian by Éva Gál, Ágota N. Goller, and Erna Páll. For a comprehensive collection of Soviet documents in Russian covering all of 1956, see E. D. Orekhova, V. T. Sereda, and A. S. Stykhalin, eds., *Sovietskiy Soyuz i vengerskiy krizis, 1956 goda: Dokumentiy* [The Soviet Union and the Hungarian Crisis, 1956: Documents] (Moscow: Rossien, 1998).

[31] Veljko Mićunović, *Moscow Diary* (Garden City, N.Y.: Doubleday, 1980), 127.

ceeded in mobilizing an ever-growing anti-Soviet uprising that spread from Budapest to the countryside. The Kremlin, despite informative cables from Mikoyan and Suslov, was not yet ready to change course. Politburo members, instead of debating alternative courses of action, jumped on each other's weak points (which is exactly what the Hungarian leaders were doing in Budapest). In Moscow, in what amounted to a revival (or continuation) of the post-Stalin power struggle, Bulganin, Molotov, Kaganovich, Malenkov, and others gave vent to their frustration by attacking the "liberal" Mikoyan, presumably to deprive Khrushchev of his most loyal supporter. Defending his absent ally, Khrushchev stated matter-of-factly that "Comrade Mikoyan supported a position of nonintervention, but our troops are there," meaning Mikoyan, even though he opposed his colleagues' decision, was loyally implementing it. "Mikoyan is acting as he said he would," Khrushchev added, no doubt sensing that he was as much the target of the Old Guard as was Mikoyan.[32]

Uncertainties and political infighting both in Moscow and in Budapest produced the Soviet attack on the Corvinites on the 28th. The party's Military Committee, together with some hard-liners at the Hungarian Ministry of Defense and the Soviet military authorities, ordered the action—despite Prime Minister Nagy's explicit objections. By then the Corvinites had developed a working relationship if not a common front with the officers at nearby Kilián Barracks, commanded by Colonel Pál Maléter; as a consequence—amazingly—the Soviet forces were unable to complete their mission and liquidate the rebels of Corvin Passage.

The revolution, in short, was approaching its first turning point. With the Hungarian Army just standing by, the war between the mighty Soviet Army and the incredibly brave and ingenious insurgents had come to a standstill.

The first phase in Washington and Munich. On the American side, no one—not the White House or the State Department, not the Central Intelligence Agency (CIA), and not Radio Free Europe—had antici-

---

[32] When the Malin Notes became available, this particular Soviet Politburo session was assumed to have taken place two days later, on October 28. However, the inimitable Mark Kramer, in his role as a detective-scholar, discovered from Malin's text that this Politburo meeting was actually the announced follow-up to an earlier one on October 26. For the translated text, see "Working Notes from the Session of the CPSU CC Presidium on 26 October 1956," in Kramer, "New Evidence on Soviet Decision-Making and the 1956 Polish and Hungarian Crises," 389.

pated the outbreak of violence in Hungary. Government analysts were quite aware of some sort of "intellectual ferment" there (and in Poland), but those who followed events more closely had considered Imre Nagy and his supporters weak-kneed Titoists, not even as energetic or shrewd as was Poland's Gomułka. When news that proved to be false reached the outside world—that Nagy had called in the Soviet troops—Washington could and did conclude that its negative view about the Hungarian reformer was correct all along.

Preoccupied with the presidential reelection campaign that was about to conclude, U.S. president Dwight D. Eisenhower saw the Hungarian uprising as a problem, not an opportunity. At a meeting of his National Security Council on October 26, he seemed mostly concerned about the danger of Moscow's overreaction to Hungary by launching a major war. Calm and prudent, the president wanted everyone to watch carefully to see if the Kremlin might not feel "tempted to resort to extreme measures and even precipitate global war."[33] At the same council meeting, Harold Stassen, Eisenhower's disarmament adviser, put forth an interesting proposal. He suggested that a message of assurance should be sent immediately to the Kremlin in which the United States would state its lack of interest in drawing Hungary into NATO but would consider the neutralization of that country on the Austrian pattern. The president promptly rejected the idea, although later that day he changed his mind and asked Secretary of State John Foster Dulles to consider it. On the 27th, Dulles alluded to the Stassen proposal in his only major speech on Hungary when he said: "We do not look upon these nations [Poland and Hungary] as potential military allies. We see them as part of a new and friendly and no longer divided Europe." If they were to succeed and become free on their own, Dulles continued, the United States would draw on its "abundance to tide [the Hungarians and the Poles] over the period of economic adjustment."[34]

In this phase of the revolution, this was all Washington managed to do diplomatically or otherwise. A message along the lines of the Dulles speech was conveyed to the Kremlin and to allied capitals. After years

---

[33] *Foreign Relations of the United States: Diplomatic Papers, 1955–1957* (Washington. D.C.: U.S. Government Printing Office, 1988), vol. 25, 299.

[34] Ibid., 318.

of preaching "liberation" and "rollback," now, with the moment of truth at hand, the United States did not know what else to do. There were no plans whatsoever on the shelves, no diplomatic initiatives had been prepared, and of course no consideration was given to any form of military assistance, let alone direct intervention. Dulles's offer, signaling to Moscow that there would be no American military support for the Hungarians, was sensible but gratuitous. C. D. Jackson, the influential psychological warfare hawk who served the Eisenhower administration and then continued to advise the president in a private capacity, had anticipated the predicament inherent in Dulles's modest message. He had warned the White House in August 1953 that "the big problem we face when we call for action behind the Iron Curtain is the extent to which we are willing to back that action if serious trouble develops. It would be both immoral and inefficient to provoke massacres, which would not only kill off the best men, but would also destroy our position in the minds of the people behind the Iron Curtain."[35]

An alternative to Washington's feeble reaction was advanced in a column by Walter Lippmann, the doyen of American journalism, which appeared in the October 26 issue of the *Washington Post and Times Herald*.[36] Undoubtedly reflecting the private views of many professional diplomats, Lippmann argued that "it is not in our interest that the movement in Eastern Europe should go so far that no accommodation with Russia is possible. . . . In the interest of peace and of freedom—freedom from both despotism and from anarchy—we must hope that for a time, not forever but for a time, the uprising in the satellite orbit will be stabilized at Titoism." However, with emotions coloring political judgments, no one active in the political arena in the United States or in Western Europe could risk his political career by openly endorsing, let alone working toward, a Titoist path.

---

[35] As quoted in H. W. Brands Jr., *Cold Warriors: Eisenhower's Generation and American Foreign Policy* (New York: Columbia University Press, 1988), 124. On November 17, 1956, less than two weeks after the Soviet crackdown in Hungary, Jackson, though apprehensive, bounced back and found something positive to stress: "Aggressive, imperial Communism received a terrible blow in the one-two punches of Poland and Hungary," he wrote to a White House official. "Their close to two-million-man military and paramilitary organizations in the satellites were conclusively revealed as unreliable for the purposes of their Soviet masters. The international mystique and omnipotence of Communism was sorely cracked if not shattered." Ibid., 132.

[36] Walter Lippmann, "How Far in Eastern Europe?" *Washington Post and Times Herald*, October 26, 1956.

True, Washington officials were not necessarily unsympathetic to the idea of stepping back from the brink and accepting only a modest step forward. Had they thought of it, they could have drawn on a seldom-noticed passage of Dulles's original, 1952 formulation. "We do not want a series of bloody uprisings and reprisals," the future secretary of state stated in his famous article in *Life* magazine in which he promoted the idea of rollback and liberation rather than the virtues of realpolitik. "There can be peaceful separation from Moscow, as Tito showed," Dulles added, "and enslavement can be made so unprofitable that the master will let go of his grip."[37] The Eisenhower administration could have built a rationale for its new departure on such words—but it was probably too late to do so. By this time, the political climate in the United States, including the waning but still persistent impact of McCarthyism, made an explicit endorsement of Titoism all but impossible. By the mid-1950s, moreover, it was George Kennan who advocated support for Titoism in Eastern Europe—and Dulles could not bring himself to agree with his nemesis.[38] Most important, even if Washington had overcome these problems and found a way to endorse Lippmann's limitationist approach, it could not have quickly implemented an explicitly pro-Titoist stance where it mattered most: at Radio Free Europe. There, as late as July 1956, an otherwise rather convoluted policy guidance referred to "Titoism" and "national communism" as slogans or labels that "we cannot approve and will not use ourselves."[39] A largely new staff of editors, reporters, and announcers would have had to be found to tell their Hungarian audience to calm down and seek less.

In the end, the White House had little to say and nothing to offer. *The excuse of helplessness replaced the myth of liberation and the illusion of omnipotence.*

As to the Central Intelligence Agency, it was as clueless as the White House and the Department of State. Contrary to Communist propaganda and what critics of the CIA have said around the world, notably in the United States, the agency had nothing to do with the outbreak of the Hungarian revolt. Its candid and competent internal review, com-

---

[37] John Foster Dulles, "A Policy of Boldness," *Life*, May 19, 1952, 146–60.

[38] Brands, *Cold Warriors*, 11n13.

[39] "RFE/New York Special Guidance, July 9, 1956." Hoover Institution unsorted RFE Archive.

pleted in 1958, suggests that while it had one Hungarian-speaking agent in place in Budapest on October 23, elsewhere—outside Hungary—it only "had a pool of seven or so Hungarian speakers . . . of varying capabilities."[40] In this phase of the revolt, "there was no team" whose members could have cooperated with each other; thus, each "border visit"—presumably to the Austro-Hungarian border area—"was an independent probe."[41] The personnel sent there waited for eyewitnesses to show up, who would tell their stories to the assorted journalists, Austrian welfare officials, and others, including intelligence officers from different countries. Because information reaching the area tended to relate happenings in West Hungarian towns and cities, it rounded out the news coming from Budapest from such superb reporters as John McCormack of the *New York Times*. With its sole representative in Budapest mostly cut off from the outside world, the CIA was "not getting news from the storm center of the revolution at Budapest or on a country-wide basis" either.[42]

Sometime between October 26 and November 4, two CIA contract agents entered Hungary. One, with "partial use of the language . . . took a spin around Hungary and came out and wrote an excellent report on what he had seen." The other went in twice, met with students, and got out just in time before the second Soviet intervention on November 4.[43] More generally, reporting to CIA headquarters from the border area was minimal (one report a day between October 24 and 26), but then on the 27th two reports were sent to headquarters. "Previous to this day [the 27th]," the CIA review notes, "they [i.e., CIA headquarters] had no information which was not likewise available in the U.S. through radio and newspapers, and had been engaged in marshalling their forces and attempting to orient themselves to a situation for which, as has already been pointed out, they were completely unprepared."[44]

---

[40] CIA, *Clandestine Services Historical Series (CSHP 6): The Hungarian Revolution and Planning for the Future, 23 October–4 November 1956, Volume I of II* (MORI DocID: 1203072; parts declassified at my request in March 2005), 78. On the identity of the sole CIA agent assigned to work in Budapest, see chap. 1, fn. 4, above.

[41] Ibid., 79. Those who visited the border region must have been inexperienced people on contract to the agency, because "staff members . . . were prohibited" even from going there. Ibid., 80.

[42] Ibid., 83.

[43] Ibid., 85.

[44] Ibid., 90.

As the last of these cables requested guidance from headquarters about what else to do, "particularly in regard to sending arms and ammunition shipments into Hungary," the reply that came on the 28th was specific. The instructions stated that "we must restrict ourselves to information collection only, that agents sent to the border must *not get involved in anything that would reveal U.S. interest or give cause to claim intervention,* that [*word excised*] should try to *get the identities of activists,* and that there might be the possibility of passing in radio equipment a little later." The next day, a subsequent instruction made it clear that "*it was not permitted to send U.S. weapons in.*" In practice, headquarters' prohibition against transferring weapons or ammunition made no difference at all because "at this date no one had checked precisely on the exact location and nature of U.S. or other weapons available to CIA [presumably somewhere in Western Europe]. This was done finally in December."[45]

As for Radio Free Europe, broadcasting from Munich, what it said mattered far more to Hungarians than anything the CIA or Washington officials said or did. And what the Hungarians heard from the beginning was that *they should not trust Imre Nagy and they should press ahead vigorously for all they sought—up to and including, of course, the overthrow of Nagy's government.* The programs did not advise prudence. The programs did not quote Western press reports explaining Nagy's predicament. The programs did not speak of a possible Titoist scenario, or of the Soviet Army's might and determination, or of the dilemmas of choice in the West. The programs did not hint that the Eisenhower administration, in the midst of a presidential campaign, was not even considering extending military help (though, contrary to RFE's critics, only one program that was broadcast after the second Soviet intervention on November 4 claimed that military help would be forthcoming).

With the tapes of the actual broadcasts unavailable for four decades but finally found and released in the mid-1990s,[46] there can no doubt

---

[45] Ibid., 91–92. Italics in the original.

[46] The history of RFE's Hungarian broadcasts is illustrative of American and especially German concerns about their content in late 1956 and in 1957. With (West) Germany a sovereign entity since 1955, the main concern was whether public discussion in that country might not show strong sentiment against RFE and endanger its operations in Munich. The muddled story of the Hungarian tapes of October–November 1956 began against that background, with the German Foreign Office borrowing them in December 1956 in order to decide if various public charges of incitement by RFE

about the inflammatory tone of many of the commentaries. In February 1957, at a closed RFE workshop devoted to an assessment of RFE's performance during the Hungarian crisis, William E. Griffith, the radio's political adviser, admitted so much when he replied to a staff member's question. He was asked if he would do anything differently in case another revolt was to occur in the region. Griffith said that in that case, according to his new instructions from New York, RFE would only broadcast news and news analyses rather than take sides or state the station's preferences. "Would we openly tell that there was no hope?" the staffer wanted to know. Griffith: "Not openly, only indirectly. We would let it be known in our news and commentary [programs]."[47]

When it comes to content, then, RFE's unprofessional treatment of the 1956 crisis is beyond serious debate. The debatable issue is who was most responsible for the debacle—CIA headquarters in Washington, RFE's center of operations in New York, the American managers and advisers in Munich, or the émigrés on the Hungarian desk?[48] Or, as noted in chapter 3, did the problem go even deeper, to America's political culture, which seemed to prompt U.S. politicians to pretend, then and always, that victory could be had?

RFE, with some justification at first, was highly skeptical of Nagy. After all, he *was* the man who introduced a state of emergency on the 24th. That day, an RFE commentary correctly observed that if Nagy was

---

were valid or not. In January 1957, after a quick review, Chancellor Konrad Adenauer announced the results: RFE had not violated its charter. The Germans promptly returned the tapes to RFE. But then, in July 1957, the German Foreign Office and RFE agreed to return the tapes to the Foreign Office in order to remove them physically from the purview of the German Labor Court. The reason for that, in turn, had to do with dismissed Hungarian broadcasters' threat to use the tapes in their case for reinstatement. The tapes ended up in the German Federal Archives in Koblenz and stayed there for almost forty years. Having been finally released to Hungarian Radio, and vastly improved by a reverse engineering project, the complete set of what was actually broadcast in October–November 1956 is now available at the Hoover Institution's RFE/RL collection, the Széchenyi Library in Budapest, and at the German Federal Archive in Koblenz. According to Gyula Borbándi, *Magyarok az Angol Kertben: A Szabad Európa Rádió története* [Hungarians at the English garden: A history of Radio Free Europe] (Budapest: Európa, 1996), 288–90, one of the thirteen dismissals was particularly puzzling as well as tragic. The editor in question was Viktor Márjás, who had strongly protested the radio's vehement and hostile denunciation of Imre Nagy during the revolt. He should have been promoted. For unknown reasons, Márjás committed suicide in 1974.

47 Borbándi, *Magyarok az Angol Kertben*, 286.

48 A detailed account of the issue of responsibility, based on examination of all available relevant records, awaits A. Ross Johnson's comprehensive study of RFE's history. Meanwhile, readers are advised to check sources identified in chapter 3, such as Arch Puddington's thoughtful and candid study. My book concerns itself less with the internal affairs of the radio than with the contents and probable impact of its broadcasts.

to continue this way, the same people who brought him to power would promptly remove him. On the 25th, after Nagy announced his intention to discuss the withdrawal of Soviet forces and also made other concessions, RFE, in an emotional comment, lectured Nagy about what he should be doing. Nagy's "casual promises" (*odavetett ígéretek*), the reporter intoned, showed that his government still had not resolved to fulfill the people's legitimate demands. Later, going further, another reporter "reminded" Nagy of how "desperately he had begged" on the radio, "how, his voice trembling, he promised amnesty." The same reporter "warned" Nagy that "yesterday's popularity was becoming today's detestation." With the text doing no justice to the incredibly arrogant tone of these broadcasts, the least that can be said is that the comments showed little or no understanding of the complexity of the Hungarian crisis and of Nagy's role and dilemmas.[49]

In a relatively more balanced commentary, Andor Gellért, head of the RFE Hungarian Desk, raised the question of whether Nagy should be blamed for calling in the Soviet troops. Gellért observed that Nagy might not have been the responsible official to have made that decision, which was a reasonable enough point to make, but then he went on to say that in the end it did not much matter—there was "no excuse" (*mentő körülmény*) either way—because Nagy accepted his predecessors' "legacy." In short, he committed "treachery" whether he called in the Soviet troops or not. Gellért also referred to Nagy as a man with "Cain's stamp on his forehead."[50] Worse yet, as time passed and Nagy got more conciliatory—even in this first phase of the revolt—RFE's attacks became more and more insistent, bombastic, and hysterical. On

---

[49] The commentaries, taken from the actual radio broadcasts, are quoted at length in Judit Katona and György Vámos, "Nagy Imre és a Szabad Európa Rádió 1956-ban" [Imre Nagy and Radio Free Europe in 1956], in *Nagy Imre és kora: Tanulmányok és források* [Imre Nagy and his era: Studies and sources] (Budapest: Nagy Imre Alapítvány, 2002), 139–90. Thanks to Gábor Hanák of the Széchenyi Library in Budapest, I have the text of several broadcasts in my files and I have also listened to them. All translations are mine.

[50] Katona and Vámos, "Nagy Imre és a Szabad Európa Rádió," 156–58. In his detailed review and assessment of RFE's programming, William E. Griffith praised Gellért's comment but then—wisely—also added this: "Gellert's commentary should at least have referred to the fact that there might be elements of complexity in Nagy's situation of which we were unaware and therefore our judgment could only be tentative." That is the mentality that should have guided RFE's Hungarian programs during the crisis. See the text of Griffith's review, dated December 5, 1956, "Policy Review of Voice for Free Hungary Programming, October 23–November 23, 1956," in *The 1956 Hungarian Revolution: A History in Documents*, ed. Csaba Békés, Malcolm Byrne, and János M. Rainer (Budapest: Central European Press, 2002), 464–84.

the 26th: "The new prime minister shouldn't be promising anything, the people have no need for his program, no need for his deceitful popular-front government, no need for his rhetorical art, not even one voice [from him]. . . . The last moment was over long ago. It was over when the first martyr, the first martyr of this fight for freedom, dropped on the pavement. Imre Nagy missed the last moment. Yet he still has a last opportunity. [He could still follow] the command of the homeland and of the people. Away with the Russians! And if not, away with him forever!"[51]

In the evening of the 26th, the hostile, anti-Nagy rhetoric reached a new crescendo. "Soviet tanks arrive at the behest of Imre Nagy whose hands are steeped in Hungarian blood," a reporter screeched and scolded. "You, Imre Nagy, must stop, drop on your knees as a penitent sinner before the nation, try to make amends for the terrible crime of forcing on us these Soviet legions. If you still want to give some meaning to your misguided life, then you have only one duty left: shout 'stop!' to the Soviet mercenaries whom you have hideously let loose on the nation! After that 'hands up'—surrender to the nation's irresistible will."[52] The only way to interpret this harangue is to assume that its author had no idea of what Hungarians of the post–World War II generation were thinking, doing, or expecting; if nothing else, the commentator should have considered the absence of an effective alternative to the prime minister.

RFE telling its listeners to fight on for maximum gain was the other controversial theme—and this was the explicit or implicit message of just about every news item and commentary. It could not be otherwise. After all, RFE was born in the spirit of America's desire for the liberation of Central and Eastern Europe, and now the collapse of Communist authority seemed at hand. This was what the editors and reporters—and their supervisors in Munich, New York, and Washington—had been waiting for. Living in exile in West Germany, many of the

---

[51] Katona and Vámos, "Nagy Imre és a Szabad Európa Rádió," 159–61. In Griffith's view, this comment was "totally lacking in refinement, subtlety, and humility," and, together with similar "blasts" against Nagy, did not conform to RFE's policies as reflected in its daily guidance. For sure, the hysterical tone of some of the broadcasts was not ordered, requested, or suggested by RFE's American management.

[52] Katona and Vámos, "Nagy Imre és a Szabad Európa Rádió," 162–63.

Hungarian-born employees were also hoping to go home. Their excitement was as understandable as it was boundless. Surprisingly, then, Griffith considered only one program as "overly excited." He observed later that on the 24th, at the beginning of the revolt, a commentator should not have explicitly urged the Hungarians to fight on; he should not have stated that "no, we cannot be pacified with words and half-solutions any more, . . . do not give up the struggle until you have received an answer to the most burning questions."[53] RFE broadcast many other comments along these lines.

Meanwhile, in Hungary itself, the first phase of the revolt was coming to an end as elements of confrontation began to mix with cautious attempts at contact and even coordination in search of a modus vivendi.

· 4 ·

On October 28, after a reasonably calm day, with the insurgents talking to officials, including Nagy himself, the coordination phase of the revolt commenced. Things were getting much better; that day, and the next couple of days even more so, Budapest was relatively quiet and there was a modicum of optimism in the air.

This phase *began* with the Corvinites' heroic defense of their turf against a Soviet-led military attack; Nagy's order for a general and immediate cease-fire; the creation of a new government that included a couple of genuine noncommunists such as Zoltán Tildy and Béla Kovács; and the formation of a six-member Communist Party presidium that was composed of four centrist Kádár supporters (Kádár, Antal Apró, Károly Kiss, and Ferenc Münnich) and two Nagy reformers (Nagy and Zoltán Szántó). This phase *ended* with the restoration of the multiparty system, patterned on the 1945–47 period; the founding of a new National Guard composed of police, army, *and* insurrectionist groups; and a significant statement by the Soviet government declaring its intention to withdraw Soviet forces from Budapest right away and begin negotiations with Hungary (and Romania) about removing its military from the territories of these two countries. Yet, on the 30th, there was also a major setback when a group of angry rebels attacked the Communist

---

[53] Griffith, "Policy Review," 473.

Party's municipal headquarters, which ended up in the gruesome lynching of a dozen or more real or presumed party officials and secret policemen. That dreadful, and shameful, scene was shown in newsreels around the world, projecting a misleading impression of the revolution—particularly as it seemed to be moving in a peaceful direction.

The second phase in Budapest: Imre Nagy and the government. In the afternoon of the 27th, there was a dramatic encounter between Nagy and some of his old supporters. The meeting happened as a result of a trick by such radical Nagy allies as Gimes, Szilágyi, Tamás Aczél, and others who could not get an appointment to tell Nagy that he must change course. They figured that Nagy would be much more likely to receive them if they made themselves part of a delegation from the working-class district of Angyalföld. So they found two workers from that district and together they all went to see Nagy. It was a tense encounter. The delegation—composed of ten men and one woman—tried to tell Nagy to leave the main party building and set up his office either at Budapest police headquarters or in the Parliament. They told him about his lack of popularity; how he was being identified now as "Imrov" rather than Imre, suggesting that he had become a Soviet puppet. They wanted the "real" Imre Nagy to stand up. Whether the conversation only shook up the apparently very tired Nagy or he actually cried too (as Gimes later testified[54]) is uncertain.

The meeting did have an impact on Nagy's behavior, however. In its immediate aftermath, Nagy pushed the cause of change forward. The Politburo met; consultations took place. Nagy had turned the corner and—significantly—Kádár appeared supportive. Kádár's new approach —in particular, his reluctance to use military force against workers— made an impression both on the Soviet emissaries and on his centrist Hungarian adherents. Much of the party's Central Committee followed Kádár's lead. Nagy and Kádár talked with Mikoyan and Suslov at the Soviet Embassy. Nagy sent a message to his intellectual allies, including Donáth, Losonczy, and Vásárhelyi, to come in next morning to help.

---

[54] Testimony before his interrogators on March 22, 1957; Hungarian National Archive, XX-5-h, vol. 33, 16–29. For a fine summary, see also Sándor Révész, *Egyetlen élet: Gimes Miklós története* [Unique life: The story of Miklós Gimes] (Budapest: 1956-os Intézet and Sík Kiadó, 1999), 309–12.

Not much is known about who said what to whom at every meeting, but at a critical Politburo gathering in the morning of the 28th, Nagy, for the first time, argued vigorously and effectively for change. There as a "guest," a skeptical but not very hostile Mikoyan said: "We respect Comrade Nagy, we consider him a sincere man, but at times he very easily gets under the influence of others. To be firm, one must take a decisive position." Feeling confident and apparently unafraid, Nagy replied that he was not going to "stand firm" when the party's interests demanded that he take a step forward.[55]

Still a Marxist-Leninist, Nagy just turned into an inadvertent revolutionary.

He had come to understand that what mattered most was an ideological reassessment of the situation. He concluded, at long last, that a popular uprising rather than a counterrevolution was taking place. He was ready to make common cause with the workers, students, and soldiers who sought independence from the Soviet Union, a coalition government rooted in political pluralism, and a socialist economic order. This was more than the "reforms" he had expected to implement, but he was beginning to find the new goals quite acceptable if not appealing. Because he had also received the green light at the Soviet Embassy that morning, Nagy, with the help of a dozen or so of his old allies, began to phrase the text of a radio speech he was going to deliver later that day.

In his speech, Nagy rejected the old view that a "counterrevolution" was taking place; we were witnessing, he declared, a "broad democratic mass movement." He put himself, and his government, at the head of a struggle that aimed at "guaranteeing our national freedom, independence, and sovereignty, of advancing our society, our economic and political system on the way of democracy—for this is the only foundation of socialism in our country." He announced a general cease-fire. He promised no reprisals against those who took part in the revolt. He said he had ordered the Hungarian military "not to shoot unless attacked," and he expressed his readiness to discuss matters with the insurgents. He pledged to dissolve the hated secret police. He said his government

---

[55] For the minutes of this critical session, see *Ötvenhat októbere és a hatalom*, ed. Horváth and Ripp, 101–7.

and the Soviet government agreed about the immediate withdrawal of Soviet forces from Budapest. On a matter of great symbolic import, he said he would propose to the country's legislature the reinstatement of the traditional Emblem of Kossuth as the national emblem and the restoration of March 15 as a national holiday.[56]

Given the large number of "moderate" Communists still in the leadership, the public did not yet have a sense of the magnitude of changes under way. Many of the almost-new faces were hardly known; it was not clear who was gone. Though Nagy's speech was quite forthcoming, it was not particularly well received because people had lost faith in words during the preceding days of fighting and chaos and lies. The public might have been more appreciative of what was being announced if it had been informed of the departure from the country of four of the notorious and much despised members of the Old Guard—Gerő; Hegedüs; László Piros, the former minister of internal affairs; and István Bata, the former defense minister. Under cover of darkness that evening, they were surreptitiously taken from their homes to a Soviet military airport in an armored car and flown to the Soviet Union.[57]

On the 29th, Prime Minister Nagy left party headquarters at Alkotmány Street and moved back to his old office in the Parliament Building. Symbolically, he was trying to free himself from his old comrades who kept pulling him back; he also wanted to find time to go home. For the first time since the revolution had begun almost a week earlier, he repaired for several hours to his house on Orsó Street, where he got a good night's sleep as well. When he returned to his office the next morning, on the 30th, he seemed rested and ready to take another step to meet popular demands. He consulted with Mikoyan and Suslov, who were in Budapest. Kádár also talked with Mikoyan and Suslov. Tildy, Nagy's de facto deputy, talked privately with Mikoyan for an hour, discussing the reestablishment of a multiparty system—and Mikoyan, according to Tildy, "accepted everything."[58]

---

[56] Nagy's speech is reprinted in *National Communism*, ed. Zinner, 428–32.

[57] András Hegedüs, *A történelem és a hatalom igézetében* [Spellbound by history and power] (Budapest, Kossuth, 1988), 305–7.

[58] József Kővágó, his Smallholder colleague who was the lord mayor of Budapest, reported Tildy's comments; see his *You Are All Alone* (New York: Praeger, 1959), 197–202.

For once Nagy was not far behind the people's demands when he made his historic announcement on the radio at 2:28 P.M. on October 30:

> In the interest of the further democratization of the country's life, the cabinet abolishes the one-party system and puts the country's government on the basis of the democratic cooperation between the coalition parties as they existed in 1945. . . . The members of the new [smaller] cabinet are Imre Nagy, Zoltán Tildy, Béla Kovács, Ferenc Erdei, János Kádár, Géza Losonczy, and a person to be appointed by the Social Democratic Party [who, as it turned out, was Anna Kéthly].[59]

Past or present party affiliations aside, genuine democrats in the cabinet were now in the majority. They were Tildy, Kovács, Losonczy, and Kéthly; Nagy was clearly moving in that direction; Erdei, who was nominally of the National Peasant Party but in fact a secret Communist Party member, was an effective administrator and a political survivor with no identifiable convictions; and Kádár, of course, was a centrist Communist who would soon betray his colleagues and friends. Though the government was thus made up of strange bedfellows, it had the makings of a new Hungary patterned on the era of the "democratic interlude" of 1945–47. *And it came into being with Mikoyan's explicit approval.* The revolution appeared victorious.

After Nagy, a fragile, jubilant, and yet calm Tildy expressed the sentiments many felt. Once a Calvinist minister, he found the right words to say on this momentous occasion:

> Hungarian Brothers! I stand before the microphone deeply moved. I don't have a prepared text, my speech may be disjointed, but with my heart overflowing with love and joy I salute the beloved youth of Hungary. . . . We are a small nation, but we want to live in this country in our Hungarian way and in freedom. I'm convinced that once the peoples and leaders of the Soviet Union face not a humiliated but a free nation and its representatives, they will see how different our relationship can be, how much more understanding, respect, and affection there will be. . . . Let there be no more sacrifice, no more destruction. Let us all be

---

[59] The text of Nagy's speech, "Proclamation of Imre Nagy on the Restoration of a Multiparty System and a Coalition Government, October 30, 1956," is reprinted in *National Communism*, ed. Zinner, 453–54.

faithful to ourselves, to this historic moment, let us make peace and order in our country. Rejoice my Hungarian brothers and let's go to work.[60]

The second phase in Budapest: The insurgents. The "street" viewed the
cease-fire and truce announced by Nagy on the 28th with understandable skepticism. After all, the previous phase of the revolution had not
offered any proof to the rebels of the sincerity or moderation of the
party's leadership or the government. The insurgents were not yet prepared to lay down their arms, because even those who believed that the
announcements were serious had to wait for their implementation.
That took time, all the more so because the party's Military Committee and assorted groups of secret policemen did not subscribe to the
terms of Nagy's new policies. However, despite an occasional shot here
and there, the fighting actually came to a halt.

In this coordination or transitional phase, two key developments
took place—one very promising and the other ugly and fateful. The
promising one was the formation of the National Guard under General
Béla Király's command. Király was a professional soldier who had been
jailed on fabricated charges by Hungary's Stalinist regime. Freed on the
eve of the revolution, he put his considerable organizational skills at the
service of Nagy. Acting on his own but with Nagy's concurrence, Király's
goal was to unite the forces of the ordinary police, the Hungarian armed
forces, and the more responsible elements from various groups of insurgents. The task was made difficult not only because of the suspicion
that permeated the relationship between the insurgents on the one
hand and uniformed army and police officers on the other. There was,
in addition, tremendous rivalry among the insurgent groups; the leaders of each group and regular members who did not always trust their
leaders; and between such pro-Nagy military chiefs as Király and
Colonel Pál Maléter of the Kilián Barracks (who was to become minister of defense in a few days).[61] Despite various professional and per-

---

[60] *Magyar Nemzet*, October 31, 1956.

[61] General Király—who left for the United States after the Soviet intervention, obtained a Ph.D. in
military history from Columbia University, enjoyed a distinguished academic career in the United
States, and then returned to Hungary in 1989—published extensively about the military aspects of
the 1956 revolution. Among his many contributions in English is *The Hungarian Revolution in Retrospect*, ed. Béla K. Király and Pál Jónás (Boulder, Colo.: East European Monographs, 1977).

sonal rivalries, the National Guard did come into being and appeared headed toward a key role in consolidating the revolution's gains.

Of course, difficulties remained. It was particularly hard to manage József Dudás, self-appointed head of something called the "National Revolutionary Council," who was one of the more colorful if not especially helpful characters in 1956. Once an anti-Moscow, nationalist Communist, Dudás was arrested as early as 1947 and kept in jail until 1954. He was among the very first to form a rebel group, with which he then occupied the headquarters of the Communist Party daily *Szabad Nép.* Even though Nagy eventually sat down to talk with him (on October 30), Dudás was unwilling to recognize the Nagy government; in fact, he proclaimed the existence of a rival government headed by himself. (In the end, during the last phase of revolt, he was detained, but then quickly released, on Nagy's order.)

Far more significant, and damaging to the cause of the revolt, was the lynching of secret police officers and possibly others in front of the party's municipal headquarters on Köztársaság (Republic) Square on October 30. Rumors had spread that morning throughout Budapest that there were secret, underground catacombs under the pavement in front of the building. Soon enough a huge crowd gathered, and some people claimed to hear the cry of prisoners calling for help. Armed rebels tried to enter the building to find the secret corridor to the underground jails, but they were arrested. In the ensuing battle, members of the secret police guards sent there to protect the building opened fire on the crowd in the square. Army tanks arrived; the shooting escalated; secret policemen were dragged out of the building and lynched; and Imre Mező, head of the Budapest party committee and a Nagy supporter, was also killed. There were no underground catacombs, and no political prisoners were found in the vicinity.[62]

In this phase, then, the insurgents developed contact with government representatives, and there was even a modicum of understanding

---

[62] A Russian source I am not authorized to name claims that someone at the Soviet Embassy apparently witnessed the lynching and reported what he saw to his superiors. According to this source, Mrs. Andropov, the ambassador's wife, was deeply affected by these reports for many years. Though I cannot verify the story, I find it quite believable because of the veracity of the source, and because as a young man I witnessed the same scene. To this day, I recall how this furious and frenzied crowd took pleasure at the mutilation of dead bodies. I hasten to add that this was an exception to the rule; to my knowledge, such disgusting misbehavior did not happen elsewhere during the revolt.

between them, but few of the fighters yet believed that the revolution was victorious. If the evolving relationship was not harmonious, and it was not, that was because the implementation of Nagy's new policies was slow and haphazard, and because various rumors contributed to lingering suspicion about the government's real intentions as well as about the Kremlin's willingness to let the Hungarians sort out their problems on their own.

The second phase in Moscow. The Soviet Politburo devoted much of its time to Hungarian events between October 28 and 30. Whatever other sources of information it might have had, the Politburo relied heavily on reports from Mikoyan and Suslov; from Ivan Serov, the head of the KGB; and from the Soviet Embassy in Budapest, notably Ambassador Andropov.[63]

On the 28th, most members of the Politburo continued to complain not only about Mikoyan and Imre Nagy but about Kádár as well. They saw him—correctly—as Nagy's new partner who was ready to deal with the situation without Soviet help and without using force if at all possible. Proud and fearful of being seen as weak, the Politburo was particularly insistent that the Hungarians' call for the withdrawal of Soviet forces should not degenerate into "capitulation." Kliment Voroshilov, who seldom missed an opportunity to be wrong and who was upset by Mikoyan's and Suslov's passive behavior, drew on Serov's unsubstantiated report to claim that "American secret services" were more active in Budapest than his Politburo colleagues. Because he was unprepared to decide what to do, Khrushchev reviewed the available options, of which he appeared to favor words, that is, "appeals" to be sent by the Chinese, Bulgarians, Poles, Czechs, and Yugoslavs to the Hungarians suggesting loyalty to their common cause. More important, however, a very reluctant Soviet Politburo—clearly unhappy about the Hungarian Communist Party's new approach to what it now called a "national uprising" and

---

[63] For the most important records, notably the Malin Notes and Mark Kramer's reconstruction of what transpired in the Kremlin, see *Cold War International History Project Bulletin*, issues 8–9 (Winter 1996–97), with two of Kramer's articles: "New Evidence on Soviet Decision-Making and the 1956 Polish and Hungarian Crises," 358–84, and "The 'Malin Notes' on the Crises in Hungary and Poland, 1956—Translated and Annotated by Mark Kramer," 385–410. In the account that follows, I make use of his translation of the "Malin Notes."

also concerned about the new camaraderie between Nagy and Kádár—nonetheless chose to support the Hungarians' latest stance.

Khrushchev, who could not make up his mind one way or another on the 28th, was a different person on the 30th. On the basis of his talks with Mikoyan, he said that Kádár was now "behaving well." Khrushchev devoted most of this session to a discussion of a Draft Declaration about Soviet relations with Eastern Europe. Others also spoke up. Maxim Saburov: "We must reexamine our relations. Relations must be built on an equal basis." Georgi Zhukov: "Restructuring [our relations with Eastern Europe] was thwarted after the Twentieth Congress. . . . We should say the Twentieth Congress condemned the disregard for principles of equality." Dmitri Shepilov: "The course of events reveals the crisis in our relations with the countries of people's democracy. . . . With the agreement of the government of Hungary, we are ready to withdraw troops." Nikolai Bulganin: Don't soften the self-criticism. Mistakes were committed." Surprisingly, Molotov was also on board: "We should issue the Declaration and explain our position." Khrushchev: "There are two paths. A military path—one of occupation. A peaceful path—the withdrawal of troops, negotiations." Khrushchev announced the verdict in favor of a nonmilitary, political approach: "We are unanimous. As a first step we will issue the Declaration."

The declaration,[64] in a nutshell, was an extension of de-Stalinization to the realm of Moscow's relations with the countries in the Soviet bloc. Previously, the Soviet leaders had spoken about "socialist legality" at home and "peaceful coexistence" with the West. While they also improved relations with Tito's Yugoslavia, the Kremlin never reconsidered its government-to-government or party-to-party relations with its putative allies. Such reconsideration with respect to Poland and Hungary might have been germinating since July 1956, perhaps since the aftermath of the Poznan uprising, but it was issued now to provide a formal statement explaining the Soviet decision to let the Hungarians and the Poles work out their problems—without Soviet advisers and without stationing Soviet troops on the territories of Hungary and Poland as well

---

[64] "Declaration of the Government of the USSR on the Principles of Development and Further Strengthening of Friendship and Cooperation between the Soviet Union and Other Socialist States, October 30, 1956," in *National Communism*, ed. Zinner, 485–89.

as Romania. (The declaration made no mention of Soviet troops in East Germany.) With respect to the immediate issue at hand, the Soviet government stated its willingness "to withdraw the Soviet military units from the city of Budapest as soon as this was considered necessary by the Hungarian Government." The declaration also affirmed that negotiations could begin about the whole "question of the presence of Soviet troops on the territory of Hungary."[65]

When the Soviet declaration was published in *Pravda* on October 31, it created a sensation around the globe. Did the Soviet leaders really mean what they said? The declaration was hailed in Hungary and throughout the Soviet bloc, of course, and Western analysts also considered it a major step in the right direction. It was seen as genuine and significant. As the minutes from Russian archives now prove, that judgment was accurate; *the declaration was indeed authentic.* Deception was not the name of the game—not yet.

The second phase in Washington and Munich. The United States could not rise to the occasion. It acknowledged the Soviet declaration, but it offered nothing in response. On October 28, with Budapest entering a period of relative calm, attention shifted to the Middle East as the first reports of a British-French-Israeli mobilization reached the capital. Secretary of State Dulles told the British and the French that their action would damage the West's case against Moscow; however, it could not be inferred from open sources then, and it cannot be inferred from the declassified record of secret deliberations now, whether the emerging "Suez crisis" made much difference in the end. My reading of the evidence is that it did not make a difference in either Washington or Moscow. After all, Washington never had any plans under consideration to engage Moscow diplomatically or otherwise with respect to Hungary. As for the Soviet leaders, they appeared unaware at first of the division in Western ranks concerning the Suez crisis.

Meanwhile, the U.S. Legation still did not have high-level personnel to do its job of observing and reporting on Hungarian developments. (A new minister, Edward T. Wailes—who was quite unprepared for his assignment—arrived in Budapest on November 2.) The State Depart-

---

[65] Ibid., 488.

ment, having "welcomed" the partial cease-fire that began on October 28, seemed hopeful that the situation would take care of itself. Assessing the Soviet declaration of the 30th, Washington concluded that the Kremlin, in seeking a political solution to the crisis in Hungary and Poland, had decided to make the best of its predicament.

President Eisenhower recalled later that he was more skeptical than his advisers; he said he was unsure of the declaration's—of the Kremlin's—honesty.[66] The president was also more skeptical than most of his aides about both the feasibility and desirability of changing the European status quo. He was a military man who calculated the balance of forces, and who had learned to appreciate the Red Army's actual and psychological strengths during World War II. He had little interest in and few illusions about "moral victories"; he lacked John Foster Dulles's missionary zeal. Besides, Eisenhower's focus of attention—understandably so—was the presidential race that was coming to an end the following week.[67]

The CIA's response to the Hungarian crisis remained unchanged in this phase of the revolt—except for the preparation of a superb assessment on Eastern Europe. On the 30th, the intelligence community, led by the CIA's analytical division, issued a Special National Intelligence Estimate (SNIE 12-2-56)—"Probable Developments in Eastern Europe and Implications for Soviet Policy"—that did not yet reflect on the latest developments in Budapest or elsewhere. However, the analysts displayed a profound understanding of the choices ahead: "If the rebels refuse to make an accommodation with Nagy," the report stated, "the Soviet Union will be faced with the alternatives of risking the development of a non-Communist and independent Hungary or of intervening with large scale military forces to take over the country by force."[68]

---

[66] Dwight D. Eisenhower, *Waging Peace* (Garden City, N.Y.: Doubleday, 1964), 79.

[67] John Lukacs has written, incisively, that Eisenhower and Dulles were passive during the Hungarian crisis because they did not want "to tamper with the division of Europe or to suggest to the Russians that if they really withdrew from Hungary, there would be a corresponding American withdrawal" from a small NATO ally Western Europe. Thus, they were actually "relieved when the Russians came back and squelched the Hungarian Rising" (because of its public relations value to the United States). Lukacs added that Eisenhower and Nixon "were not merely hypocrites but dishonest." In fact, Vice President Richard Nixon's remarks behind the scenes, cited in chapter 3 above—to which Lukacs had no access when he wrote his book—lend credence to his blunt but astute conclusions. John Lukacs, *A Thread of Years* (New Haven, Conn.: Yale University Press, 1998), 390–91.

[68] CIA Electronic Reading Room, http://www.foia.cia.gov/search.

In other words, the critical issue was whether the revolution would or would not go beyond Titoism or the kind of deal that Poland's Gomułka was just then in the process of negotiating with his people. In this sense, the estimate's detached, analytical language paralleled Walter Lippmann's observation about the need to "stop at Titoism." It is another question whether anyone in position of authority actually read, or considered drawing the policy implications from, the estimate's wise insights.

By October 30 and 31, the agency's staff in Europe had gathered enough information—relying largely on "border contacts . . . broadcasts of local rebel radios and rumors trickling up from Budapest"[69]—that two "think-pieces" were sent to headquarters. The two papers, according to a summary, *"deplored the lack of unified leadership in the revolution,* debated whether the Soviets would or would not interfere with what was going on in Hungary, stated that *the revolution was losing momentum,* that *Imre Nagy was discredited as a future leader* and proposed that *a national leader must come forth around whom the whole revolutionary movement and its gains could be solidified."*[70] Dated October 30, the first of these reports seems to have described the Hungarian situation as it appeared before October 28. Very possibly because of the absence of good sources or because of excessive reliance on RFE's monitoring service, these observations were both confused and out of date.[71]

In a critical vein, the 1958 in-house CIA review pointed to "the relative uselessness of conventional clandestine sources as against unusual and unconventional sources in a crisis period."[72] That was a polite way of saying that careful readers of good newspapers—in John McCormack the *New York Times* had a particularly enterprising correspondent in Budapest—might have had as much up-to-date information during the revolt as did the CIA. Speaking of sources, the review further noted the

---

[69] CIA, *CSHP* 6, 92.

[70] Ibid., 92–93. Italics in the original.

[71] At this time—aside from Geza Katona, its resident in Budapest (see chapter 1, fn. 4, above)—the CIA still did not have a full-time professional agent in Hungary. Its search for Hungarian-speaking agents on home leave, on vacation, or on assignment elsewhere continued. "Among others, headquarters attempted to find the exact address of a former [word deleted] agent who had been resettled. . . . This was a little like the scene in an old comedy where in the frantic search for a missing person, people begin to ransack the bureau drawers." CIA, *CSHP* 6, 92.

[72] Ibid., 97.

agency's extensive reliance on Radio Free Europe's radio-scanning service, especially its excellent monitoring of various rebel stations.[73] Other sources mentioned were diplomats and journalists. Echoing customary bureaucratic rivalries, the review pointedly concluded that "between the American Legation and journalists, the latter understandably take the prize. . . . Reporting from the American Legation was at best sporadic and laced with premature analysis and assumptions (of the sort that diplomats feel their government stands in need of)."[74]

In Munich, Radio Free Europe continued to attack Prime Minister Nagy in this phase, too, despite the major concessions he made on the 28th (and more on the 30th). RFE's October 29, 1956, New York Guidance, reflecting U.S. policy, took no notice of Nagy's evolution. Identifying itself with militant rebel radio stations, the guidance instructed broadcasters to repeat these radios' radical demands. The guidance also stated: "Radio Free Europe will avoid to the utmost extent any explicit or implicit support of individual personalities in a temporary government [*sic*]—especially of Communist personalities such as Imre Nagy or Kádár"—even though, the guidance went on, "many of [the rebel groups] seem to believe that Imre Nagy can and will further their wishes."[75] In other words, RFE management chose to embrace the insurgents' radical demands when they aimed *against* Nagy's "temporary" government, but they declined to repeat the insurgents' avowal of support *for* Nagy and his government.[76] In this respect, as in so many other ways, too, RFE closely followed Washington's lead (and not just the Hungarian émigré staff's "anticommunist" instincts). Speaking at about the same time, Secretary of State Dulles showed absolutely no interest in Nagy.[77]

---

[73] Ibid., 99.

[74] Ibid., 101.

[75] RFE/RL unsorted documents, Hoover Institution Archive. Italics added. RFE usually referred to these stations as Freedom Radios or Freedom Stations.

[76] In 1996, on the fortieth anniversary of the Hungarian revolution—and soon after RFE's 1956 tapes were released—William E. Griffith, RFE's political adviser, conceded at a scholarly workshop in Budapest that "RFE's coverage of Imre Nagy and its polemics against him were probably its major policy error during the Revolution, although *they were in accordance with guidance from RFE New York and Munich.*" See Griffith, "RFE and the Hungarian Revolution and the Polish October," paper prepared for the international conference "Hungary and the World, 1956: The New Archival Evidence," Budapest, September 26–29, 1996, 3. Italics added.

[77] Dulles did not think the Nagy government would last; he was fully dismissive of its efforts and prospects. For more on this point, see fn. 109 below.

The Hungarian Desk readily obliged its New York and Munich supervisors. On the 28th, minutes after Nagy offered his first set of concessions—calling the revolt a democratic mass movement, for example—RFE all but dismissed the speech by lecturing the audience to demand more: "Those hundreds and thousands of martyrs [*sic*] did not sacrifice their lives for such shabby (*felemás*) concessions, for such cosmetology," said one editorialist. Later that evening, another commentator thundered his admonitory, know-it-all polemics against Nagy: "Why does he notice this [the revolt's democratic character] only now, and why did he not notice it when he identified this great national movement as a reactionary, plunderous, counterrevolutionary disturbance, and [when] he turned loose on Budapest the Soviet army [committed to] the destruction of life and property?"[78]

And so it went. There was nothing Nagy could do that deserved RFE's consideration. As Griffith acknowledged in 1996, the Hungarian Desk "was politically too right wing, that is, not only anticommunist but many of them too sympathetic to the pre-1945 Horthy regime."[79] Raised on the interwar era's fervent anti-Bolshevism that was subsequently reinforced by the horrors of Stalinism and Washington's (as well as RFE's) misleading rhetoric about the liberation of Eastern Europe from Communist oppression, most members of the Hungarian Desk—unlike their counterparts on the Polish Desk—could not and did not draw distinctions between "orthodox" and "revisionist" Communists. Writing in December 1956, Griffith took particular exception to a broadcast on October 30 that, at a time of Nagy's abandonment of the one-party system, attacked the prime minister for having Communists and regular criminals [*sic*] in his government and for implying that Nagy had "perfidious motives in misleading the people about the true situation."[80] Commenting on still another "shrill" broadcast delivered on the 30th, an obviously furious Griffith—maintaining that these programs were prepared behind his back—stated that "there are so many internal contradictions that it is often impossible to discover one singly consistent line; one gets the impression that these programs must often

---

[78] Katona and Vámos, "Nagy Imre és a Szabad Európa Rádió," 166–67.

[79] See Griffith, "RFE and the Hungarian Revolution," 2.

[80] Griffith, "Policy Review," 472.

have sounded to listeners as emotional outpourings without any consistent line."[81]

Hard as it is to divide responsibility between management and staff for programs that assailed Nagy and issued threatening demands and sweeping ultimatums, it is still noteworthy that various American and German blue-ribbon commissions found no fault with RFE's Hungarian broadcasts; to his credit, Griffith did. Yet personnel changes were made, and they told a different story. Richard Condon, the main administrator in Munich, was fired, for example. In 1959, Griffith, a world-famous scholar on communism, left RFE and so did his deputy, Paul Henze. Perhaps to muddy the waters a bit, the several editors, reporters, and editorialists on the Hungarian Desk who were dismissed belonged to the left and to the right alike, implying no penalty for reckless programming. With the aftereffects of McCarthyism still felt, it was all but impossible to be wrong on the right; extremism on behalf of "anticommunism" was no vice. Imre Mikes, the man identified by Griffith as the single most "shrill" commentator, remained a full-time member of RFE's Hungarian Desk till his retirement in 1967, and he was even allowed to continue on a part-time basis until 1976.

It is still difficult to be sure exactly how influential RFE was in this (or any other) phase of the revolt. In a country of 9.5 million people, about 500,000 radios could pick up its signals; many of the editorials and press surveys were repeated again and again; and RFE was the only station that was on the air practically around the clock. The fact that RFE also rebroadcast what the rebel stations in the countryside reported added interest to its own programs. *Evidence about RFE's activities and impact on its audience during Imre Nagy's reform era in 1953–55, presented by a detailed internal Hungarian document in 1955, points to the radio's enormous impact on the Hungarian population.*[82] Anecdotal evidence suggests a similar impact just before and during the revolt as well.

---

[81] Ibid., 473.

[82] Cf. Béla Révész, "A Belügyminisztérium SZER-képe 1955-ben" [The Ministry of Internal Affairs' Image of RFE], *Múltunk*, no. 2 (1999): 170–222. Like bureaucracies of this type elsewhere, Hungarians at the ministry paid to listen to RFE tended to inflate its impact. To justify the significance of their own work, they made "the enemy" appear to be far more dangerous and especially far more interested in Hungary than was the case. Readers of this and similar papers could have easily got the impression that many of the world's top leaders, such as President Eisenhower and Secretary of State Dulles, spent much of their time worrying about, and dreaming up schemes against, Hungary's "socialist order."

In the very complex second phase of the revolt—from October 28 to 30—there was plenty of good news (and some bad news). This was the time when Nagy broke with his past, when the insurgents and the government began to talk, and when the Kremlin opted for a political rather than a military solution to the crisis. Yet RFE could not accept yes for an answer. By focusing on the likelihood of deception by both the Soviet and the Hungarian governments, RFE reinforced existing doubts about the possibility of finding a modus vivendi.

· 5 ·

The third phase in Moscow. Even more so than earlier, the focus of interest in the third phase of the revolution shifted from Budapest to Moscow. For its morning editions on October 31, *Pravda* was getting ready to print millions of copies carrying a conciliatory Soviet declaration on changing the character of Soviet–East European relations. But during an anxious and sleepless night from October 30 to 31, Khrushchev had second thoughts about the declaration and indeed about the decision he and his colleagues had made on the 30th. "I could not sleep," he recalled later. "Budapest was like a nail in my head."[83] Supposedly twisting and turning in his bed, he changed his mind. The next day, at Khrushchev's urging, the Politburo reversed itself. By the time *Pravda* reached its readers, the declaration was null and void.

The reversal was less surprising than the initial decision. For what the Politburo's session on the 30th had revealed, and the declaration confirmed, was the Kremlin's willingness to treat Hungary and others the way it was treating such neutral countries as Austria, Finland, or Yugoslavia. The declaration lacked a specific timetable, but it offered to remove Soviet forces from the region after consultation with appropriate local government officials. Had the Kremlin implemented that decision, a major cause of the Cold War—Soviet domination of Eastern Europe—would have been removed. Loose talk of détente in 1955 and early 1956 would have turned into serious talks between Moscow and the West about a new future for Europe.

---

[83] There is no better guide to Khrushchev than William Taubman's tour de force, *Khrushchev: The Man and His Era* (New York: Alfred A. Knopf, 2003); on 1956, see esp. 270–99 (the quotation appears on 296).

The Kremlin's initial, conciliatory step—foreshadowing Mikhail S. Gorbachev's decision in 1988–89 to withdraw the Soviet military from Central and Eastern Europe *in order to save the cause of socialism in the Soviet Union*—represented a unilateral commitment to extend the spirit of the Twentieth Congress of the Communist Party to the Warsaw Pact area. In 1956, Khrushchev wanted to save communism from its Stalinist heritage and return to what he and others were calling "Leninist norms." To achieve that goal, they launched a series of half-measures to reshape Soviet policies and institutions immediately after Stalin's death in 1953. They closed many Soviet labor camps[84] and introduced "socialist legality" (but not the rule of law), and they also embraced a new approach to the West they called "peaceful coexistence" (which differed from the unqualified pursuit of peace). *These were genuine half-measures that signified abandonment of Stalinism but not of communism;* after all, neither "socialist legality" nor "peaceful coexistence" meant the end of the class struggle at home and abroad.

The declaration of October 30 was based on similar thinking. It did not envisage full independence or freedom for the countries of Eastern and Central Europe. It represented a rejection of the kind of imperialist relations that Stalin had built, not because they were wrong but because they were counterproductive: They neither strengthened bloc cohesion nor advanced the cause of socialism. The system of relations among putative allies that Stalin had forged failed the Soviet Union because the political and economic cost of maintaining the empire was prohibitive—which was why Khrushchev and a few of his anti-Stalinist colleagues contemplated revision. Just as domestic terror had disrupted the elite's work and confrontation with the West harmed Soviet interests, in the same way Stalin's domination of other Communist countries had also turned into a burden. To lift that burden for the sake of Soviet interests, changes had to be made—but they were supposed to seem less encompassing than they were so as not to upset the delicate balance of forces in Soviet politics.

Once Soviet troops withdrew from Hungary over a period of several years, Hungary could have evolved into something resembling

---

[84] Required reading on this subject is Anne Applebaum, *Gulag: A History* (New York: Doubleday, 2003), esp. 476–505.

Gomułka's Poland or even Tito's Yugoslavia. On October 30, after his confrontation a week earlier with Gomułka, this was what Khrushchev had in mind. In Warsaw, it will be recalled, Khrushchev had ultimately backed down when he decided that though Gomułka was a proud Pole, he was a good Communist, too (which in Khrushchev's mind meant a loyal Soviet ally). On the 30th, having heard encouraging reports from Mikoyan and Suslov, Khrushchev drew on his dramatic Polish encounter when he put his faith in Nagy and Kádár. He was going to have good relations with Poland despite reduced Soviet presence in the Polish military and intelligence services; despite having to allow two or three little political parties to function; despite considerable freedom of action on religious matters being given to the Catholic Church; despite the granting of minor outlets for young people to hear their kind of music and read what they wanted to read in small-circulation weeklies; and despite the permission obtained for private agriculture or private mom-and-pop stores to operate. Moscow would have to loosen the leash on Poland, with Comrade Gomułka in charge but Soviet and Polish agents keeping an eye on him near his office.

Hungary, as Khrushchev and especially Mikoyan saw it, would need to be on an even longer leash. Add the gradual removal of Soviet troops and a more representative multiparty system to "Gomułka's Poland"—that was to be Hungary under Soviet tutelage, not under Soviet domination. Eventually, the Kremlin would transform its sphere of domination into a sphere of influence. Eventually, the withdrawal of Soviet troops to nearby camps in the Soviet Union itself might be matched by the removal of American troops from the continent of Europe. Eventually, a neutral Germany would end up inching away from the United States and toward the Soviet Union. Eventually, this was going to be the beginning of a good deal for the Soviet Union. As a Leninist, Khrushchev knew that he had to take a step back—perhaps a big one like Lenin's New Economic Policy in the 1920s—to gain ground and move ahead.

What changed Khrushchev's mind was *that Hungary was not going to be another Poland.* Hungary did not want to be on a longer leash; it wanted to be on no leash at all. In Poland—because of signs of realism and the coincidence of cooperation among the Communist Gomułka, the Catholic Stefan Cardinal Wyszynski, and Radio Free Europe's calm Jan Nowak—the people, despite their strong idealistic tradition, accepted the half-measures that were being offered to them. In Hungary, Nagy was no Gomułka, Mindszenty was no Wyszynski, and RFE's Hungarian Desk was not led by a Nowak. On October 30, Hungarian Communists were not in charge of their country; worse yet, they no longer tried to be in charge. Two critical events of the day in Budapest—the lynching of secret police officers in Republic Square in the morning and announcing the return to the multiparty system after lunch—appear to have convinced Khrushchev that Nagy and other Communists were too weak to maintain order. (Of course, Mikoyan, without his colleagues' full backing, had assured both Nagy and Tildy that the Kremlin had no objections to the formation of a multiparty political order.)

On the 31st, according to the Malin Notes,[85] Khrushchev opened the Politburo meeting by mentioning a previous telephone conversation he had had with Gomułka. The Malin Notes did not indicate what the two leaders had discussed, but Gomułka was definitely on Khrushchev's mind as he shared his revised perspective on Hungary with his Politburo colleagues. First he proposed a high-level meeting with Gomułka the next day in Brest, and then Khrushchev made his case for reversing the decision they had all made the day before:

> We should reexamine our assessment and should not withdraw our troops from Hungary and Budapest. We should take the initiative in restoring order in Hungary. If we depart from Hungary, it will give a great boost to the Americans, English, and French—the imperialists. . . . They [the imperialists] will perceive it as weakness on our part and will go onto the offensive. . . . We would then be exposing the weakness of our positions. . . . Our party will not accept it if we do this. . . . We have no other choice. . . . If this point of view is supported and endorsed, let's consider what we should do.[86]

This was a historic reversal, the negation of a possible extension of the processes of de-Stalinization to relations with members of the bloc. Only Saburov seemed concerned: "After yesterday's session this discussion is pointless," he said. "It will vindicate NATO." But several participants urged rejection of "the view that we are reexamining our posi-

---

[85] I continue to rely here on Kramer's annotated translation, "The 'Malin Notes,'" 393–94.
[86] Ibid., 393.

tions." In other words, the party was supposed to claim that nothing had changed; after all, "the party" was always consistent (and correct). Everyone agreed to the revised approach, and the Politburo turned to details of implementation. Zhukov was authorized to work out the military plans. As for Hungary's future government, there was a consensus in favor of making Kádár the leader, heading a provisional revolutionary government, but Ferenc Münnich was also listed as premier and minister of both defense and internal affairs. Amazingly, Khrushchev left the door open to Nagy, too: If he agreed to cooperate, "bring him in as dep. Premier."[87]

While the Politburo made its decision, Mikoyan and Suslov were on their way from Budapest to Moscow. Khrushchev talked to them on the phone several times, and it was obvious that these two key figures no longer agreed with each other on what to do. That difference was displayed at the next Politburo session—on November 1. With new Soviet troops entering Hungary and Khrushchev discussing the situation with Gomułka in Brest, Mikoyan still pleaded for more time. "We should enter into negotiations. For 10–15 days. . . . We should wait another 10–15 days and support this [Nagy] government. . . . In current circumstances it is better now to support the existing govt. Right now, the use of force will not help anything." But then Mikoyan added this: "If the regime slips away, we'll need to decide what to do. We simply cannot allow Hungary to be removed from our camp."[88] By contrast, Suslov strongly supported the case for intervention: "The danger of a bourgeois restoration has reached its peak," he declared. "I don't believe that Nagy organized the uprising, but his name is being used. . . . Only by means of occupation can we have a government that supports us."[89]

Mikoyan, by now the only Politburo member holding out against intervention, did not yet give up. He seemed to believe that *his colleagues*

---

[87] Ibid. Münnich was a key figure at this point. He was an early intermediary between the Kremlin and the Hungarian centrist faction around Kádár. Even as he was still a member of the Nagy government, according to Khrushchev, he was "appealing to us [Moscow] with a request for assistance." The next day, on November 1, he convinced Kádár to betray Nagy and defect to the Soviet Union.

[88] Ibid., 394. An intriguing question is whether Mikoyan's assertive stance about keeping Hungary in "our camp" was a rhetorical device to show his colleagues he was as tough as any of them, or he really believed in the importance of keeping the bloc together come what may.

[89] Ibid. Careful readers will recall that less than a week earlier, after Nagy collapsed from exhaustion, it was Suslov who happened to have had the right medicine with him, as well as the presence of mind, and saved Nagy's life.

were reacting to their fears of what might happen rather than to what was actually happening at this time: "If Hungary becomes a base for imperialism, that's a different matter," he argued. "What we're talking about here is the current situation. There are still 3 days [till the November 4 date set for intervention] to think it over."[90] He also pleaded his case with Khrushchev privately. As reported by Khrushchev and summarized by William Taubman, Mikoyan returned to Moscow in the evening of October 31. He phoned Khrushchev late at night and called the planned intervention a "terrible mistake." Khrushchev said it was too late to go back to the original plan. The next morning, Khrushchev asked Mikoyan: "Do you think it's any easier for me?" Mikoyan's response: "If blood is shed I don't know what I'll do with myself." Khrushchev, thinking Mikoyan would commit suicide, replied: " That would be the height of stupidity, Anastas." (As it happened, Mikoyan was thinking about resignation.)[91]

It was indeed too late. The Soviet military was getting ready to take over all of Hungary. On November 1, Nagy was awakened with the news of Soviet troops crossing the Soviet-Hungarian border. That day and the next, Khrushchev engaged in a bit of shuttle diplomacy. Having briefed Gomułka on the impending Soviet intervention at a late-night meeting held in Brest at the Polish-Soviet border, he then went on to Bucharest to inform Bulgarian, Czechoslovak, and Romanian officials. After a brief stopover in Moscow, Khrushchev and Georgi Malenkov continued their secret journey to the Yugoslav island of Brioni to see Tito at his palace on the Adriatic. They arrived at 7 P.M. on the evening of November 2—because of bad weather and bad flying conditions, Malenkov was quite ill—and they talked about Hungary with Tito and his lieutenants for ten hours. They left for Moscow the next morning, on November 3, at 5 A.M. Veljko Mićunović, the Yugoslav ambassador to the Soviet Union, kept detailed notes about the meeting.[92]

---

[90] Ibid., 395. On Mikoyan, see also Kramer, "New Evidence on Soviet Decision-Making and the 1956 Polish and Hungarian Crises," 371–72.

[91] Taubman, *Khrushchev*, 298.

[92] Mićunović, *Moscow Diary*, 130–42. In the next paragraph, my account of the Brioni meeting, based largely on Mićunović, draws on my description and analysis in Charles Gati, *Hungary and the Soviet Bloc* (Durham, N.C.: Duke University Press, 1986), 152–53.

Of the two leaders, Khrushchev carried the day. He said they came to inform the Yugoslavs "about the Soviet Union's decision" and to hear Tito's views. He identified one Hungarian domestic concern and four external circumstances that justified the Soviet decision to intervene: (1) Communists were being murdered in Hungary; (2) Nagy had withdrawn Hungary from the Warsaw Pact, declared neutrality, and appealed to the United Nations; (3) capitalism was about to be restored in Hungary; (4) the British-French-Israeli intervention in Suez would divert the world's attention from Soviet "assistance" to Hungary; and (5) if he failed to act, a "who lost Hungary?" debate would unite Stalinist diehards and military leaders against his anti-Stalinist faction.[93]

Tito, Stalin's old nemesis, certainly understood the need to back up Khrushchev at this point. While he would have liked to witness the rise of a Titoist Hungary next door, he also expected something positive to accrue from Soviet intervention. In the eyes of the West and the developing world, he would remain the only European Communist independent, drawing attention and support. Like U.S. vice president Richard Nixon's assessment in the summer of 1956, which foresaw huge propaganda gains for Washington after a Soviet military intervention (see chapter 3 above), Tito, another practitioner of realpolitik, would have also benefited from the enlargement of independent Communist states—but he also saw advantages in being the only show in town. This was why he not only favored the Kremlin's decision to crush the Hungarian revolt but also offered to lure Nagy into the Yugoslav Embassy in Budapest—and then let the KGB kidnap him and force him to go to Romanian exile.

Back in Moscow, members of the Soviet Politburo were meeting on November 2 with Kádár; Münnich, an old Muscovite veteran and a former Hungarian ambassador to Moscow and Belgrade; and the former defense minister, István Bata. At another meeting the next day, Imre Horváth, a foreign policy specialist, was also present instead of Bata.[94]

---

[93] As recorded by Mićunović, Malenkov's only notable contribution to the discussion was his assurance that the Soviet armed forces were ready to act. They must go in "frontally and with great force," Malenkov said, because the Soviet Union was "completely isolated from the Hungarian people." Italics added. Miæunoviæ, Moscow Diary.

[94] Kramer, "New Evidence on Soviet Decision-Making and the 1956 Polish and Hungarian Crises," 395–97 (Politburo meeting on November 2), and 397–98 (Politburo meeting on November 3). Mikoyan took part in both meetings; Khrushchev was there for the second session with the Hungarians.

Horváth, who spoke Russian well, also took notes.[95] These meetings clarified why Kádár defected to the Soviet Union. He had disappeared from Budapest in Münnich's company on November 1. Both had backed Nagy and all his decisions. Kádár was a strong supporter of the reestablishment of the multiparty system. On November 1 (see below), he voted in favor of declaring Hungary's neutrality. In a radio speech recorded earlier on that very day, he had made a reference to "our glorious revolution."

The next day, on November 2, he was in Moscow, negotiating the future of his country with the Soviet leadership.

Clearly, on November 1, after he recorded his speech for broadcast on Kossuth Rádió later that day, Kádár was informed by Münnich (who was probably told by Ambassador Andropov) that the Soviet declaration had been reversed and the Kremlin decided to crush the revolution. He and Münnich were being offered the two top jobs. They knew that leading members of the Old Guard—notably Rákosi, Gerő, and Hegedüs—were in the Kremlin eager to return and take over the country's leadership. Their choice, therefore, was either to become traitors or to effectively hand over Hungary to the Stalinist diehards. Münnich, the intermediary between the Kremlin and Kádár, immediately accepted the choice of escaping to Moscow and discussing the details of forming a new, anti-Nagy government. It took Kádár a couple of hours to make that decision. He left Budapest without telling his wife where he was going. Professional politicians and detached analysts might call it a sensible choice under incredibly difficult circumstances, adding, perhaps, that this was what a politician who was a patriot had to do. In the real world, where decency and integrity also mattered, Kádár revealed himself to be a man with a bottomless capacity for expedient rationalization—and a man without a moral compass. On many subsequent occasions over the years, Kádár indicated that he had defected in order to prevent the Stalinist Old Guard led by Rákosi from being returned to power in Soviet tanks.

Facing the Soviet Politburo on November 2 and 3, Kádár gave the impression of a troubled and confused (and very tired) man. He reviewed not only the previous days' developments but also earlier events,

---

[95] Ibid., 398.

such as the Stalinist purges of the late 1940s and early 1950s. He conceded that he had voted for every controversial decision made by the Nagy government, including its declaration of neutrality. On Nagy, all Kádár said was that his "policy has counterrev. aspects to it."[96] Especially important and revealing, Kádár sensed that the Kremlin had turned completely against Nagy; and so the next day, on November 3, he too became more critical of his former colleague. "On Nagy's behavior," the Malin Notes quote him, "They're killing Communists. The counterrev. are killing them, and premier Nagy provides a cover."[97] Münnich, playing second fiddle, fully supported Kádár's assessment and conclusions; he did not seem to seek the top position.

The die was cast. Kádár and the government the Kremlin appointed for him would return to Hungary the next day, after Soviet tanks had partly cleared the country of "counterrevolutionary elements." Khrushchev saw the intervention as a necessary setback rather than a conclusive defeat for his de-Stalinization efforts. Like Kádár, he made a choice in which the critical factor was his own political survival. Unlike his closest and more principled ally, Mikoyan, Khrushchev resolved to flex his muscles and show the Molotovs and Voroshilovs of the Politburo that he was their man too.

The third phase in Budapest: The government and the insurgents. From October 31 to November 3, the atmosphere in Budapest could not have been more misleading.[98] There were rumors going around, and a few publications reported about, Soviet troop movements, but only Nagy and a few close advisers knew what was going on. Nagy ordered a news blackout on the Soviet invasion of the country that began on Thursday, November 1. Losonczy and Szántó visited the Yugoslav Embassy and raised the question of receiving political asylum if "counterrevolutionary bands" were to threaten them or their families.[99] Given the atrocities at Republic Square just a couple of days ago, all present or former Communist officials—even if they had changed in recent years or re-

---

[96] Ibid., 395.

[97] Ibid., 397.

[98] Cf. Gati, *Hungary and the Soviet Bloc,* 148–52.

[99] *See* Kövér, *Losonczy Géza,* 298, as well as Losonczy's and Szántó's testimonies before their interrogators in 1957.

cent days—worried about their safety. However, the reason for their request might well have been altogether different. It is more likely that the two prominent Hungarian officials—by then, Losonczy was minister of state and in effect one of Nagy's two deputies, and Szántó was a member of the party's small executive committee—explored the possibility of political asylum because they knew of the ongoing Soviet invasion. As heretics, they had more to fear from the Soviet Union than from angry insurgents. In the event, Dalibor Soldatic, the Yugoslav ambassador, was not yet authorized to offer them political asylum.

As many of the insurgents and indeed the Hungarian people in general drew their conclusion from what they could observe—the evacuation of Soviet forces from Budapest—there was a curious mixture of joy and anxiety in the air. Though everyone knew that the Soviet forces were leaving Budapest, very few knew that at the same time other Soviet forces were entering the country. One unusually trenchant newspaper headline captured the mood of the day; it asked: "Are They Coming or Going?"[100] Of the few who knew the answer, only a handful could believe that they *were* coming. Nagy was one of them. He called in Ambassador Andropov several times during the day, demanding an answer. By then, all Andropov could do was to lie; he wanted Nagy to believe that all was well. He called attention to the Soviet government's historic declaration, published in *Pravda* the day before, and assured Nagy that it was still in force. On display was a deceitful diplomat who welcomed his government's decision to crush these troublesome Hungarians. As his cables over the years had shown, he had little or nothing good to say about any of them.[101] But Nagy was not

---

[100] *Igazság*, November 2, 1956. This daily was born during the revolution.

[101] Andropov did like Hungarian music and literature. On home leave in Moscow in December 1956, he gave a lecture about the Hungarian "counterrevolution" at the Soviet Diplomatic Academy, telling his audience that the crisis was sparked by American imperialists. Of course, the United States was blamed for whatever went wrong in the Soviet Union or in the Soviet bloc. After the session at the Academy, Viktor Israelyan, then a young Soviet diplomat specializing in Hungarian affairs who was assigned the task of preparing a pamphlet on the insidious role of American imperialism in the Hungarian crisis, stopped Andropov and asked him for documentary evidence. "'That's nonsense,' he laughed. 'The events in Hungary took the Americans by surprise. They came to the Soviet embassy and asked us to explain what was happening in Budapest. They played no role in the events.'" Viktor Israelyan, *On the Battlefields of the Cold War: A Soviet Ambassador's Confession* (University Park: Pennsylvania State University Press, 2003), 59. Ambassador Israelyan, who became a prominent member of the Soviet diplomatic establishment before his retirement in 1987, told me the same story at a conference in Miami (interview, November 24, 1991).

deceived. He believed the veracity of the reports from the Soviet-Hungarian border, from cities in eastern Hungary like Miskolc and Debrecen; he warned Andropov that he had no choice but to declare Hungary's neutrality, withdraw unilaterally from the Warsaw Pact, and notify the United Nations of his decisions. In a move of utter desperation, he appealed to the international community for at least some expression of support.

Nagy gained approval for his next move by party and government leaders (including Kádár), and he then addressed the Hungarian people on the radio a few minutes before 8 P.M. on November 1:

> The Hungarian national Government, imbued with profound responsibility toward the Hungarian people and history, and giving expression to the undivided will of the Hungarian millions, declares the neutrality of the Hungarian People's Republic. The Hungarian people, on the basis of equality and in accordance with the spirit of the UN Charter, wish to live in true friendship with their neighbors, the Soviet Union, and all peoples of the world. . . . The century-old dream of the Hungarian people is thus fulfilled. . . . We appeal to our neighbors, countries near and far, to respect the unalterable decision of our people. It is true indeed that today our people are as united in this decision as perhaps never before in their history.[102]

Nagy's speech was brief and dramatic. He knew that if Moscow had indeed made a final decision to crush the revolt, his declaration and appeal to the UN would fall on deaf ears in Western capitals. Still, on November 2 and 3, he called in the ambassadors of the Warsaw Pact countries, explained his policies, and asked for their help. He received none. More important, according to an English-language study prepared by the respected Institute for the Study of the Hungarian Revolution in Budapest and edited by György Litván, "Nagy informed Andropov that he was willing to rescind his appeal to the UN in exchange for a Soviet pledge not to engage in further military intervention; Nagy also requested an immediate audience with the highest-level Soviet leadership—*a request which the Soviets promptly denied*."[103]

---

[102] "Radio Address to the Nation by Imre Nagy Proclaiming the Neutrality of Hungary, November 1, 1956," in *National Communism*, ed. Zinner, 463–64.

[103] György Litván, *The Hungarian Revolution of 1956: Reform, Revolt and Repression 1953–1963* (London: Longman, 1996), 88. Italics added.

Publicly, Nagy did not explain his address beyond saying that it reflected the will of his people. He made no mention of his unpleasant encounters with Ambassador Andropov or of the profound sense of deception that he felt.[104] He did not reveal the real reason for declaring neutrality, which was to show defiance in the face of the Soviet invasion that had just commenced. Indeed, to avoid panic and perhaps unnecessary bloodshed, Nagy went out of his way to keep the fact of the invasion from the public. As a result, as described in chapter 1 above, during the last three days before the attack on Budapest on November 4, Hungarians began to enjoy themselves. Ignorance was bliss. More food was available. Several factories reopened. A few buses and streetcars ran again. The insurgents joined regular police and the military in the new National Guard. Dozens of new dailies and weeklies appeared, representing every shade of political opinion. Budapest was quiet, except for announcements about the formation of new social and political organizations and parties. One—jarring—opinion was also heard on the radio on November 3, on the eve of the capture of Budapest, which turned into a sad footnote to the revolution. Cardinal Mindszenty, recently released from years of suffering in Communist jails, delivered a rather tortuous and ambiguous speech in which—echoing Radio Free Europe's approach—he endorsed the Hungarians' struggle for freedom but declined to give his backing to the Nagy government. Whatever Cardinal Mindszenty said or meant to say did not make any difference, however; Budapest was surrounded by then, and his message did neither harm nor good.[105]

On November 3, negotiations were under way about the process and timing of Soviet withdrawals. They began at the Parliament Building in the morning and continued in the evening at the Soviet military base at Tököl. At about 10 P.M. that evening, KGB officers entered the conference room where the negotiations were taking place and arrested all the members of the Hungarian delegation. At about the same time,

---

[104] For many months to come, in Romanian exile as well as in Hungarian jails between late November 1956 and his execution in Budapest in June 1958, Nagy's refrain about the Soviet leaders remained the same: "Becsaptak . . . elárultak" [They deceived me . . . they betrayed me]. (Interview with Miklós Vásárhelyi, July 18, 1991.)

[105] For a more positive assessment of the cardinal's address, delivered at 8 P.M. on the eve of the Soviet invasion, see Ferenc A. Váli, *Rift and Revolt in Hungary: Nationalism versus Communism* (Cambridge, Mass.: Harvard University Press, 1961), 335–37.

Soviet troops closed the Austro-Hungarian border. With some of the country's military leaders, notably the just-promoted General Pál Maléter, under arrest and the country's Western borders sealed, the Soviet Army effectively prepared for all eventualities before attacking the capital next morning. When they did, they found its residents both surprised and distressed. After Nagy's brief radio address at 5:20 A.M., minutes before the arrival of the Soviet troops, the Hungarians were also confused. The speech they heard—it was Nagy's last public statement—made little sense. This was what Nagy said: "Today at daybreak Soviet forces started an attack against our capital, with the obvious intention to overthrow the legal democratic Hungarian Government. Our troops are fighting. The Government is in its place. I notify the people of our country and the entire world of this."[106] In four sentences, Nagy made three points. *One:* "Soviet forces launched an attack against our capital city." That was the shocking truth, the source of surprise and distress. *Two:* "Our troops are fighting." This was not true; Nagy had declined to order the Hungarian Army to engage in a hopeless battle against a vastly superior force. *Three:* "The Government is in its place." This was not true either. Shortly after Nagy delivered his speech, he and his entourage of forty-two colleagues and family members—all reform-Communists—left the Parliament Building and escaped to the Yugoslav Embassy. Did Nagy try to say something that no one seemed to understand, or was this only an awkward farewell? Tildy, Donáth, and Nagy had phrased the statement in a great hurry and under extraordinary circumstances, but its meaning or purpose was never clarified.[107]

With the Soviet armed forces in charge of Budapest and the prime minister and his colleagues ensconced at the Yugoslav Embassy, "1956" came to a tragic finale. The end should not obscure the fact that growing cooperation between the rebels and the government marked the last four days—the third phase—of the Hungarian revolt. That achievement

---

[106] "Statement by Prime Minister Imre Nagy Announcing an Attack by Soviet Forces on the Hungarian Government, November 4, 1956," in *National Communism*, ed. Zinner, 472.

[107] Their Hungarian interrogators spent hundreds of hours trying to find out who wrote what part of this four-sentence statement; in the end, they did not seem to know more than when they began questioning the three defendants. For Donáth's account of what happened, see his interrogation on July 27, 1957, in Archive of the Ministry of Internal Affairs, V-150.000/47. According to this account, Tildy proposed that the government issue a statement; Nagy dictated the text; Donáth served as the typist; and then Nagy took the text to a nearby radio studio and read it.

made it possible for Hungarians to claim—correctly—that, however briefly, their fight for independence was victorious.

The third phase in Washington and Munich. By now the time for diplomatic initiatives by the United States, other Western powers, or the UN had passed. Washington, having cautiously welcomed the Soviet government's statement published on October 31, adopted a wait-and-see attitude. Information was sketchy. Charles E. Bohlen, the veteran U.S. ambassador to the Soviet Union, filed a few useful and insightful observations on what he saw at various diplomatic receptions and on what his interlocutors in Moscow were saying.[108] Privately, Secretary of State Dulles told the U.S. minister-designate to Hungary that he did not need to meet with President Eisenhower, because "the present government [of Nagy] is not one we want to do much with."[109] The secretary's comment echoed Radio Free Europe's ongoing harangues against Nagy. Though the ailing Dulles did not say much during this or any other phase of the Hungarian revolt, the little he did say suggested that, like RFE, he believed that the Nagy government, led by a Communist, was temporary or transitional and therefore did not deserve America's interest, let alone support.

Because the 1956 U. S. presidential campaign was concurrently coming to an end and American diplomats were spending their time and energy trying to restrain the British, French, and Israelis in the Suez crisis, and because reports from Moscow and Budapest were confusing and contradictory, there was not very much the Department of State or especially the White House wanted to do. More than ever, the Hungarian crisis was on the officials' back burner. Even verbal support for Hungary found opponents complaining that Nagy was a Communist; others believed that too much Western interest in Nagy would only make the Kremlin more suspicious of him. Under the circumstances, the best thing to do was to lay low. With hundreds of thousands of demonstrators in New York and throughout Western Europe calling on their governments to do more—to do *something*—the United States began to

---

[108] Cf. Charles E. Bohlen, *Witness to History, 1929–1969* (New York: W. W. Norton, 1973).

[109] Record of Dulles's phone conversation as quoted in Bennett Kovrig, *Of Walls and Bridges: The United States & Eastern Europe* (New York: New York University Press, 1991), 92.

think about taking the issue to the United Nations. But the UN was the wrong place for action, not only because of its inability to counter a major power but also because it was preoccupied with Suez.

In his television address on October 31, President Eisenhower devoted most of his time to the Suez crisis. On Hungary and more generally on Eastern Europe, he rejected the utility of any action, diplomatic or otherwise. Despite the failure of "rollback" and "liberation," he praised his administration for having kept "alive the hope of these peoples for freedom."[110] Although the Hungarians had risen up against their Soviet oppressors as Washington had wished they would, in Eisenhower's view doing nothing now was in "the best interests of the Eastern European peoples" and also in line with the UN's "abiding principles." In fact, the United States decided to put the Hungarian question on the UN's agenda only after the Soviet intervention on November 4. The purpose of that diplomatic move was not to help Hungary but to put the Soviet Union on the defensive and thus exploit an obvious propaganda opportunity.

As for Radio Free Europe, several "special directives" issued on November 2 by New York and Munich were adamant on promoting programs that would advocate "continued progress toward total democracy." However, as a sign of moderation, the instructions—quite belatedly—pointed out that the pace of progress must be set by the people of Hungary; RFE management in both New York and in Munich also kept stressing that it was not for outsiders "to decide whether any individual [politician] should stay or go."[111]

Along these lines was part of a commentary broadcast that day by Andor Gellért, head of the Hungarian Desk. It was a relatively calm piece of analysis about Hungary's prospects, discussing the consequences of a possible Soviet invasion. But on the allergic and critical issue of Nagy, Gellért failed to follow management's latest instructions. "The fist of Soviet militarism once again rises frighteningly over the country," Gellért declared. He went on to do the kind of lecturing he was not supposed to do: "It is the [Hungarian] government's historic

---

[110] Council on Foreign Relations, *Documents on American Foreign Relations, 1956* (New York: Harper, 1957), 50.

[111] RFE-RL Collection, Hoover Institution.

duty to raise its voice, in the name of the nation, against the military invasion now started," he continued. Warming up, he started questioning Nagy's credibility, something the prime minister had just proved conclusively the previous day by declaring Hungary's neutrality. But this was not good enough. Gellért: "Under such circumstances, the first question is this: What moral and political right does the present prime minister have to request the nation's unity and trust?"[112] Clearly, in the last two or possibly three days of the revolt, management's directives and the actual broadcasts diverged on assessing Nagy and his role. Given Nagy's Communist past, the Hungarian broadcasters could not forgive him for what he used to be.

How different was the message RFE was sending to its Polish listeners! In 1996, Jan Nowak summarized what he and his colleagues on the Polish Desk had tried to achieve in 1956: "Our message was clear," he said at a workshop in Budapest. "If the October changes were to last, they would have to be kept within certain bounds, which could not be overstepped. The border lines were marked by the monopoly of power in the hands of the reformed Communist Party and by the 'alliance' with the Soviet Union in the Warsaw Pact."[113] Thus the Poles in Poland and RFE's Polish broadcasters in Munich accepted even less than half a loaf—and Khrushchev, initially ready to attack Poland, reversed himself and said *da* to a Poland having a modicum of semi-independence and semi-freedom. By contrast, the Hungarians in Hungary sought what they thought they were entitled to have, and RFE's Hungarian broadcasters in Munich urged them to try to get even more. Initially ready to swallow his pride and accept Nagy's Hungary, Khrushchev then reversed himself and said *nyet*. And the Hungarian revolt failed.

The CIA, meanwhile, was still looking for Hungarian-speaking personnel. On November 2, it sent a communications specialist to Budapest on temporary duty.[114] Other employees were not allowed to enter Hungarian territory; headquarters kept repeating the policy, which was that no one associated with the agency should do anything that

---

[112] Ibid.

[113] Jan Nowak, "Poles and Hungarians in 1956," paper prepared for the international conference "Hungary and the World, 1956: The New Archival Evidence," Budapest, September 26–29, 1996, 5.

[114] CIA, *Clandestine Services Historical Series (CSHP 323): Hungary External Operations 1946–1965* (MORI DocID: 1161462; parts declassified at my request in December 2004), vol. 1, 69.

could possibly justify charges of intervention in Hungary's domestic affairs.[115] Much time was devoted to "the position and disposition of Ferenc Nagy [a former Smallholder leader, living in exile, unrelated to Imre Nagy], who was at that time in Paris trying to get into Austria."[116]

Information did begin to reach the CIA from Hungarian citizens, such as railroad personnel using teletype. As the agency review noted, "Some of the people we talked to at the border brought with them reports received in their towns via railroad teletype from other areas."[117] In this phase of the revolt, the CIA was keenly interested in signs of Soviet troop movements. Making use of RFE's excellent monitoring of rebel radio broadcasts, the agency picked up valuable information on October 30 and 31 about Soviet military activities near the Soviet border. In another case, useful tidbits of information reached Győr, a city near Hungary's western border, from stationmasters in eastern Hungary.[118] The CIA was also able to draw on a Hungarian truck driver or two sent to Vienna for supplies, but the drivers had little time to tell what they knew because they "were naturally in a great hurry to return."[119]

As a result of being unprepared for the revolt, lacking appropriate personnel, and prohibited from dispatching its agents to Hungary, the CIA—like the rest of the Washington bureaucracy—did not anticipate the second or ultimate Soviet intervention on November 4. This was strange because information was pouring in from outside Budapest, and especially the country's "Eastern Corridor," near the Soviet frontier, about troops entering Hungary in large numbers. On the night of November 3, "one border contact stated his conviction that that the Russians were ready to attack. However, after the attack, some agents reported that until the night of 3 November none of their contacts had predicted this intervention."[120] In the event, the agency failed to predict the coming crackdown. It believed the revolt to have been victorious.

---

[115] CIA, *CSHP 6*, vol. 1, 95.

[116] Ibid., 96. The U.S. government, including the CIA, did not want Ferenc Nagy to go to Vienna out of concern that he might then try to go on to Hungary, where his presence would create additional confusion.

[117] Ibid.

[118] Ibid., 105.

[119] Ibid., 84.

[120] Ibid., 96.

The CIA review concluded with a sardonic note about the revolt's aftermath. "On 4 November," it stated, "headquarters cabled [word deleted] that it should try to line up escaping resistance leaders for appearance before the UN, and that measures would be taken to hasten the entry of such into the U.S. *On 6 November we were already talking about the mechanics and methods of exploiting refugees.* And that was that."[121] Thus the new U.S. agenda would feature slogans that condemned the Soviet crackdown, replacing the old and now inoperative slogans that had promoted liberation and rollback.

Did it have to end this way?

---

[121] Ibid. Italics added.

6

The Revolt That Did Not Have to Fail

> In the interest of peace and freedom—freedom from both despotism and anarchy—we must hope that for a time, not forever but for a time, the uprising in the satellite orbit will be stabilized at Titoism.
>
> —*Walter Lippmann, October 26, 1956*

· 1 ·

Professional students of the 1956 Hungarian revolt have seldom pondered—and when they did, they tended to dismiss—the possibility of a successful outcome, saying that what happened reflected the correlation of forces in the Cold War and was therefore foreseeable and inevitable. For both the Soviet Union and the United States, in this view, the division of Europe was preferable to the incalculable consequences of changes in the postwar status quo. The revolt had to fail. Case closed.

In less formal settings, and especially after a drink or two, Hungarians and Americans remembering or interested in '56 have never stopped considering the chances for a different finale to the Hungarian crisis. After all, history is not only a series of "facts" or "events" but also a matter of interpretation; there is room for informed speculation on the roads not taken. As long as the alternatives to what happened are *plausible* rather than farfetched, it is a legitimate and a useful intellectual enterprise to discuss and debate other conceivable outcomes. We continue to think about the origins of World War II, for example, wondering about the possible consequences of an active rather than an isolationist America, or of Winston Churchill rather than Neville Chamberlain leading the United Kingdom in the 1930s, or of a successful conspiracy against Hitler. With respect to the case of Hungary, it is equally reasonable to ask: *What if* Nikita Khrushchev, for the sake of regional stability, had extended the processes of de-Stalinization to the Soviet bloc by allowing Titoist-like changes? *What if* the Hungarian party, following the Polish example, had let Imre Nagy vigorously support such changes from the beginning? *What if* the United States had pursued a policy of peaceful engagement toward Central and Eastern Europe already in the 1950s, seeking incremental gains, as America began to do in the 1960s? *What if* during the Hungarian crisis the United States had proposed a mutual reduction of forces from Central Europe?

In 2002, the prominent Hungarian historian Csaba Békés published a systematic, tightly argued essay, "Could the Hungarian Revolution Have Been Victorious in 1956?"[1] Relying on the teachings of the realpolitik school of political analysis, Békés argued that it would be ahistorical to question the inevitability of the revolt's downfall. Making use of both public and the latest archival evidence, Békés considered four major variables—the role of the Suez crisis, of the United States, of the United Nations, and of course of the Soviet Union—in the Hungarian crisis. He concluded (correctly, I think) that Suez was but a convenient distraction for Washington; if it had not occurred, the United States would not have acted differently toward Hungary. The United Nations was deadlocked and thus useless. As for the Kremlin, Anastas Mikoyan did seem to be more tolerant toward the Hungarians than his colleagues in the Soviet Politburo—he believed that a government led by Nagy would probably make a Soviet military intervention unnecessary—but

---

[1] Csaba Békés, "Győzhetett volna-e a magyar forradalom 1956-ban?" [Could the Hungarian revolution have been victorious in 1956?], in *Mítoszok, legendák, tévhitek a 20. századi magyar történelemből* [Myths, legends, delusions in 20th-century Hungarian history], ed. Ignác Romcsis (Budapest: Osiris, 2002), 339–60. See also his pioneering work, *The 1956 Hungarian Revolution and World Politics*, Cold War International History Project Paper 16 (Washington, D.C.: Woodrow Wilson International Center for Scholars, 1996).

in the final analysis, no Soviet leader could have let Hungary join the West and also keep his job. Therefore, in Békés's view, what mattered was the frozen relationship between Moscow and Washington and thus the logic of the Cold War. And that logic signified the unchangeable division of Europe between East and West that could not be altered without war between the major antagonists. Hence the revolt was doomed from the beginning; what happened had to happen. According to Békés, the Hungarians—as well as much of the American public—did not understand that the two sides had reached an implicit understanding about the division of Europe, believing instead in the empty slogans of liberation perpetrated by hypocritical Western politicians and propagandists. He reported a poll conducted in February 1957 that showed—incredibly—that no fewer than 96 percent of Hungarian refugees then in Austria had expected some form of U.S. help during the revolt.[2]

As to the rebels' excessive zeal and the role of Radio Free Europe (RFE) in goading them, others have occasionally voiced similarly fatalistic assessments on the issue of whether moderation by the Hungarians and by RFE might have made a difference. "It is one of the imponderables of history," wrote Bennett Kovrig in his classic *The Myth of Liberation*, "whether, had the Hungarian people been more pragmatic and compromising, the revolution could have ended with the consolidation of [Nagy's] regime."[3] Though Kovrig declined to answer his question, Gyula Borbándi, the author of a comprehensive and thoughtful history of RFE's Hungarian Desk, categorically denied the very possibility of restraint by RFE or by the insurgents under the circumstances.[4] In an interview with Arch Puddington, Borbándi put it this way:

> What were we to say to the Hungarians: "Be moderate; go back to your homes, be restrained"? We had from the beginning of RFE been urging Hungarians to resist Communism. Should we now have told the workers to return to the factories? Or the soldiers to return to their barracks? We couldn't say to the Hungarians: "Please be moderate." The Soviet

---

[2] This poll of uncertain origin should not be taken at face value. It is a safe bet, however, that a majority of Hungarians—fighters and supporters alike—did anticipate some sort of U.S. help.

[3] Bennett Kovrig, *The Myth of Liberation: East-Central Europe in U.S. Diplomacy and Politics since 1941* (Baltimore: Johns Hopkins University Press, 1973), 182.

[4] Gyula Borbándi, *Magyarok az Angol Kertben: A Szabad Európa Rádió története* [Hungarians at the English Garden: A History of Radio Free Europe] (Budapest: Európa, 1996).

army was in Budapest. . . . The revolution was anti-Communist; Nagy
was a Communist. Some wondered how a Communist could lead an
anti-Communist revolution.[5]

One ought to be understanding, and even sympathetic, toward such
comments. RFE's managers and broadcasters had indeed been regaled
for nearly four years with Washington's persistent and loud rhetoric
about liberation and rollback. Moreover, when the revolt began, they
were operating in the context of limited information and considerable
uncertainty. They also believed their hard work on behalf of the Hungarian people was now, finally, bearing fruit.

That said, the upshot of Békés's views is that by 1956, despite persistent ideological hostility and continuing crises over Berlin, the Cold
War in Europe had in fact produced a stalemate. The language of rollback by the United States and professed Soviet faith in the ultimate triumph of socialism notwithstanding, the status quo could not and would
not be changed. On one level of reality, Washington, implicitly acknowledging the division of the old continent into two camps, understood that Moscow would not let go of a country bordering on a neutral but pro-Western Austria and an independent Yugoslavia, and so it
shed crocodile tears over Soviet brutality and exploited propaganda opportunities as they emerged. On another level, Washington urged on anticommunist activities in Eastern Europe while Moscow financed pro-
communist activities in Western Europe. Under the circumstances,
moreover, the insurgents could not be more moderate; after all, they
were insurgents against one side in the Cold War, while the other side
manipulated their distress as if they were pawns in a grand chess game.
And with a Communist—Nagy—heading the Hungarian government,
RFE could not counsel the revolutionaries to temper their demands.

These sensible if unduly fatalistic observations deserve scrutiny.
What looks self-evident in retrospect might not have been self-evident
then; arguably, the revolt's failure was neither predestined nor inex-
orable. Thus, to gain a better understanding of what happened and why,

---

[5] Arch Puddington, *Broadcasting Freedom: The Cold War Triumph of Radio Free Europe and Radio Liberty* (Lexington: University Press of Kentucky, 2000), 108. On the same page, Puddington adds: "Although admitting that some of the criticism directed at the Hungarian staff was justified, Borbandi
believes that the RFE management contributed to the problem by failing to exercise firm political
leadership."

the "imponderables of history" need to be explored: Why did the four major players in the Hungarian drama—the Kremlin, the insurgents, the Hungarian government, and Washington (including RFE in Munich)—do what they did? Could they have done something else? Might it have made a difference?

▪ 2 ▪

There is no mystery about why, after thirteen dramatic days, the revolt collapsed. It collapsed because Moscow had allowed itself to be guided by fear of losing its satellites; because Budapest—the insurgents, and eventually the Hungarian government, too—had pursued goals unacceptable to the Kremlin; and because Washington, though unprepared to help, put no alternatives on the table and even allowed RFE to push for an unrealistic outcome. Put another way, the insurgents pressed for all they sought; the Hungarian government was too feeble to envisage a viable deal; Washington failed to tender wise advice about applying restraint; and the Kremlin, undeterred by a weak adversary in Budapest, decided to defeat the Hungarians.

This is not to say that if only three of the four major players in the Hungarian drama—the revolutionaries, the Hungarian government, and the United States—had proceeded more creatively or more cautiously, Moscow would have allowed the revolt to achieve all its objectives. If those three key players had acted more prudently—seeking to gain a few yards instead of risking all for a touchdown—the Kremlin might not have even allowed a semi-free and a semi-independent Hungary to emerge. We will never know. What we know is that in 1956 illusions and pent-up frustrations guided all four participants' actions. Cool heads did not prevail in Budapest, in Washington, or of course in Moscow. Emotions reigned, and wisdom was in short supply. In the end, instead of winning a bit of elbow room, as happened in Poland, the Hungarians ended up with little or nothing to show for their extraordinary bravery.

▪ 3 ▪

The ultimate outcome of the 1956 Hungarian revolt depended on

- the Kremlin's choice between its old imperial instincts and new if uncertain post-Stalin stance,

- the insurgents' fortitude as well as their political skill,
- the Hungarian government's ability to satisfy both the insurgents and the Soviet leadership, and
- Washington's restraining influence, so that each side—the insurgents, the Hungarian government, Moscow, and Washington itself—would accept less than it had hoped or expected to gain.

Each of these factors deserves separate treatment.

▪ 4 ▪

As to the Kremlin's choice of what to do about Hungary, the main questions are the following: What could have convinced the Kremlin to continue to uphold the policy of nonintervention it adopted on October 30, announced on October 31, and then also canceled on October 31? What could have persuaded the majority of the Soviet Politburo to side with Mikoyan and continue for a few more days its support for Nagy's efforts to restore order? What, if anything, could the Hungarians have done that might have influenced Soviet behavior?

Three answers to these questions—first about the history of Soviet–East European relations, second about the concurrent Soviet-Polish crisis, and third about the Soviet Union's stunning decision on October 30 *not* to intervene—tend to discredit the received wisdom about the inevitability of the revolt's failure.

First: Contrary to widely shared assumptions, the Kremlin, in its dealings with the satellites before or after 1956, was never particularly trigger-happy; at times, it made prudent if tactical adjustments to new realities. True, on critically important occasions it was unwilling to allow its putative allies to be different—witness, in particular, Soviet military interventions in East Germany in 1953 and Czechoslovakia in 1968. It is equally true, however, that the Kremlin was occasionally if grudgingly willing to tolerate divergence—witness, despite its obvious displeasure, the absence of military intervention against Yugoslavia, Poland, Albania, and Romania, where largely united, independent-minded Communist leaderships resisted intransigent Soviet demands.

In the fall of 1956, the history of Soviet foreign policy indicated the probability but not the certainty of military intervention against Hungary. The presence of Soviet forces on Hungarian territory—as in the East German and Czechoslovak cases—as well as Hungary's proximity to a Western-oriented if neutral Austria pointed to the likelihood of intervention. However, the anti-Stalin campaign launched earlier in 1956 pointed to a less violent campaign by Moscow—as was the case, in the end, with respect to Poland. Because of de-Stalinization and the ongoing process of courting Tito, the Kremlin had good reasons in late 1956 to stress the goal of "regime viability" rather than the goal of "bloc cohesion."[6] Allowing for "regime viability" would have signified policies granting Central and Eastern European leaders at least a modicum of legitimacy so that they could obtain a measure of support from their own people; the goal of "bloc cohesion" signified the imperative of the satellites following the Soviet lead in every important respect. All in all, then, the history of Soviet–East European relations suggests a somewhat more nuanced political mentality in the Kremlin than commonly assumed; Soviet policies toward Central and Eastern Europe show dissimilar reactions to crisis situations in general and the threat of defection in particular.[7]

Second: It is an incontestable fact rather than a matter of interpretation that under comparable though certainly not identical circumstances in Poland, the Kremlin chose not to intervene. Some details are discussed in chapter 5. What needs to be stressed here is that Poland, then as always, was far more important to Moscow than Hungary. Poland mattered because of its location between Germany and the Soviet Union, its size, its common Slavic roots and historical relationship with Russia, and as a showcase for the much-advertised gains of socialism. Hungary mattered only because it was part of the Kremlin's

---

[6] For a brilliant analysis of these two then-original concepts, *see* J. F. Brown, *Relations between the Soviet Union and Its Eastern European Allies: A Survey* (Santa Monica, Calif.: RAND, 1975).

[7] Though each circumstance was different, anti-Soviet movements and revolts in Central and Eastern Europe fell into three broad categories. Some, as in East Germany (1953), Hungary (1956), Poland (1956, 1968, 1976, and the 1980s) were popular outbursts against Communist oppression, aimed primarily against Soviet domination and partly against hard-line domestic Communist bosses and factions. Others, such as Yugoslavia (1948), Albania (1961), and Romania (1964), were led by hard-line, oppressive, and nationalist Communist parties and leaders who were trying to eliminate or curb Soviet domination. Finally, Czechoslovakia in 1968 was a case in which a reform-minded regime initiated far-reaching liberalization from above and earned widespread popular support, much to the dismay of the Soviet leaders. Admittedly, interventions in East Germany, Hungary, and Czechoslovakia suggest the Kremlin's geopolitical concern about frontline states—those that bordered on the West.

claim to "socialism in one region." And yet the Soviet Army intervened in Hungary, not in Poland.

In Soviet eyes, the question of authority was a critical consideration. Poland's Władysław Gomułka knew what he was doing. He was in charge. He was not torn about his loyalties: He was a Pole, he was a Communist, and he was a friend though not a stooge of the Soviet Union. Once Poland's Communist leaders, notably Edward Ochab, stepped aside in his favor, and both the Catholic Church and RFE signaled their support for his nationalist Communist course, Gomułka's authority—despite his Communist beliefs and policies—was assured. Clearly, Khrushchev understood Gomułka well, and appreciated him, too; this was why, after their initial confrontation, the two consulted as often as they did both on the phone and in person. Khrushchev wanted Gomułka to find a political solution to the Polish crisis and believed that he could.

As for Hungary, Khrushchev had expected Nagy to take charge and control his country as much as and as soon as possible. Reports reaching Khrushchev during the early days of the revolt were discouraging, but then came a period of relative calm, and the Soviet Politburo decided to withdraw its military from Budapest. Alas, Nagy was less decisive than Gomułka. For almost five days, Nagy was a confused and troubled man who (reluctantly) supported Soviet intervention against what he regarded as counterrevolutionary elements. Then (at first, again, reluctantly) he shifted to the insurgents' side, but he was too ineffective to prevent the slaughter of party workers and secret policemen on Republic Square on October 30. For Khrushchev, and indeed all Soviet officials with the exception of Mikoyan, this—the killing of Communists under chaotic conditions—was what they could not accept. Other factors obviously influenced them as they changed their minds again and decided to crush the Hungarians, but *fear of disorder* and similar disorder elsewhere in their orbit—deeply ingrained in Russian political culture—sparked a strong and visceral response. If Nagy had been able to prevent that one atrocious incident from taking place on Republic Square, and if he had been able to present himself to the rulers of the Kremlin as a decisive, resolute, and calculating if independent-minded Communist, chances are that Khrushchev would have seen him as another Gomułka and given him an opportunity to restore order on his own. Instead, Nagy seemed to his Soviet visitors to be harried and vacillating.

Third: It is also an incontestable fact that the Soviet Politburo unanimously decided—on October 30—*not* to intervene militarily in Hungary. That decision showed Khrushchev's reluctance to risk de-Stalinization at home and the possibility of détente with the West abroad for the sake of enforcing Stalinist-style "stability" over a troublesome part of his empire. The intriguing question is why he and his colleagues changed their mind—why they opted for the goal of "bloc cohesion" over "viability"—*when they did*. To recall: By October 30, Hungarians from the two sides of the barricades had patched up most of their differences and reaffirmed their widely shared socialist values, and the country had begun to enjoy a period of relative calm. Was the Soviet intervention in response to that one ugly anticommunist atrocity committed earlier on the 30th? Alternatively, was it the promise of stability rather than the record of instability that sparked the Soviet decision to intervene? Was it Western preoccupation with Suez rather than anything happening or not happening in Budapest, that made the Kremlin majority reverse itself and reject Mikoyan's passionate calls for delay?

My reading of the rather incomplete record of the Kremlin's deliberations, several Soviet leaders' memoirs, and contemporary exchanges between Moscow and Budapest suggest that when members Soviet Politburo approved nonintervention, they were counting on Nagy to guide Hungary toward a socialist future. They knew him well and they trusted him, and his popularity with Hungarians was a big plus. As Ambassador Yuri Andropov revealed to a trusted aide in December 1956, they knew that the United States, its propaganda notwithstanding, was in fact only a passive observer.[8] And most important, they knew that if Nagy did not work out—if he allowed Hungary to slip away—they would find ways to remind him of the limits of their tolerance (as they were to remind Gomułka later on).

The timing of the Kremlin's change of heart suggests the critical importance of the deteriorating relationship between Mikoyan and Mikhail Suslov, the two Soviet emissaries who shuttled between Moscow and Budapest during the Hungarian crisis. By Soviet standards,

---

[8] See chapter 5, fn. 101.

Mikoyan was an anti-Stalinist moderate and Suslov was a dogmatic hard-liner. Yet, until now, they had worked together well, preferring to rely on Nagy rather than on Soviet intervention. However, on October 30 their paths diverged; it happened when Suslov stopped believing that Nagy was capable of assuring Hungary's socialist future within the confines of the Soviet orbit. That day Mikoyan (not Mikoyan and Suslov) told Nagy's deputy, Zoltán Tildy, that the Kremlin had approved the formation of a multiparty political system, but Mikoyan was acting on his own authority. The Soviet Politburo did not support that move, and by then Suslov was no longer Mikoyan's alter ego. As the two emissaries were flying back to Moscow, late on October 30, and despite Mikoyan's objections, the Politburo reversed itself and voted for intervention.

Mikoyan and Suslov were in Budapest when the atrocities occurred on Republic Square. They were still in Budapest when the Hungarian government, following Mikoyan's discussion with Tildy, began to prepare for the introduction of a Western-style multiparty system. This was the day—October 30—when Mikoyan and Suslov talked to Nagy and found him to be a different man; by now, after a week of hesitation and vacillation, this once-Muscovite prime minister had turned into a Hungarian patriot and a revolutionary. This was also the day—the beginning of the revolt's third phase—when Nagy ceased being a hesitant bystander. Though even then he remained a Marxist-Leninist, for Suslov that was not enough. He wanted subservience. It is not known whether or how Suslov signaled that he no longer agreed with Mikoyan, and to whom he spoke in Moscow, but it is clear from the record that Suslov did not object to the Politburo's decision of October 31 overturning the previous day's commitment to nonintervention. It may be that, by then, Khrushchev took his cue from Suslov as well as from Ambassador Andropov and KGB Chief Ivan Serov rather than from Mikoyan, his most loyal anti-Stalinist comrade and supporter; Khrushchev, sensing political problems, did not want to be isolated from his colleagues. Precisely because Suslov had endorsed all of Khrushchev's moves with respect to Hungary, he had at least as much credibility with the Soviet leader as he did with all of the Kremlin's contentious, hard-line factions.

In the end, Nagy became a reluctant revolutionary who could not control that sudden outburst of violence on October 30, and this was the main reason why he lost whatever confidence Moscow had had in him. Contributing to the Kremlin's change of mind, and to its decision to crush the revolt by military means, was China's acquiescence in Khrushchev's verdict. A high-level Chinese delegation in Moscow had initially urged the Soviet leaders not to intervene in Poland and Hungary, no doubt because of China's growing concern about its own independence from the post-Stalin Soviet leadership. However, the Chinese reversed themselves about Hungary to show solidarity with the Kremlin, and because they were also frightened by the sight of a spontaneous outburst of popular fury against Communist officials. Thus, the Chinese did not initiate the change; they supported Khrushchev both when the Soviet leader opted for nonintervention on October 30 and when he opted for intervention on October 31.

The ultimate Soviet decision to intervene was prompted primarily by the violence on Republic Square; by the emerging unity of purpose between most insurgents and the Nagy government; by the misunderstanding triggered by Mikoyan's acceptance of a Hungarian political order that brought about Nagy's declaration reinstituting Hungary's postwar multiparty system in the early afternoon of October 30, or about sixteen to eighteen hours before the Kremlin's change of policy the next morning; and by the Kremlin's fear of spreading disorder in the Soviet bloc. Under these circumstances, what could have convinced Moscow to postpone military action? Clearly, the absence of bloodshed on Republic Square and Nagy's refusal to embrace demands to end the one-party system would have allowed Moscow to continue to implement the historic decision of October 30—a post-Stalin approach to the Soviet orbit in Central and Eastern Europe.

▪ 5 ▪

If the Hungarian insurgents gave the world a lesson about bravery but not very much about their political skill, the Hungarian government—facing Soviet duplicity and the beginning of Soviet military action—had few options left in the last days of the revolt.

The previous discussion about what mattered to the Soviet Union indicates, of course, what the Hungarians might have done to give themselves a chance to be victorious: First, the insurgents should have focused even more than they did—particularly on October 30 on Republic Square—on avoiding participation in or association with atrocities. Second, the government should not have wasted five crucial days before identifying itself with the revolt—and once it did, so it should have prevailed on the insurgents to moderate their demands and delay implementation.

That the movement for reform of the system turned into a revolt against the system was a unique feature of the Hungarian uprising. The students, together with the young workers and soldiers who joined them, believed in socialist ideals; they also believed in an independent Hungary. The initial demands they advanced on October 23, which approximated existing realities in Tito's Yugoslavia, could have been broadcast on Rádió Kossuth without the collapse of the Communist regime. The utter stupidity of Rádió Kossuth's president, who refused to put these demands on the air, was surpassed only by that of the Communist Party leadership, then headed by Ernő Gerő; knowing only the black-and-white categories of Communist ideology and politics, they believed that those who were not 100 percent with them were 100 percent against them. In the process, they managed to radicalize the country's youth. To make matters worse, they also managed to damage the reputation of Nagy by identifying him with antirevolutionary measures. Unfortunately, a rather confused, deferential, tired, and nervous Nagy allowed himself to be co-opted and discredited at a time when he was the only man who had a chance to avert bloodshed and keep Hungary on a socialist path acceptable to the Kremlin. Nagy's behavior did not reflect his credibility and popularity; in fact, he held all the high cards needed if the party leaders and their Soviet masters wanted a noninterventionist resolution of the crisis.

The first time when a chance for a Titoist dénouement was lost was when Rádió Kossuth refused to air the students' demands and thereby radicalized them and their supporters. Another chance was lost when Nagy did not publicize his quiet though profound disagreement with Gerő and his acolytes. Still another chance was lost when, with the exception of General Pál Maléter, no one from the new, more broadly based government visited the insurgents to explain to them the need to press ahead gradually, without offending too many Soviet sensibilities. In his various speeches, Nagy did ask for calm, but that was in the context of requesting the rebels to put down their arms. He could have explained that bravery without wisdom amounted to childish romanticism, and what was needed was both courage to shake off the Communist oppressors and shrewdness to make them give up their positions without a fight.

If Nagy was not forthcoming enough during the first phase of the revolt, he sought to compensate for his passivity during the third phase. Having first distanced himself from the insurgents, he went on to support all or almost all of their increasingly radical demands. The excuse the rebels had for their excessive if understandable zeal was their youth, but Nagy did not have that excuse. He was an experienced, sixty-year-old politician who should have known that in politics there is a time to move ahead and a time to slow down, a time to listen to your heart and a time to use your head, and above all a time when you accept less than what you think is your due. For a small country like Hungary, in particular, partial victory *is* victory. If from Day One of the revolution Nagy had set his sights on a Titoist or Gomułkaist outcome, fully understanding the need for a compromise solution and thus steering a course between the insurgents' hopes and the Kremlin's fears, the initial—reformist, socialist—goals of the country might well have been achieved.

His engaging if often stubborn personality notwithstanding, Nagy was a romantic Hungarian as well as a product of Communist ideology—both offering strict categories of good and bad and right and wrong. He had an encyclopedic knowledge of Hungarian history, and every now and then he quoted a favorite poet or politician. He tended to favor brave heroes and selfless martyrs, not calm, wise, compromise-seeking statesmen. He was more impressed by the likes of Sándor Petőfi (the radical poet and hero of the 1848–49 revolution against Hungary's foreign oppressors, for whom the only choice was between slavery and freedom) than he was by the likes of Ferenc Deák of the 1867 compromise with Austria, whose opportunism did not yield Hungary full independence yet sparked not only an economic boom but also an extraordinary architectural renaissance in Budapest that is visible to this day.

Nagy's background and political mentality did not prepare him to be a leader capable of delivering a Grand Compromise in 1956. His single-handed efforts as prime minister in 1953–55 to reform the Stalinist system, his decency and good intentions in 1956, and his immense courage and ultimate martyrdom in 1957–58 need not obscure his flawed political performance during the revolt. In the end, he did not rise to the challenge of convincing the proprietors of power in Moscow and the Hungarian insurgents in Budapest that they should accept less than what they sought—but gain enough to satisfy their minimal expectations.

▪ 6 ▪

More than anything else, hypocrisy characterized the U.S. approach to Hungary. Hypocrisy revealed itself in the gap between the public rhetoric of liberation and rollback on the one hand and the lack of any follow-up on the other. But hypocrisy also revealed itself in the gap between secret decisions reached behind closed doors on the one hand and the lack of any follow-up on the other. The inexplicable truth—inexplicable, that is, by standard political analysis—is that the U.S. government did not only mislead the outside world about its intentions in order to put the Communists on the defensive; it also misled itself. American officials from President Eisenhower to the Central Intelligence Agency's Frank Wisner to Radio Free Europe's William Griffith were all deeply and sincerely surprised and disappointed when their words of hope did not deliver freedom to the Hungarians. It seems that they had an excessive, almost religious faith in the power of words. In that sense, they were genuine idealists, victims of their own illusions. Other officials, meanwhile, were simply cynical. As cited at the start of chapter 3, Vice President Richard Nixon did not believe Soviet intervention would be an "unmixed evil" (because it would help the United States exploit the Kremlin's brutality),[9] and yet he subsequently visited with Hungarian refugees both in Austria and at Camp Kilmer in New Jersey. His cynicism was probably a function of political considerations. He was interested in liberating Congress from the Democrats.

---

[9] On one level, Nixon was of course right. The Soviet intervention shook up a number of communist parties in Western Europe, and Moscow's standing among the nonaligned countries of the developing world also suffered a setback. On another level, however, Nixon's apparent lack of interest in helping the Hungarians, combined with his eagerness to benefit from their bravery and sacrifice, strike me as particularly cynical.

Hypocrisy, and the question of motivation, aside, the United States committed three major errors in its policy toward Hungary in the 1950s.

First, Washington flirted with but eventually rejected the idea of promoting Titoism in Central and Eastern Europe. Stories about internal administration debates surfaced in U.S. newspapers, notably in C. L. Sulzberger's columns in the *New York Times*, but the notion of seeking partial or limited gains did not fall on fertile political soil. In 1956, under explicit order from its headquarters in New York and from supervisory officials at the Department of State and at the Central Intelligence Agency in Washington, Radio Free Europe urged its Hungarian listeners not to moderate their radical objectives—and then, adding insult to injury, also advised them how to make weapons (i.e., "Molotov cocktails") for their encounter with the Soviet intruders. If RFE did not "incite" the Hungarians to fight, it certainly "encouraged" them to pursue nothing less than maximalist objectives.

Second, and related, the United States barely noticed Nagy—and then did not like what it saw. This was the case during Nagy's first prime ministership, and it continued during the revolt. Unwilling to accept this Muscovite's genuine appeal and popularity, Washington and Munich dismissed him as just another Communist, neither better nor worse than the rest. If U.S. officials had had information about Nagy's ties to the NKVD in the 1930s and possibly later on, too, they might have had a plausible reason for not supporting him in 1953–55 and again in 1956. As much as it can be ascertained, however, such information about Nagy's background was unavailable. Therefore, what turned Washington and Munich against him was the false notion of Communist unity, which reflected official blindness to the new reality of the polycentrism exemplified by Tito's Yugoslavia.

Third, during the revolt, U.S. diplomacy failed to put anything on the table that might have appealed to the Kremlin—and at least delayed the day of reckoning. The only message conveyed to Moscow was contained in Secretary of State John Foster Dulles's October 27 speech that meant to assure Khrushchev of America's disinterest in Hungary as a potential military ally. In other words, the United States clarified what it did *not* want and did *not* plan to do. But nothing was said or proposed about what Washington *did* plan to do. For good reason! For even as the world press reported information on November 1 about the beginnings of the second and ultimate Soviet invasion, the United States did not recommend that someone like the secretary general of the United Nations fly to Budapest and use his presence to deter or to delay a Soviet crackdown. U.S. officials did not think of proposing a mutual reduction of forces from Europe, or the withdrawal of the U.S. military from a small Western European country in exchange for the withdrawal of the Soviet military from Hungary. In other words, various options could have been considered to give the Kremlin an incentive to shelve or delay its planned offensive. But Washington, for reasons discussed earlier in this book, missed an opportunity to keep faith with the Hungarians—and with itself.

· 7 ·

Too many members of the Soviet political elite entertained illusions about building a viable state by relying on coercion rather than persuasion. Too many Hungarians entertained illusions about their courageous insurgency forcing the Soviet Union to retreat. Too many Americans entertained illusions about their strident rhetoric forcing the Soviet Union to retreat.

Too many Hungarians and Americans believed that they would prevail because they were right.

The proper antidote for such illusions was not, and should not be, realpolitik based on the acceptance of what is because it has been, but a mature willingness to seek limited change.[10] If the key actors in the Hungarian drama of 1956 had been guided by idealists who did not entertain illusions—who, accordingly, did not set their sights too high—the revolt might well have succeeded. The evidence strongly suggests that if the United States had successfully counseled the Hungarians to exercise restraint and seek limited objectives, the historic Soviet decision of October 30, 1956, not to intervene would not have been reversed the next day.

---

[10] The generalization here and elsewhere in this book is about 1956. At that time, international circumstances argued for limited change. In 1989, by contrast, international circumstances—notably the Kremlin's decision to let go of the Soviet Union's so-called outer empire—made it possible to seek fundamental change.

That said, whereas Americans and Hungarians made serious mistakes of commission and omission during the course of 1956, and before 1956 too, the responsible party for the failure of this noble effort to achieve Hungarian independence resided, of course, in Moscow rather than in Washington or Budapest.

7

Epilogue: Memories
Repressed and Recovered

How could you [Hungarians] live without freedom
for thirty-three years?

*—Imre Mécs, a university student whose death sentence for his
role in the 1956 revolt was commuted, June 16, 1989*

· 1 ·

The year 1956 was a defining political moment in my life; to this day
it remains a vivid, memorable experience. Yet, because of my personal
ties to 1956 and the people who shaped it, I waited almost three
decades before publishing a chapter called "Moscow and Imre Nagy,
1953–1956" in my 1986 book, *Hungary and the Soviet Bloc.* Only then
did I feel confident that I could treat the subject fairly and objectively.

In the early 1990s, when the once-secret archives opened up after
the collapse of communism, I decided to take another look. I was curious if new documents confirmed what I had experienced and what I
had learned from open sources. The answer turned out to be mixed. In
very general terms, many of the documents I read and at least some of
the interviews I conducted with Hungarians on opposite sides of the
barricades tended to confirm what we knew or suspected. Of course,

documentary evidence and firsthand confirmation by participants was helpful. On the other hand, the details were revealing about the insurgents; the deliberations of Nagy's revolutionary government; the behavior of the Soviet Union, Yugoslavia, and the United States during the crisis; Radio Free Europe's broadcasts; and the creation of János Kádár's pro-Soviet, postrevolutionary government. What was particularly striking was the portrait that emerged of Imre Nagy, this central figure in the drama of 1956. I was among the first to gain access to documents about his Romanian exile in late 1956 and early 1957, his dealings with his post-1956 accusers, and his fearless behavior before two secret Hungarian tribunals in February and June 1958.

Nagy, who was uncertain of himself during the revolution, became—on the road to the gallows in 1957–58—decisive, resolute, strong-willed, and unyielding. As he bravely confronted his interrogators and the so-called judges of the Hungarian kangaroo courts, he showed himself to be a genuine hero and a patriot who stood up for his beliefs. This is all the more remarkable not only because of his Muscovite past but also because if, after the Soviet intervention, Nagy had formally resigned and accepted Kádár's Moscow-installed government, he would have been allowed to live; he might have even played a role in Hungarian political or academic life. Instead, he did not cooperate with his jailors; he did not confess his political sins. On several occasions, he stubbornly refused to sign the minutes of his testimony and went on a hunger strike when his tough interrogator did not allow him to relate his side of the story.

Nagy's February 1958 trial was interrupted at Soviet request; Moscow did not want the publicity of his death sentence to stifle its ongoing efforts to hold a summit with the United States. At his second, and last, trial, in June 1958, he is seen on film—only a segment of which has surfaced—to defy the Kafkaesque abnormality of being the main defendant in a secret show trial that was played out before a court with a judge, two prosecutors, and a small team of meek defense lawyers—all acting as if they were following normal judicial procedures. During the course of this sham trial, which also featured a small audience made up of trusted secret police officers and a camera held by one of these officers taping the grim proceedings, Nagy never broke down. As if he had expected the record of the trial to become public one day, he fought for his legacy. He declined to ask for clemency. In his last memorable words, he appealed to "the international working-class movement" to clear his name. He died a genuine martyr and the only good Bolshevik the world has ever known.

Thus the simple truth about Nagy is that he was a Communist true believer who became a loyal Hungarian. The more complex truth is that he was a Communist who became a patriot while remaining a Communist.

· 2 ·

On June 16, 1989—thirty-one years after they were hanged and buried at an unmarked grave—Imre Nagy and four other martyrs of the 1956 revolt were reburied at a ceremony that began at Heroes Square and was attended by some 250,000 people and watched on live television by millions in Hungary and elsewhere. The collapse of the Communist one-party state, which was a key demand in 1956, was imminent. I was there at a place reserved for dignitaries and the press, not because I was a dignitary or a reporter but because I went there in the company of Mark Palmer, the energetic and effective U.S. ambassador to Hungary, and the late Peter Jennings of ABC News and his wife, Kati Marton.

There was an air of unreality about the scene. The honor guard was made up of Hungary's Communist leaders, who were trying to claim Nagy as their own. The crowd, acquiescing in Communist rule for years, kept arriving at the square from all over the country, anticipating the brief moment of 1956 to turn into lasting reality. Members of the honor guard pretended not to recall how they had suppressed even the memory of 1956 for three long decades. The crowd did not want to remember years of quiet cooperation with Kádár's oppressive, postrevolutionary regime. And Ambassador Palmer, cheerful as ever, did not discuss how his superiors at the White House and the Department of State had warned him to show less enthusiasm for the immense changes taking place.

The speeches by distinguished survivors and a few emerging opposition leaders were mercifully brief. "How could you [Hungarians] live without freedom for thirty-three years?" asked Imre Mécs, a university student in 1956 who spent years on death row.[1] The young Viktor Or-

---

[1] *Magyar Nemzet,* June 17, 1989.

bán, who became Hungary's prime minister in less than a decade, shattered the façade of camaraderie between the old regime and its critics: "We cannot understand," he said, "that those who were eager to slander the Revolution and its prime minister have suddenly changed into great supporters of Imre Nagy. Nor can we understand that the party leaders, who made us study from books which falsified the Revolution, now rush to touch the coffins as they were charms of good luck."[2] Paradoxically, Orbán, then a fiery anticommunist and deeply pro-Western liberal, changed his spots and became a fiery anticommunist nationalist in a few years.

Although neither at Heroes Square nor in the years that have passed since have Hungarians fully come to terms with the unsettled legacy of 1956, the mood at the square was surely encouraging, even inspiring. The people, having taken pride in living in what was widely called the "best barrack in the Communist camp" and enjoying the meager freedoms granted to them by Kádár's semiauthoritarian regime, suddenly appear to have recovered the long-suppressed memories of real freedom in 1956. Did they finally stand tall, or did it only seem that way? More than a single teardrop rolled down my face. For the second time in my life, I experienced history in the making.

■ 3 ■

For several years, I studied tens of thousands of pages of documents in various archives in Budapest, Moscow, as well as in the Washington area; visited the cells where the prisoners of 1956 were kept; obtained a copy of the film made of the last phony trial of Imre Nagy and his associates; and, like a detective, pursued and interviewed more than a hundred participants, including surviving victims, members of the Hungarian Politburo then and later, several police officers, and even a couple of informers. I have mentioned or described a few of these encounters in this book, though I have relegated them to footnotes; I have integrated other conversations into the narrative.

The single most memorable and by far the most contentious interview I had, lasting some forty hours altogether, was in 1991 with Gen-

---

[2] *New York Times,* June 17, 1989.

eral Sándor Rajnai of the Hungarian secret police. In 1957, Rajnai had taken possession of Nagy and his fellow exiles outside Bucharest, brought them to Budapest in handcuffs and with welders' goggles over their eyes, supervised their interrogations, maintained liaison with the KGB's local "advisers," and wrote the script on which the charges were based. He was the playwright and the stage manager of the last bloody show trial in the history of the Soviet bloc.

A mixture of lies, evasions, and an occasional insight, Rajnai's stories seldom conformed to facts I knew. He told me he had come to regret the harsh sentences, but what was he supposed to have done? As far as he knew, for example, the judge handed down the sentences on his own. *This was untrue. Rajnai prepared the script. Kádár and his Politburo, after consultation with Nikita Khrushchev and the Soviet Politburo, decided who would live and who would die.* Did he know why some of the co-defendants received harsher sentences than others? No, he did not. *Inconceivable. Imre Nagy, General Pál Maléter, and Miklós Gimes were sentenced to death; the police chief, Sándor Kopácsi, was sentenced to life imprisonment; Zoltán Tildy, Ferenc Donáth, Ferenc Jánosi, and Miklós Vásárhelyi received sentences ranging from twelve to five years. Separated from his comrades, József Szilágyi was also sentenced to death, while Géza Losonczy, who did not get proper medical and psychological attention in jail, was "allowed" to die. Rajnai was intimately involved with every aspect of the trial.* What role did he play then? He said he only supervised the investigation at the beginning, through August 1957. He did not attend the trial and did not even know it was being held until it was over. *Untrue. He was present at the phony trial and watched the grim proceedings.* Who was there from the higher-ups? No one he knew. *Untrue. Several officials from the secret police and the Ministry of Justice listened to the proceedings in a secret hideaway near the courtroom. Rajnai was one of two trusted police officials allowed in there to visit with their bosses. Among other relevant documents, I found the caterer's invoice in a Hungarian archive.* Who gave him his instructions? He knew his job and knew what to do. He reported to the deputy minister of internal affairs. *Partly true. Circumstantial evidence strongly suggests that he was also the liaison between the Hungarian masterminds of the trial and the Soviet secret police.*

To get under Rajnai's skin, I said at our next-to-last encounter that his answers reminded me of the Nazis' defense; they did not accept any responsibility for what they had done either. My wife, who was present at this last interview held at the outskirts of Budapest at Rajnai's villa, was even more direct. She reminded Rajnai how lucky he was that the new, postcommunist Hungarian authorities decided not to treat him and his likes as war criminals. Our harsh, confrontational approach did not do the trick; his face turning red, Rajnai deeply resented the comparison with the Nazis and did not tell me more than he had set out to tell. In fact, in all the conversations we had, he told me little of substance I did not already know from the documents and other interviews. As we walked to the bus stop to return to Budapest, my wife wondered if I was wasting my time. I did not think so. His obvious need to talk to me so many times and at such length, together with all the details he did recount, offered revealing insights into the mentality of this calm, well-educated, articulate, even sophisticated, and yet ultimately evil man. By the time we met, he was experiencing a serious inner conflict, wavering from one day to the next between defiant self-justification and repentance. He was eager to talk but he was equally reluctant to tell what he knew. He once related what he felt about Nagy not to me but to the notorious Markus "Mischa" Wolf, East Germany's onetime spymaster: "'Mischa,' Rajnai said, according to Wolf, 'that sort of thing must never happen again.'"[3]

In a letter I received from Rajnai in 1993, a couple of years after our last interview, he asked for my help to obtain an American visa. He had no greater desire, he wrote, than to visit his daughter who lived in the United States. Because of the forty or so hours he had spent with me, and because in America I thought I might tempt him to tell me more, it occurred to me that I should try to help. I did not. I owed that much to the memory of his victims—the brave heroes of 1956 and of Imre Nagy, in particular.

· 4 ·

Why Nagy and several of his associates were sentenced to death and who decided who will live and who will die are intriguing and impor-

---

[3] Markus Wolf, *Man without a Face: The Autobiography of Communism's Greatest Spymaster* (New York: Times Books–Random House, 1997), 85.

tant questions that can now be answered. The answer is that in the summer of 1957 the focus of decisionmaking shifted from Moscow to Budapest and in Budapest to János Kádár. In the end, it was Kádár rather than the Soviet leadership that carried the case—with fanatic if methodical tenacity—to its ultimate finale.

The archives contain plenty of information about decisionmaking in Budapest and Moscow. From November 1956 through June 1958, someone, somewhere, discussed the Nagy case almost every day, some days for hours and in different settings. The minutes, reports, and memoranda are extensive and detailed, showing what was said and when, and who met whom and where. The names of the select few involved in the secret preparations, consultations, and decisions—as well as the interrogations of the defendants—were neither omitted nor erased. What emerges from the documents about the rationale for harsh punishment echoes public statements made by Soviet and Hungarian leaders: Nagy had "paved the way" to the counterrevolution, allowed innocent Communists and workers to be killed, betrayed the people's democracy, and so on. The wielders of power in Moscow and Budapest alike considered Nagy a traitor and an enemy who had caused irreparable harm to Hungary, the Soviet bloc, and indeed the "cause of socialism." Accordingly, they wanted the sentences to reflect the serious crimes committed, and to set an example so that no one would be tempted to follow Nagy's independent path.

The arguments advanced both publicly and behind closed doors for making the Nagy group pay for its alleged crimes revealed an interest in and a commitment to protecting the party's monopoly of power. Among many others things, he was held responsible for the killing of Communists on Republic Square on October 30. What is missing in the documents is the answer to a subjective question: What personal motives prompted some of the Hungarian or Soviet leaders to make the judgments and reach the conclusions they did? Also missing is a satisfactory answer to a factual question: If Nagy's alleged crimes were as heinous as claimed, why was the trial postponed several times and why was it held only in mid-1958?

The question of repeated delays—why it took a year and a half to try Nagy and only then "set an example"—matters because political circumstances in the immediate aftermath of the revolution were so very different from those prevailing in mid-1958. In December 1956 or January 1957, Hungary was most unstable. Some of the worker's councils were still active; writers circulated letters of protest; Western embassies were bombarded with urgent requests for action against or condemnation of Kádár's puppet regime. Elsewhere in the Communist world, particularly in Poland, the situation remained tense, potentially volatile. Under the circumstances, the summary proceedings and courts-martial held at the time against hundreds of insurgents served a rational if ignoble purpose. They were meant to scare the population into submission. In fact, several small fry, accused of far lesser crimes than Nagy and his associates, were executed immediately after the Kádár regime's installation, and their punishment was widely publicized, to "set an example."[4] Meanwhile, although Nagy was being blamed for just about everything that had happened during the revolution, and a group of investigators began to set the proceedings against him in motion, he remained in an elegant Romanian resort under conditions of house arrest. Mainly because of Kádár's ambivalence at this time, the opportunity was missed to punish the so-called chief instigator of the 1956 revolution early on.

By sharp contrast, when Nagy was eventually tried and executed in June 1958, Hungary was quiet, the spirit of resistance spent. By then János Kádár had consolidated his authority. Władysław Gomułka, Nagy's counterpart in Poland, had trimmed his reformist sails and begun to repair to the Soviet fold. In the Soviet Union, Khrushchev was riding high, having defeated a year earlier his Stalinist opponents, the so-called antiparty group led by Molotov, Malenkov, and Kaganovich. The time when he was under great pressure to prove his tough credentials—during the Hungarian revolt and in the first half of 1957—had passed. Increasingly, this "Butcher of Budapest" was once again seen,

---

[4] In the aftermath of the Soviet intervention, Hungarian courts sentenced 229 individuals to death; the charge against half of them (51 percent) was participation in the armed rebellion. The next largest group (15 percent) was accused of taking part in the anticommunist, postrevolutionary resistance movement. Hungarian civilian and military courts operating between November 4, 1956, and April 1, 1958, handed out prison sentences to 14,378 individuals. There are no reliable figures on the number of people taken to the Soviet Union, but they appear to have been fewer than the thousands originally rumored. Data from Attila Szakolczai, *Az 1956-os forradalom és szabadságharc* [The 1956 revolution and freedom fight] (Budapest: 1956-os Intézet, 2001), 92–93.

and wanted to be seen, as an anti-Stalinist with whom the West could do business. By late 1957, he sought a summit meeting with the United States, expressing interest in reaching arms control accords and pursuing the general idea of "peaceful coexistence." Nagy was certainly not among his top priorities. While the Soviet press continued to attack Nagy and his "revisionist" sins, for Khrushchev the case had outlived the political usefulness it had once had.

Khrushchev's changing political circumstances account for Moscow's changing approach to Nagy. In the first half of 1957, the Soviet side, led by Molotov, took the initiative, pressing the deliberate and perhaps somewhat reluctant Kádár to speed up the process and bring it to closure. Marshal Voroshilov told Kádár at that time that if he was not ready for the task, they would consider returning the Stalinists in Soviet exile, including Mátyás Rákosi, to positions of power in Budapest. In the second half of 1957, however, Soviet interest in the Nagy affair began to fade. In August, contrary to the customs of the day, only midlevel Soviet officials received Béla Biszku, the Hungarian minister of internal affairs and one of Kádár's deputies, who flew secretly to Moscow. Biszku told Andropov, the former hard-line Soviet ambassador in Budapest who became a department head in the party hierarchy, and two other officials—Roman A. Rudenko, the chief Soviet procurator, and General Petr I. Ivashutin of the KGB—that preparations for the Nagy trial were complete and that his Politburo had considered "the most severe sentences" for seven of the eleven defendants: Nagy, Losonczy, Donáth, Gimes, General Maléter, Szilágyi, as well as General Béla Király in absentia. Sounding almost indifferent, the three Soviet officials dutifully reported the substance of their consultation with Biszku to their superiors on the Central Committee.[5]

---

[5] For the key documents in English, see two "letters" to the Soviet Communist Party's Central Committee, of which one, dated August 29, 1957, was cosigned by former ambassador to Hungary, Yuri Andropov, who was by then head of the Soviet party's department dealing with the bloc's Communist parties; Rudenko; and Ivashutin, the KGB's deputy head. The second document, dated August 29, 1957, was written by Andropov. Both documents—translated by Svetlana Savranskaya and Malcolm Byrne, respectively—appeared in *The 1956 Hungarian Revolution: A History in Documents*, ed. Csaba Békés, Malcolm Byrne, and János M. Rainer (Budapest: Central European Press, 2002), 539–42. These letters reflected the substance of conversations the three officials had just had with Béla Biszku, the Hungarian minister of internal affairs who supervised preparations for the forthcoming Nagy trial.

After mid-1957, the Hungarian tail began to wag the Soviet dog. It was now Kádár's turn to take the initiative and close the book on Nagy once and for all. Kádár had good political reason to do so. With renewed confidence, diehards in the party and especially in the secret police emerged from the woodwork to voice disapproval of his past and present conduct. For them, Kádár was "too soft." Nagy's interrogators told their prisoner, for example, that in time Kádár would also be behind bars. They recalled gleefully that only a few hours before Kádár had defected to Moscow on November 1, 1956, he had hailed the Hungarian people for "our glorious revolution." We know Kádár is not different from you, the prisoners were told.[6]

To neutralize his hard-line opponents who demanded more bloodletting, Kádár decided in August to let the trial begin in September. Staying in their cells with nothing to do, the defendants no longer had to reply to the same questions they had answered so many times. But the trial did not begin. Before it could get under way, Moscow—claiming it would prejudice the September debate of the "Hungarian Question" at the United Nations—requested a postponement. Kádár had to wait.[7] Then the Hungarian Politburo ordered the judicial authorities to start the proceedings once again. But when on February 5, 1958, the trial—held at the Fő utca (Main Street) Prison's courtroom in Buda in great secrecy behind closed doors—actually began, it ran for only one and a half days. As soon as the prosecution concluded its initial presentation, the trial was suddenly suspended—supposedly because of unspecified procedural problems but in fact because the Soviet Union had requested another postponement. This time, Moscow explained, the trial and the protests it would spark in Western capitals would strengthen the case of American hard-liners, such as Secretary of State John Foster Dulles, against a summit with the Soviet leadership—a farfetched if not altogether unbelievable proposition.[8] Told of the post-

---

[6] Interview with Lieutenant General József Szalma and Miklós Vásárhelyi.

[7] As late as December 1957, Khrushchev asked Kádár through Y. I. Gromov, the new Soviet ambassador to Hungary, what the Hungarians were planning to do with Nagy—"Is it going to be prison, reprimand, or what?" See Kádár's account of the conversation in Hungarian National Archive, 288. f. 5/69.

[8] In point of fact, the Soviet Politburo met that very day, on February 5, 1958, and discussed the trial of Nagy and his associates. The record of the meeting is brief but revealing: "1. On the trial of Imre Nagy. Khrushchev, Voroshilov, Mikoyan, Aristov, Kyrychenko. Adopt the proposals (show firmness and generosity). Do not record it in the protocol." The source of this meeting is "Protokol No. 138

ponement in the courtroom in front of the defendants, the presiding judge fell ill (or so he claimed); he promptly checked into a hospital and withdrew from the case. Kádár waited a few months but did not give up. In June, by then with Soviet support, a new, hanging judge brought the case of Imre Nagy and his associates to a bitter conclusion.

The punishment was so untimely and excessive, and it was so unusual if not unique in the post-Stalin era, that it cannot be explained simply by the damage that Nagy and his associates had supposedly done to the "cause of socialism." If Kádár could not let Nagy go, he did not have to order him hanged. But even if Nagy had to be sacrificed for reasons of high politics, what about Géza Losonczy, one of Nagy's two de facto deputies, who was driven to death in prison? What about Miklós Gimes, the editor, who supported the revolution only with his pen? What about General Maléter, who did not order his troops into battle against the invading Soviet Army? And what about József Szilágyi, Nagy's chief of staff and bodyguard, whose main crime was that he told his interrogators exactly what he thought of them and of Kádár, his old friend from the Communist underground?

Kádár, in consultation with a few Hungarian Politburo colleagues, guided the work of the prosecutors and the judges of the kangaroo court, and made all the decisions about the sentences. He had known the defendants long and well, not only the particularly defiant and tactlessly blunt Szilágyi. They had shared many common experiences. Surely he remembered the years he had spent in Rákosi's torture chambers as a political prisoner with his friend Géza Losonczy and his close personal friend Ferenc Donáth. Did he remember—and if he did, did it matter?—that the three of them were arrested by Rákosi's thugs the same day in May 1951 and freed by Imre Nagy, the man he was about to send to the gallows, the same day in July 1954? What combination of fear and hatred, envy, jealousy or feelings of inferiority, what sort of need for revenge for what his victims were and he would not or could not be, made him decide to sacrifice them for the "cause of socialism"?

Prezidiuma TsK KPSS: Zasedanie 5 fevralya 1958 g.," 5 Fe. 1958, in RGANI, F.3, Op. 12, D. 1008, L. 48. It does not take a brilliant Kremlinologist to figure out that by this time the Kremlin was far less interested in punishing Nagy than were Kádár and his Hungarian Politburo colleagues. In the spring, when Khrushchev's relationship with Yugoslavia's Tito worsened, the Kremlin gave Kádár the green light to punish Nagy—as a way of punishing Tito.

• 5 •

That the Nagy case kept haunting Kádár's life came into sharper focus in 1989 when, afflicted by a variety of physical ailments, he experienced a serious mental breakdown. On April 12, 1989, in effect coming out of retirement, and appearing unexpectedly at a Central Committee meeting, Kádár asked for the floor. To a stunned audience of his comrades aware of his condition, he delivered a long, convoluted, and indeed nonsensical monologue in which he kept referring to "a certain man," who was Imre Nagy. To the extent anyone could even begin to decipher the meaning of what he was trying to say, Kádár was particularly preoccupied with the deceitful pledge of safe conduct he had given that "certain man" in November 1956. For he had permitted Nagy, his family, and a bus full of associates and their families to leave the Yugoslav Embassy, where they had received political asylum, and go home—but in fact he had conspired with the Soviet secret police to have them all taken off the bus, arrested, and sent to Romanian house arrest. Clearly, the memory of treachery haunted him all his life.

Although many Hungarians and most Western politicians would come to appreciate Kádár, and his "goulash Communism" that commenced in the early 1960s, others could never forgive him for being a traitor in 1956 and a quisling for years thereafter.

On July 6, 1989, three weeks after Nagy, his nemesis, had been publicly exonerated and less than three months after addressing the Central Committee in a state of mental and physical disintegration, Kádár died on the very day the Hungarian Supreme Court began a televised hearing to acquit Imre Nagy and his fallen associates. As the Nagy hearing got under way, two pieces of paper from an unidentified source were passed around from hand to hand—one among the judges and another among members of the audience. Both had the same message:

KÁDÁR DIED, PASS IT ON

The judges were expressionless, the audience gasped. The news sparked no celebration in the courtroom, but it made for a moment of reflection. Who was this man who, having ruled Hungary with considerable skill since the 1960s, had sent his onetime comrades and friends to the gallows?

Only the initiated few knew that Kádár had fallen sick both physically and mentally since the issue of Nagy's exoneration arose the previous year. Even fewer knew that he was tortured by guilt that gave him no peace, that he was experiencing nightmares, that he was consumed by fear for his life, that he trusted only his wife. And almost no one knew then that as he expected to be arrested and killed, he asked his wife to pack a small suitcase for him that he then placed by the door near one of his house's exits, and on occasion he also went into hiding under the dining room table. Given his state of mind, did Kádár die of natural causes (as his doctors would testify) or commit suicide? Did he simply give up living just before—minutes before—Nagy's exoneration? Could it be that he wanted the news of his death and of Nagy's formal, judicial "rehabilitation" to coincide?

What happened that morning in the courtroom was the epilogue to a political drama worthy of Shakespeare's imagination, except that it was for real.

▪ 6 ▪

For the United States, the Soviet crackdown on Hungary was a shocking setback, and yet it offered an opportunity, too. Those who had expected the post-Stalin Kremlin to behave better were disappointed. Others used the occasion to make sure everyone understood how awful and devious Moscow was. Still others, perhaps compensating for Washington's passivity, reached out to the refugees, of whom close to 50,000 came to the America and received heartfelt, generous support from government agencies and private organizations alike. I benefited greatly from the kindness of many Americans, notably at Indiana University, where I began to learn English in 1957 and stayed on to receive my undergraduate and graduate degrees. The second best decision I have ever made was when I chose to settle in America. (My best choice was when I married Toby.)

In the immediate aftermath of the Hungarian crisis, there was a good deal of Monday morning quarterbacking in the United States. The prominent and very-well-connected Kremlinologist, Richard Lowenthal, argued forcefully in *The New Republic* that the West could have offered to make the loss of the satellite empire strategically tolerable for Russia by matching a Soviet withdrawal from Eastern Europe with an American withdrawal from Western Europe. The old Soviet proposal for a simultaneous dissolution of the Warsaw and Atlantic Pacts has never been acceptable to the West, basically because the Soviet control of Eastern Europe does not depend on the Warsaw Pact but on the Communist regimes, and because while Eastern Europe remains under Soviet control, Western Europe cannot defend itself by its own strength. But in a situation where Soviet Communist control of Eastern Europe was actually crumbling, the offer of an American withdrawal [from Western Europe] on condition of full freedom for Eastern Europe would have transformed the situation. . . . It would have added to the calculations of the Soviet leaders the one consideration which might have induced them to give in.[9]

Writing in *The New Leader*,[10] Frank A. Lindsay, the former Central Intelligence Agency official who in the early 1950s resigned his post because he saw no prospects for successful operations in Eastern Europe, offered a detailed list of policy measures by the United States and the United Nations, which would have combined demonstration of U.S. strategic superiority with the dispatch of a UN delegation to Budapest. Lindsay maintained that there was a window of opportunity after November 1, when Nagy declared Hungary's neutrality, renounced the Warsaw Pact, and asked Secretary General Dag Hammarskjold for UN protection. The key assumption behind Lindsay's proposal was the Kremlin's reluctance to crush Hungary while a representative UN observer team was on the scene. That, certainly, was a possibility in view of what we now know about the debates taking place in the Soviet Politburo.

Going beyond the specific case of Hungary toward shaping a new policy toward Eastern Europe, Zbigniew Brzezinski, then a professor at Columbia, and William E. Griffith, the former Radio Free Europe policy director, coauthored an article in *Foreign Affairs* in 1961. Drawing the lessons of the Hungarian crisis, the article was based on the recognition that the "liberation" of Eastern Europe in the foreseeable future was a pipedream and therefore the United States should pursue only limited objectives. The objectives they outlined had to do with stimu-

---

[9] Richard Lowenthal, "Hungary—Were We Helpless? *New Republic*, November 26, 1956.

[10] Franklin A. Lindsay, "What Might Have Happened in Hungary," *The New Leader*, December 24–31, 1956.

lating diversity in the Communist world (*note:* not democracy but diversity); encouraging a greater measure of independence from Moscow (*note:* not independence but a greater measure of it); and creating a neutral, Finnish-like belt of states that would be free domestically without joining Western alliances (*note:* free internally but not in foreign affairs). Urging the adoption of a course between what was desirable and what was possible, the authors proposed a series of specific steps for the United States to take—such as liberalized trade agreements and the expansion of educational exchanges—as a way to lure the satellites into making genuine if limited concessions over a period of many years.[11]

As the Kennedy administration began to translate these and similar ideas into policy, the U.S. approach to Eastern Europe became increasingly pragmatic, replacing the fundamentalist rhetoric of liberation of the 1950s. Because of the Hungarian tragedy, Washington reached the conclusion that foreign policy required not only "inspiring" words but also wisdom and finesse. Stressing evolutionary change rather than a quick victory, the United States embraced a sensible set of modest policies that would come to fruition—and help promote genuine independence—in the years ahead. What a pity that in 1956 so many Hungarians and others in the Communist orbit began to doubt America's credibility, and suffered for their illusions, before Washington understood what it could do, and what it could not, to effect change in Central and Eastern Europe.

· **7** ·

This book was not meant to inspire, it was meant to explain; it is a book of historical analysis, not a political or religious sermon. Whenever possible, I have used pastel shades rather than poster colors. My intention has not been to celebrate bravery or cry out against injustice, but to clarify how much more could have been achieved if valor had been coupled with wisdom and circumspection. Nor have I tried to endow the main actors of the Hungarian drama with qualities they did not have. Imre Nagy, for example, in 1956 became a man of integrity—and he

---

[11] Zbigniew Brzezinski and William E. Griffith, "Peaceful Engagement in Eastern Europe," *Foreign Affairs* 39, no. 4 (1961): 642–54.

was a genuine patriot, too—but he was not an effective leader. Finally, I have not repeated the conventional wisdom about how the Hungarians turned into ultimate winners in 1989, and I have avoided judgments about "moral victory." This was not meant to deny that in addition to Gorbachev and Reagan, Pope John Paul II and Poland's Solidarity, the heroes of 1956 and those who upheld its legacy did not make a contribution to Hungary's eventual liberation. I believe they did.

In the final analysis, sober-minded realism about the past cannot and does not mean abandonment of hope for justice and a fair deal. It goes without saying that neither Americans nor Hungarian can be, or should be, deprived of wanting to improve their lot and indeed to do some good. What they needed in 1956, and what the world needs now, is the ability to steer prudently between that which is desirable and that which is possible—the ability to be idealists without illusions.

Acknowledgments

I am pleased to acknowledge my gratitude to those who helped me carry out this project. It began in 1991 as an inquiry into the life and death of Imre Nagy, with some emphasis on his kidnapping after the Soviet intervention, his interrogations by Hungarian political police officers, and his 1958 trials and execution. Although *Failed Illusions* is, of course, a more comprehensive study that deals with Nagy as well as with the Hungarian insurgents, with Soviet decisionmaking, and with the policies of the United States, it could not have been written without the generous initial support I received from the Ford Foundation and the Smith Richardson Foundation in the early 1990s. It allowed me to work in newly opened Hungarian and—to the extent I was allowed— Russian archives. Paul Balaran, then of the Ford Foundation, was a particularly knowledgeable and supportive presence. I appreciate his confidence and patience.

This book would not have been written except for Jim Hershberg's intellectual and even emotional encouragement. No one could ask for a better editor who could, and did, combine enthusiastic support and deep interest with rigorous standards. Jim, the ebullient (as I call him) and my unofficial chapter-by-chapter reader, Mark Kramer, both offered advice, criticism, and much-appreciated praise. I am awed by their knowledge of Cold War history in general and the circumstances of 1956 in particular. At the publisher's request, Malcolm Byrne evaluated the book; his generous praise, given his immense knowledge of 1956, was, I confess, music to my ears. When the manuscript was almost finished, several friends and colleagues read it and gave me both intellectual nourishment and helpful criticism; they included Ivan Berend, Zbigniew Brzezinski, Woodrow Kuhns, Tom Lantos, and Fred Starr. My wife, Toby Gati, also read the book at that time and offered very useful, line-by-line suggestions for improvement. She also took on additional family responsibilities during the last year or two, which given her own busy schedule was and is much appreciated. This book is dedicated to her.

When I wrote the first, second, and third drafts of chapter 1, I needed more feedback than usual about the wisdom of combining a traditional introduction with personal recollections about what I had experienced as a young man in 1956. Mainly for this reason, I asked another group of friends, experts, and colleagues to review that chapter; I am grateful for the good advice I received from Frank Gado, Miklós Haraszti, John Lukacs, Attila Pók, Edit Pór, Bob Sharlet, and Steve Szabo. In November 2004, as I was in the process of writing one of my many drafts of that chapter, I presented its main propositions and my main findings at a seminar in Budapest at the Institute for the Study of the 1956 Hungarian Revolution. The session was organized by János Rainer and Csaba Békés; participants included the cream of Hungarian scholars devoted to the study of 1956, such as Magdolna Baráth, László Eörsi, János Kenedi, György Litván, Zoltán Ripp, and Éva Standeisky. I felt honored to be invited to this remarkable institution of learning; I greatly benefited from the participants' probing questions and helpful advice.

At Johns Hopkins University's Paul H. Nitze School of Advanced International Studies, where I teach in the European Studies Program, I have had the good fortune of getting considerable help from a number of gifted and diligent graduate research assistants. They included in recent years Allison McCoy, who spent several weekends checking out U.S. military intelligence files at the National Archives for me; and Ryan Miller, who during the last phase of putting together the manuscript was always on call and always available. Their work, and mine, was made easier by the ever-cheerful and efficient cooperation of Nancy Tobin, the European Studies Program's able coordinator.

Finally, I would like to thank Ferenc Glatz and Tibor Zinner for helping me make contact and conduct interviews with former officials who might not have talked to me otherwise. Those I interviewed in Budapest who were associated, in one way or another, with the Kádár regime included György Aczél, László Bencze, Miklós Béres, Béla Biszku, József Bognár, Éva Erlich, Jenő Fock, Sándor Gáspár, Antal Gyenes, József Horváth, Gyula Kállai, József Köböl, Rezső Nyers, Mrs. Zoltán Radó, Sándor Rajnai, Ágnes Ságvári, József Szalma, and Gyula Thürmer. I also spoke with my childhood friend, Vilmos Sós, about the activities of his father, the Budapest police chief György Sós. From the other side of the barricades, I had the pleasure of interviewing Ferenc Donáth, Éva Bozóki (Mrs. Ferenc Donáth), László Donáth, Árpád Göncz, Alíz Halda, Mária Haraszti (Mrs. Géza Losonczy), Béla Király, Sándor Kopácsi, Mrs. Pál Maléter, Éva (Mrs. Miklós) Molnár, Miklós Molnár, Mrs. József Szilágyi, Júlia Szilágyi, Szilárd Ujhelyi, Miklós Vásárhelyi, and Erzsébet Vészi (Erzsébet Nagy). In Moscow, where it was much more difficult to have candid conversation about 1956, I was able to conduct several interviews on the record with Valerii Musatov and Aleksandr Yakovlev, and talked about 1956 with Vladimir Lukin and Andrey Kozyrev. In the United States, I benefited from helpful conversations with Avis Bohlen, Robert Gabor, William E. Griffith, A. Ross Johnson, Geza Katona, Frank Lindsay, James McCargar, and Ellis Wisner.

It goes without saying that I could not have written this book without all the information, insights, and especially "the feel" about 1956 that I have gained from those who were willing to talk to me, and I am deeply indebted to all of them. However, the responsibility for all the facts and conclusions presented in this book is mine alone.

Washington, D.C.
May 2006

Selected Bibliography

Archives

Budapest

Archive of the Political Science Institute.
Archive of the Ministry of Internal Affairs (State Security).
Archive of the Hungarian Supreme Court.
Hungarian National Archive.
Institute for the Study of the 1956 Hungarian Revolution.
New Hungarian Central Archive.

Moscow

Archive of the Russian Foreign Ministry.
Archive of Russian State Security (KGB).

Washington and Vicinity

Center for the Study of Intelligence (CIA).
National Archives (Washington and Maryland).
National Security Archive (George Washington University).

Books

Aczél, Tamás, and Tibor Méray. *The Revolt of the Mind: A Case History of Intellectual Resistance behind the Iron Curtain.* New York: Praeger, 1959.
Andrew, Christopher. *For the President's Eyes Only: Secret Intelligence and the American Presidency from Washington to Bush.* New York: HarperCollins, 1995.

Andrew, Christopher, and Oleg Gordievsky. *KGB: The Inside Story of Its Operations from Lenin to Gorbachev.* New York: HarperCollins, 1990.

Andrew, Christopher, and Vasili Mitrokhin. *The Sword and the Shield: The Mitrokhin Archive and the Secret History of the KGB.* New York: Basic Books, 1999.

Applebaum, Anne. *Gulag: A History.* New York: Doubleday, 2003.

Azrael, Jeremy R. *The KGB in Kremlin Politics.* Los Angeles: RAND and University of California, Los Angeles, 1989.

Bain, Leslie B. *The Reluctant Satellites: An Eyewitness Report on East Europe and the Hungarian Revolution.* New York: Macmillan, 1960.

Balogh, Sándor, ed. *Nehéz esztendők krónikája 1949–1953: Dokumentumok* [Chronicle of difficult years 1949–1953: Documents]. Budapest: Gondolat, 1986.

Baráth, Magdolna, ed. *Szovjet nagyköveti iratok Magyarországról 1953–1956: Kiszeljov és Andropov titkos jelentései* [Soviet ambassadors' documents about Hungary 1953–1956: Kiselyov's and Andropov's secret reports]. Budapest: Napvilág Kiadó, 2002.

Barron, John. *KGB: The Secret Work of Soviet Secret Agents.* London: Hodder and Stoughton, 1974.

Becker, Theodore L., ed. *Political Trials.* Indianapolis: Bobbs-Merrill, 1971.

Békés, Csaba. *Európából Európába: Magyarország a konfliktusok kereszttüzében* [From Europe to Europe: Hungary in the crossfire of conflicts]. Budapest: Gondolat, 2004.

———. *The 1956 Hungarian Revolution and World Politics.* Cold War International History Project Working Paper 16. Washington, D.C.: Woodrow Wilson International Center for Scholars, 1996.

———. *Az 1956-os magyar forradalom a világpolitikában* [The 1956 Hungarian revolution in world politics]. Budapest: 1956-os Intézet, 1996.

Békés, Csaba, Malcolm Byrne, János M. Rainer, eds. *The 1956 Hungarian Revolution: A History in Documents.* Budapest: Central European University Press, 2002.

Beszélő Összkiadás [The Complete Edition of Beszélő]. Budapest: A-B Beszélő Kiadó, 1992.

Bethell, Nicholas. *Betrayed.* New York: Times Books, 1984.

Bibó, István. *Democracy, Revolution, Self-Determination (Selected Essays),* ed. Károly Nagy. New York: Columbia University Press, 1991.

Bohlen, Charles E. *Witness to History, 1929–1969.* New York: W. W. Norton, 1973.

Borbándi, Gyula. *Magyarok az Angol Kertben: A Szabad Európa Rádió története* [Hungarians at the English Garden: A history of Radio Free Europe]. Budapest: Európa, 1996.

Borhi, László. *Hungary in the Cold War 1945–1956.* Budapest: Central European Press, 2004.

Bowie, Robert R. *Suez 1956: International Crisis and the Role of Law.* London: Oxford University Press, 1974.

Brown, J. F. *Relations between the Soviet Union and Its Eastern European Allies: A Survey.* Santa Monica, Calif.: RAND, 1975.

Brzezinski, Zbigniew. *The Soviet Bloc: Unity and Conflict,* rev. ed. New York: Praeger, 1961.

Burke, Michael. *Outrageous Good Fortune.* Boston: Little, Brown, 1984.

Carson, William R. *The Armies of Ignorance: The Rise of the American Intelligence Empire.* New York: Dial Press, 1977.

Chester, Eric Thomas. *Covert Network: Progressives, the International Rescue Committee and the CIA.* Armonk, N.Y.: M. E. Sharpe, 1995.

Colby, William, and Peter Forbath. *Honorable Men: My Life at the CIA.* New York: Simon & Schuster, 1978.

Conquest, R. *Power and Policy in the USSR: The Study of Soviet Dynastics.* London: Macmillan, 1962.

Cookridge, E. H. *Gehlen: Spy of the Century.* New York: Pyramid Books, 1971.

Council on Foreign Relations. *Documents on American Foreign Relations, 1956.* New York: Harper, 1957.

Dallin, Alexander, Fridrikh Igorevich Firsov, and Vadim A. Staklo, eds. *Dimitrov and Stalin, 1934–1943: Letters from the Soviet Archives.* Annals of Communism Series. New Haven, Conn.: Yale University Press, 2000.

De Silva, Peer. *Sub Rosa: The CIA and the Uses of Intelligence.* New York: Times Books, 1978.

Documents on International Affairs, 1955. London: Oxford University Press, 1958.

Donáth, Ferenc. *A Márciusi Fronttól Monorig: Tanulmányok, vázlatok, emlékezések* [From the March Front to Monor: Studies, outlines, recollections]. Budapest: Századvég Kiadó, 1992.

Dorril, Stephen. *MI6: Inside the Covert World of Her Majesty's Secret Intelligence Service.* New York: Simon & Schuster / Touchstone, 2002.

Eisenhower, Dwight D. *Waging Peace.* New York: Doubleday, 1964.

Eörsi, László. *A Corvinisták 1956: A VIII. kerület fegyveres csoportjai* [The Corvinites 1956: Militant groups in the 8th district]. Budapest: 1956-os Intézet, 2001.

————. *Mítoszok helyett, 1956* [Instead of myths, 1956]. Budapest; Noran, 2003.

————. *A Széna tériek 1956* [The Széna Square (fighters) 1956]. Budapest: 1956-os Intézet and Állambiztonsági Szolgálatok Történeti Levéltára, n.d.

Fact-Finding Commission. *Törvénytelen szocializmus* [Lawless socialism]. Budapest: Zrinyi Kiadó/Új Magyarország, 1991.

Fazekas, György. *Forró ősz Budapesten: Életinterjú* [Hot autumn in Budapest: Memoir interview]. Budapest; Magyar Hirlap, 1989.

Fehérváry, István. *Börtönvilág Magyarországon* [The world of prisons in Hungary]. Center Square, Pa.: Alpha Publications, 1978.

Felix, Christopher. *A Short Course in the Secret War.* New York: Dell, 1963.

Fulbright, J. W. *The Arrogance of Power.* New York: Vintage Books, 1967.

Gábor, Róbert. *Az igazi szociáldemokrácia: Küzdelem a fasizmus és a kommunizmus ellen, 1944–1948* [Genuine social democracy: Struggle against fascism and communism, 1944–1948]. Budapest: Századvég, 1998.

Gál, Éva, András B. Hegedüs, György Litván, and János M. Rainer, eds. *A "Jelcin Dosszié": Szovjet dokumentumok 1956-ról* [The "Yeltsin Dossier": Soviet Documents about 1956], trans. from Russian into Hungarian by Éva Gál, Ágota N. Goller, and Erna Páll. Budapest: Századvég Kiadó-56-os Intézet, 1993.

Gati, Charles. *Hungary and the Soviet Bloc.* Durham, N.C.: Duke University Press, 1986.

Granville, Johanna C. *The First Domino: International Decision Making during the Hungarian Crisis of 1956.* College Station: Texas A&M University Press, 2004.

Grose, Peter. *Gentleman Spy: The Life of Allen Dulles.* Boston: Houghton Mifflin / Richard Todd, 1994.

———. *Operation Rollback: America's Secret War behind the Iron Curtain.* Boston: Houghton Mifflin, 2000.

Gyurgyák, János. *A zsidókérdés Magyarországon: Politikai eszmetörténet* [The Jewish Question in Hungary: History of political thought]. Budapest: Osiris Kiadó, 2001.

Gyurkó, László. *A bakancsos forradalom* [roughly: Revolution in Worn Boots]. Budapest: Kossuth, 2001.

Halda, Aliz. *Magánügy* [Private Matter]. Budapest: Noran, 2002.

Hay, Julius. *Born 1900: Memoirs.* La Salle, Ill.: Library Press, 1975.

Hazard, Elizabeth W. *Cold War Crucible.* Boulder, Colo.: East European Monographs, 1996.

Hegedüs, András. *Élet egy eszme árnyékában* [Life in the shadow of an ideal]. Vienna: Zoltán Zsille, 1985.

———. *A történelem és a hatalom igézetében: Életrajzi elemzések* [Spellbound by history and power: Autobiographical assessments]. Budapest: Kossuth, 1988.

Hershberg, James G. *James B. Conant: Harvard to Hiroshima and the Making of the Nuclear Age.* New York: Alfred A. Knopf, 1993.

Ioanid, Ileana, ed. *Nagy Imre, Însemnāri de la Snagov: Corespondenþā, rapoarte, convorbiri* [Imre Nagy, Notes from Snagov: Correspondence, reports, conversations]. Bucharest: Polirom, 2004.

Iratok az igazságszolgáltatás történetéhez [Documents on the history of the administration of justice]. Budapest: Közgazdasági és Jogi Könyvkiadó, 1993.

Irving, David. *Uprising!* London: Hodder and Stoughton, 1981.

Israelyan, Viktor. *On the Battlefields of the Cold War: A Soviet Ambassador's Confession.* University Park: Pennsylvania State University Press, 2003.

Izsák, Lajos, and Miklós Kun, eds. *Moszkvának jelentjük—Titkos dokumentumok 1944–1948* [Reporting to Moscow—Secret documents 1944–1948]. Budapest: Századvég, 1994.

Javorniczky, István. *Eljő az a nagy, szép idő* [Beautiful times are still ahead]. Budapest: A Héttorony Könyvkiadó, n.d. but c. 1991.

Kaplain, Karel. *Report on the Murder of the General Secretary.* Columbus: Ohio State University Press, 1990.

Kennan, George F. *Memoirs, 1925–1950.* Boston: Atlantic–Little, Brown, 1967.

Kopacsi, Sandor. *In the Name of the Working Class: The Inside Story of the Hungarian Revolution.* New York: Grove Press, 1987.

Kővágó, József. *You Are All Alone.* New York: Praeger, 1959.

Kövér, György. *Losonczy Géza 1917–1957* [Géza Losonczy 1917–1957]. Budapest: 1956-os Intézet, 1998.

Kovrig, Bennett. *Communism in Hungary: From Kun to Kádár.* Stanford, Calif.: Hoover Institution Press, 1979.

———. *The Myth of Liberation: East-Central Europe in U.S. Diplomacy and Politics since 1941.* Baltimore: Johns Hopkins University Press, 1973.

————. *Of Walls and Bridges: The United States & Eastern Europe* (New York: New York University Press / Twentieth Century Fund, 1991.

Kryuchkov, Vladimir. *Lichnoye delo* [Private case]. Moscow: Olimp-Akt, 1996.

Lewis, Flora. *A Case History of Hope.* Garden City, N.Y.: Doubleday, 1958.

Lippmann, Walter. *U.S Foreign Policy: Shield of the Republic.* Boston: Little, Brown, 1943.

Litván, György. *The Hungarian Revolution of 1956: Reform, Revolt and Repression 1953–1963.* London: Longman, 1996.

Loftus, John. *The Belarus Secret.* New York: Alfred A. Knopf, 1982.

Lukacs, John. *A Thread of Years.* New Haven, Conn.: Yale University Press, 1998.

Lundestad, Geir. *The American Non-Policy towards Eastern Europe 1943–1947.* New York: Humanities Press, 1975.

Marshall, Charles Burton. *The Exercise of Sovereignty: Papers on Foreign Policy.* Baltimore: Johns Hopkins University Press, 1965.

————. *The Limits of Foreign Policy.* New York: Henry Holt, 1954.

Mastny, Vojtech. *Russia's Road to the Cold War.* New York: Columbia University Press, 1979.

Marchio, Jim. *Rhetoric and Reality: The Eisenhower Administration and Unrest in Eastern Europe, 1953–1959.* Washington, D.C.: American University Press, 1990.

Marton, Endre. *The Forbidden Sky.* Boston: Little, Brown, 1971.

Matthews, John P. C. *Tinderbox: East-Central Europe in the Spring, Summer, and Early Fall of 1956.* Tucson: Fenestra Books, 2003.

McCargar, James. *A Short Course in the Secret War.* New York: Dell, 1988.

Méray, Tibor. *Thirteen Days That Shook the Kremlin: Imre Nagy and the Hungarian Revolution.* New York: Praeger, 1959.

Meyer, Cord. *Facing Reality: From World Federalism to the CIA.* New York: Harper & Row, 1980.

Mićunović, Veljko. *Moscow Diary.* Garden City, N.Y.: Doubleday, 1980.

Mindszenty, Josef Cardinal. *Memoirs.* New York: Macmillan, 1974.

Miscamble, Wilson D. *George F. Kennan and the Making of American Foreign Policy, 1947–1950.* Princeton, N.J.: Princeton University Press, 1992.

Mitrovich, Gregory. *Undermining the Kremlin: America's Strategy to Subvert the Soviet Bloc, 1947–1956.* Ithaca, N.Y.: Cornell University Press, 2000.

Morgenthau, Hans. *In Defense of the National Interest.* New York: Alfred A. Knopf, 1951.

Nagy, Imre. *On Communism: In Defense of the New Course.* New York: Praeger, 1957.

————. *Viharos emberöltő, 1896–195 . . . ?* [Stormy generation, 1896–195 . . . ?]. Budapest: Nagy Imre Alapítvány, 2002.

Ostermann, Christian F., ed. *Uprising in East Germany 1953: The Cold War, the German Question, and the First Major Upheaval behind the Iron Curtain.* Budapest: Central European University Press, 2001.

Pongrátz, Gergely. *Corvin köz 1956* [Corvin passage1956]. Chicago: author's edition, 1982. (Reprinted in Budapest in 1985, samizdat; 1989; and 1992.)

Puddington, Arch. *Broadcasting Freedom: The Cold War Triumph of Radio Free Europe and Radio Liberty.* Lexington: University Press of Kentucky, 2000.

Prados, John. *Presidents' Secret Wars: CIA and Pentagon Covert Operations from World War II through Iranscram.* New York: Quill / William Morrow, 1986.

Radzinsky, Edvard. *The Last Tsar: The Life and Death of Nicholas II.* New York: Doubleday, 1992.

Rainer, János M. *Nagy Imre: Politikai életrajz* [Imre Nagy: Political biography], 2 vols. Budapest: 1956-os Intézet, 1996.

Rákosi, Mátyás. *Visszaemlékezések 1940–1956* [Memoirs 1940–1956], vols. 1–2. Budapest: Napvilág, 1997.

Révész, Sándor. *Egyetlen élet: Gimes Miklós története* [Unique life: The story of Miklós Gimes]. Budapest: 1956-os Intézet and Sík Kiadó, 1999.

Richardson, John H. *My Father the Spy: An Investigative Memoir.* New York: Harper-Collins, 2005.

Rocca, Raymond G., and John J. Dziak. *Bibliography on Soviet Intelligence and Security Services.* Boulder, Colo.: Westview Press, 1985.

Romsics, Ignác. *Magyarország története a XX. században* [Hungary's history in the 20th century]. Budapest: Osiris, 1999.

———, ed. *Wartime American Plans for a New Hungary: Documents from the U.S. Department of State, 1942–1944.* New York: Columbia University Press, 1992.

Rositzke, Harry. *The KGB: The Eyes of Russia.* London: Sidgwick & Jackson, 1981.

Saunders, Frances Stoner. *The Cultural Cold War: The CIA and the World of Arts and Letters.* New York: New Press, 1999.

Sawatsky, John. *For Services Rendered.* Toronto: Penguin Books, 1982.

Sayer, Ian, and Douglas Botting. *America's Secret Army: The Untold Story of the Counter Intelligence Corps.* New York: Franklin Watts, 1989.

Sereda, Vyacheslav, and Jámos M. Rainer, eds. *Döntés a Kremlben, 1956: A szovjet pártelnökség vitái Magyarországról* [Decision in the Kremlin, 1956: The Soviet Politburo's debates about Hungary]. Budapest: 1956-os Intézet, 1996.

Sereda, Vyacheslav, and Aleksandr Stikhalin, eds. *Hiányzó lapok 1956 történetéből: Dokumentumok a volt SZKP KB levéltárából* [Missing pages from the history of 1956: Documents from the former CPSU Central Committee's archive]. Budapest: Zenit, 1993.

Simpson, Christopher. *Blowback: The First Full Account of America's Recruitment of Nazis, and Its Disastrous Effect on Our Domestic and Foreign Policy.* New York: Weidenfeld & Nicholson, 1988.

Sovyetskiy Soyuz I Vengerskiy krizis—1956 goda: Dokumenti [The Soviet Union and the Hungarian crisis in 1956: Documents]. Moscow: Rosspen, 1998.

Spulber, Nicolas. *The Economics of Communist Eastern Europe.* Cambridge, Mass.: MIT Press, 1957.

Sudoplatov, Pavel, and Anatoli Sudoplatov, with Jerrold and Leona Schecter. *Special Tasks: The Memoirs of an Unwanted Witness—A Soviet Spymaster.* Boston: Little, Brown, 1994.

Sulzberger, C. L. *The Last of the Giants.* New York: Macmillan, 1970.

Szigethy, András. *Kegyelem* [Mercy], Budapest: published by author, n.d.

Taubman, William. *Khrushchev: The Man and His Era.* New York: W. W. Norton, 2003.

Thomas, Evan. *The Very Best Men: Four Who Dared—The Early Years of the CIA*. New York: Simon & Schuster / Touchstone, 1995.

Thorne, Thomas C., Jr., and David S. Patterson, eds. *Foreign Relations of the United States, 1945–1950: Emergence of the Intelligence Establishment*. Washington, D.C.: U.S. Government Printing Office, 1996.

Tóbiás, Áron, ed. *In Memoriam Nagy Imre*. Budapest: Szabad Tér Kiadó, 1989.

Tucker, Robert C., and Stephen F. Cohen, eds. *The Great Purge Trial*. New York: Grosset & Dunlap, 1965.

Unwin, Peter. *Voices in the Wilderness: Imre Nagy and the Hungarian Revolution*. London: Macdonald, 1991.

Urban, George R. *Radio Free Europe and the Pursuit of Democracy*. New Haven, Conn.: Yale University Press, 1997.

Váli, Ferenc A. *Rift and Revolt in Hungary: Nationalism versus Communism*. Cambridge, Mass.: Harvard University Press, 1961.

Varga, László, ed. *Kádár János bírái előtt: Egyszer fent, egyszer lent 1949–1956* [János Kádár before his judges: Once up, once down 1949–1956]. Budapest: Osiris, 2001.

Vásárhelyi, Miklós. *Ellenzékben* [In opposition]. Budapest: Szabad Tér Kiadó, 1989.

Warner, Michael, ed. *The CIA under Harry Truman*. Washington, D.C.: Center for the Study of Intelligence, 1994.

Yergin, Daniel. *Shattered Peace: The Origins of the Cold War and the National Security State*. Boston: Houghton Mifflin, 1977.

Zinner, Paul E. *Revolution in Hungary*. New York: Columbia University Press, 1962.

Essays and Articles

Békés, Csaba. "Győzhetett volna-e a magyar forradalom 1956-ban?" [Could the Hungarian revolution have been victorious in 1956?]. In *Mitoszok, legendák, tévhitek a 2O. századi magyar történelemből* [Myths, legends, delusions in 20th-century Hungarian history], ed. Ignác Romcsis. Budapest: Osiris, 2002.

Bell, Daniel. "Ten Theories in Search of Reality: The Prediction of Soviet Behavior in the Social Sciences." In *Soviet Conduct in World Affairs: A Selection of Readings*, comp. Alexander Dallin. New York: Columbia University Press, 1960.

Binder, David. "'56 East Europe Plan of C.I.A. Is Described." *New York Times*, November 30, 1976.

Brogan, D. W. "The Illusion of American Omnipotence." *Harper's Magazine*, December 1952, 21–28.

Deák, István. "Jews and Communism: The Hungarian Case." In *Dark Times, Dire Decisions: Jews and Communism*, ed. Jonathan Frankel. Studies in Contemporary Jewry, Avraham Harman Institute of Contemporary Jewry and Hebrew University of Jerusalem. Oxford: Oxford University Press, 2004.

Dravis, Michael W. "Storming Fortress Albania: American Covert Operations in Microcosm, 1949–54." *Intelligence and National Security* 7, no. 4 (1992): 425–42.

Dulles, John Foster. "A New Foreign Policy: A Policy of Boldness." *Life*, May 19, 1952, 146–48.

"Eastern Europe: The Situation in Hungary." *Current Intelligence Digest—CIA FOIA*, October 24, 1956.

Földes, György. "Buharin és Nagy Imre" [Bukharin and Imre Nagy]. *Múltunk* 37, no. 4 (1992): 15–25.

Földvári, Rudolf. "Egy ungvári kéretlen 'vendéglátás'" [Uninvited 'hospitality' in Ungvár]. *Új Tükör*, no. 53 (1989): 6–8.

Gati, Charles. "Another Grand Debate? The Limitationist Critique of American Foreign Policy." *World Politics* 21, no. 1 (October 1968): 133–51.

———. "From Liberation to Revolution, 1945–1956." In *A History of Hungary*, ed. Peter F. Sugar, Péter Hanák, and Tibor Frank. Bloomington: Indiana University Press, 1994.

———. "New Russia, Old Lies." *New York Times* [op-ed], July 11, 1992.

Gehler, Michael. "From Non-Alignment to Neutrality? Austria's Transformation during the First East-West Détente, 1953–1958." *Journal of Cold War Studies* 7, no. 4 (Fall 2005): 104–36.

Gluchowski, G. L. "The Defection of Józef Światło and the Search for Jewish Scapegoats in the Polish United Workers' Party, 1953–54." Paper presented at Fourth Convention of the Association for the Study of the Nationalities, Harriman Institute, Columbia University, New York, April 15–17, 1999. Available at http://www.columbia.edu/cu/sipa/regional/ECE/gluchowski.pdf.

Gluchowski, L. W. "Poland, 1956: Khrushchev, Gomułka, and the 'Polish October.'" *Cold War International History Project Bulletin*, issue 5 (Spring 1995): 1, 38–49.

Gosztonyi, Péter. "Az Ideiglenes Nemzeti Kormány megalakulásának előtörténetéhez" [To the prehistory of the founding of the Provisional National Government]. *Uj Látóhatár* 15, no. 3 (August 1972): 228–29.

Granville, Johanna. "Imre Nagy, aka 'Volodya'—Dent in the Martyr's Halo?" *Cold War International History Project Bulletin*, issue 5 (Spring 1995): 34–37.

Griffith, William E. "Policy Review of Voice for Free Hungary Programming, October 23–November 23, 1956" (review dated December 5, 1956). In *The 1956 Hungarian Revolution: A History in Documents*, ed. Csaba Békés, Malcolm Byrne, and Janos Rainer. Budapest: Central European University Press, 2003.

Hajdú, Tibor. "Az 1956. október 24-i moszkvai értekezlet" [The October 24, 1956 Moscow meeting]. In *Évkönyv 1992* [Yearbook of the Institute for the Study of the 1956 Revolution, 1992]. Budapest: 1956-os Intézet, 1992.

———, ed. "The Interrogation of László Rajk, 7 June 1949: The Transcript of the Secret Recording." *New Hungarian Quarterly*, Spring 1996, 87–99.

"Hungary Heralds 'New Era' of Independent Communism." *Current Intelligence Digest—CIA FOIA*, October 12, 1956.

"Hungary: Resistance Activities and Potentials." *U.S. Department of the Army Project No. 9570—Georgetown University Research Project*, January 5, 1956.

Kajári, Erzsébet. "Az egységesitett belügyminisztérium államvédelmi tevékenysége, 1953–1956" [State security activities of the Unified Ministry of Internal Affairs]. In *Államvédelem a Rákosi-korszakban* [State security in the Rákosi era], ed. György Gyarmati. Budapest: Történeti Hivatal, 2000.

Katona, Judit, and György Vámos. "Nagy Imre és a Szabad Európa Rádió 1956-ban" [Imre Nagy and Radio Free Europe in 1956]. In *Nagy Imre és kora: Tanulmányok és források* [Imre Nagy and his era: Studies and sources]. Budapest: Nagy Imre Alapitvány, 2002.

Kende, Péter. "Elkerülhetetlen volt-e a magyar forradalom, és mi volt a haszna?" [Was the Hungarian revolution unavoidable, and what was gained by it?]. *Világosság* 37, no. 10 (October 1996): 3–22.

Kramer, Mark. "The Early Post-Stalin Succession Struggle and Upheavals in East-Central Europe: Internal-External Linkages in Soviet Policy Making, Part 2." *Journal of Cold War Studies* 1, no. 2 (Spring 1999): 3–38.

———, translator and annotator. "The 'Malin Notes' on the Crises in Hungary and Poland, 1956." *Bulletin of the Cold War International History Project*, issues 8–9 (Winter 1996–97): 385–410.

———. "New Evidence on Soviet Decision-Making and the 1956 Polish and Hungarian Crises." *Bulletin of the Cold War International History Project*, issues 8–9 (Winter 1996–97): 358–84.

———. "The Soviet Union and the 1956 Crises in Hungary and Poland: Reassessments and New Findings." *Journal of Contemporary History* 33, no. 2 (April 1998): 163–214.

Kuzmichev, P. "Eszli ne zakruvat' glaza . . . " [If one doesn't close one's eyes . . .]. *Literaturnaya Rossiya*, December 20, 1991, 22–23.

Lippmann, Walter. "How Far in Eastern Europe?" *Washington Post and Times Herald*, October 26, 1956.

Litván, György. "Mítoszok és legendák 1956-ról" [Myths and legends about 1956]. In *Évkönyv 2000* [Yearbook 2000]. Budapest: 1956 Institute, 2001.

Lukacs, John. "The Night Stalin and Churchill divided Europe." *New York Times Magazine*, October 5, 1969, 36–50.

Lukes, Igor. "The Slánský Affair: New Evidence." *Slavic Review* 58, no. 1 (Spring 1999): 16–187.

McCargar, James. "Their Man in Budapest: James McCargar and the 1947 Road to Freedom." *Hungarian Quarterly* 42 (Spring 2001): 38–62.

McCormack, John. "Reporter in Budapest Tells How Protest Grew into War." *New York Times*, October 27, 1956.

Marchio, Jim. "Resistance Potential and Rollback: U.S. Intelligence and the Eisenhower Administration's Policies toward Eastern Europe, 1953–56." *Intelligence and National Security*, April 1995, 219–41.

"Memorandum from the Assistant Director for Policy Coordination (Wisner) to Director of Central Intelligence Hillenkoetter" (October 29, 1948). In *Foreign Relations of the United States, 1945–1950: Emergence of the Intelligence Establishment*, ed. C. Thomas Thorne Jr. and David S. Patterson. Washington, D.C.: U.S. Government Printing Office, 1996.

Murányi, Gábor. "Születésnap az Orsó utcában: Nagy Imre köszöntése vagy 'politikai demonstráció'?" [Birthday party at Orsó Street: Greeting Imre Nagy or "political demonstration"?] *Magyar Nemzet*, June 6, 1991.

Muszatov, Valerij. "Kádár János és M. Sz. Gorbacsov találkozója Moszkvában, 1985. szeptember 25-én" [Meeting between János Kádár and M. S. Gorbachev in Moscow, September 25, 1985]. *Történelmi Szemle*, nos. 1–2 (1992): 133–49.

Nelson, Anna K., ed. "The Attitude of this Government toward Events in Yugoslavia," PPS/35 dated June 30, 1948. In *The State Department Policy Planning Staff Papers*, vol. 2 (1948). New York: Garland Press, 1983.

Ostermann, Christian F. "Keeping the Post Simmering: The United States and the East German Uprising of 1953." *German Studies Review* 15, no. 2 (Spring 1996): 61–89.

Palasik, Mária. "Látlelet a magyar függetlenségről" [Diagnosis of Hungarian independence]. *Kapu*, May 1989, 4–10.

"Rákosi Mátyás 1945. szept. 3-i jelentése Dimitrovnak" [Mátyás Rákosi's report to Dimitrov on Sept. 3, 1945]. *Múltunk*, nos. 2–3 (1991): 287.

Rainer, János M. "Döntés a Kremlben, 1956: Kísérlet a feljegyzések értelmezésére" [Decision in the Kremlin, 1956: An attempt to interpret the notes]. In *Döntés a Kremlben, 1956: A szovjet pártelnökség vitái Magyarországról* [Decision in the Kremlin, 1956: The Soviet Politburo's debates about Hungary], ed. Vyacheslav Sereda and János M. Rainer. Budapest: Intézet, 1956.

Révész, Béla. "A Belügyminisztérium SZER-képe 1955-ben" [The Ministry of Internal Affair's image of RFE]. *Múltunk*, no. 2 (1999): 170–222.

Ripp, Zoltán. "A pártvezetés végnapjai" [The last days of the party leadership]. In *Ötvenhat októbere és a hatalom* [October fifty six and power], ed. Julianna Horváth and Zoltán Ripp. Budapest: Napvilág, 1997.

Stout, Mark. "The Pond: Running Agents for State, War, and the CIA." *Studies in Intelligence* 48, no. 3 (2004): 69–82.

Szabó, Miklós. "A magyar Buharin" [The Hungarian Bukharin]. Unpublished manuscript, c. 1989.

"Their Man in Budapest: James McCargar and the 1947 Road to Freedom." *Hungarian Quarterly* 42, no. 161 (Spring 2001): 38–62.

Thomas, Evan. "A Singular Opportunity: Gaining Access to CIA's Records." *Studies in Intelligence* 39, no. 5 (1996): 19–23.

"Transcript of the Conversation between the Soviet Leadership and a Hungarian United Worker's Party Delegation in Moscow on 13 June 1953," trans. Mónika Borbély. *Cold War International History Project Bulletin*, issue 10 (March 1998): 81–86.

Urbán, Károly. "A Nagy Imre-kormány megalakulása (1953)" [The formation of the Imre Nagy government (1953)]. In *Nagy Imre és kora* [Imre Nagy and his age], ed. József Sipos and Levente Sipos. Budapest: Nagy Imre Alapítvány, 2002.

Varga, György T., comp. "Dokumentumok: Jegyzőkönyv a szovjet és a magyar párt- és állami vezetők tárgyalásairól (1953. Június 13–16)" [Documents: Transcript of negotiations between Soviet and Hungarian party and state leaders, June 13–16, 1953]. *Múltunk* 37, nos. 2–3 (1992): 234–69.

———. "Nagy Imre politikai levelei 1954, Dec. 14–1956 okt. 9" [Imre Nagy's political letters, Dec. 14, 1954–Oct. 9, 1956]. *Új Fórum*, no. 4 (1989): 11–39.

———, ed. "A Politikai Bizottság 1955. január 13. ülésének jegyzőkönyve" [Minutes of the meeting of the Political Committee on January 13th 1955]. In *Jalta és Szuez között: 1956 a világpolitikában* [Between Yalta and Suez: 1956 in world politics]. Budapest: Tudósítások Kiadó, 1989.

Zsitnyányi, Ildikó. "Egy 'titkos háború' természete: A Magyar Harcosok Bajtársi Közössége tagjaival szemben lefolytatott internálási és büntetőeljárási gyakorlat, 1948–1950" [The nature of a 'secret war': The practice of internment and criminal procedure against members of the Hungarian Veterans' Association, 1948–1950]. *Hadtörténelmi Közlemények*, 2002–4, 1086–1101.

INDEX